STRANGE WORLD
of
THE BRONTËS

Marie Campbell

W0009739

Published by Sigma Leisure – an imprint of
Sigma Press, 1 South Oak Lane, Wilmslow, Cheshire SK9 6AR, England.

British Library Cataloguing in Publication Data
A CIP record for this book is available from the British Library.

ISBN: 1-85058-758-2

Typesetting and Design by: Sigma Press, Wilmslow, Cheshire.

Cover Design: Graham Beech

Cover photograph: The ruins of Top Withens in the moorland above Haworth – the possible inspiration for the setting of 'Wuthering Heights' *(photographed by Simon Warner)*

Printed by: MFP Design & Print

Foreword

By Peter Underwood – Life President of the Ghost Club Society

Here indeed is a very strange world, the hitherto virtually unknown world of the Brontës. Charlotte who used to talk about 'a voice of wild and wailing music' coming into her mind; Emily who had a 'strong faith in ghosts'; and Anne whose novels contain violence and sexual passion thought unseemly in Victorian England. No wonder the writings of the Brontë sisters belong to the literature of feeling.

I have always found Haworth Parsonage to be an inhospitable-looking place, even today and even in summertime; one shudders to think what it must have been like to the Brontë family. Emily wrote 'The house is old, the trees are bare' and 'The mute bird sitting on the stone, the dank moss dripping from the wall' and 'The garden-walk with weeds o'ergrown ...' But she loved the place passionately. I remember in particular the tiny notebooks in minuscule handwriting that requires a magnifying glass to decipher.

Bleak and remote it may have been but that was only the half of it. 'A killing place' one author has called it and indeed Mrs Brontë died there soon followed by two of her daughters – Maria aged eleven and Elizabeth aged ten and, before very long, the only son Branwell and then Emily, refusing medical treatment to the last. Anne died the following year, at Scarborough where she had gone hoping to improve her health. Now only Charlotte and her father remained and she cared for him devotedly as his sight failed and as he grew cantankerous at the thought of her marriage but marry she did and after less than a year of happiness died at her old home and eventually at the age of eighty-four the unsuccessful author and curate Mr Brontë died there too. The entire family, except for Anne, lie buried covered in concrete in the vault at the foot of one of the pillars at the entrance to the present church, built eighteen years after the Revd Brontë's death.

Everyone should visit Haworth and its surroundings at least once during their lifetime and if they do with this volume of *Strange World of the Brontës* in their pocket the visit will be considerably enriched.

Among other interesting sites nearby, The Old Silent Inn at Stanbury is mentioned and some of its ghostly associations. I once stayed there in the company of David Kossoff and Sandy Gall (I had just missed Bing Crosby who had been there a couple of days earlier) after the three of us had been Special Guests at a Yorkshire Literary Dinner. We saw no ghosts, although David Kossoff asked to change his room. Next morning we enjoyed an Authors' Coffee Morning at the historic establishment that has been the scene of murder, mysterious bell-ringing, unexplained movement of objects and ghostly figures including that of a tall man in old-fashioned clothing and an unidentified young girl – who didn't visit me!

There is, however, far more than ghost stories in this entertaining volume. There is a wealth of information on all sorts of subjects: the Order of the Golden Dawn, the Theosophical Society, fairy lore, local soothsayers, witchcraft, superstitions, astrology, numerology, stone circles, reincarnation, murders and mysterious deaths – even Jack the Ripper in Bradford, and a lot more besides. And it is always interesting to learn the probable originals of fictional properties mentioned in the Brontë novels and here there are many surprises and some little-known aspects of such properties.

Marie Campbell has succeeded in unearthing a wealth of lore and legend, of mysterious history, and of ghosts and hauntings concerning Haworth and its surroundings. It is all the result of considerable research and for the first time we have a comprehensive and exhaustive examination of the subject. The author is to be congratulated on a unique and lasting achievement.

The Savage Club,
1, Whitehall Place
London SW1A 2HD

Preface

Strange World of the Brontës is for the most part a light-hearted look at the life and times of all those gone before who have created their own legends famous or otherwise. I very much hope readers will enjoy the contents of this book containing both true and legendary stories relating to Haworth and its environs, before, during and after the time of the Brontë family.

Romer Wilson believed members of this family suffered from various types of depression and delusions – especially Charlotte whom she said endured a certain type of religious mania. Wilson claimed that Charlotte almost lost her mind because she believed she was eternally damned.

The same author suggests too that the great Emily suffered from a persecution complex fuelled by a deep sense of failure – she was never to know the impact her novel *Wuthering* or *Sobbing Heights* was to have upon the world.

Astrological clues within the text of this work may provide some insight to the family's inner personalities contained in their birth and name charts drawn up by astrologer Angela Pearl Curtis who has been described as "an extraordinary gifted clairvoyant/medium."

Was Bradford town, where Branwell once lived, and the home of a secret and mysterious occult sect named the Golden Dawn, visited by the real 'Jack the Ripper' at the close of 1888 when the horribly dismembered, mutilated corpse of little Johnnie Gill was discovered in James Berwick's stable early one dark foggy morning? His injuries were deemed so bad that women were actually banned from the courtroom. The true assailant was never brought to justice but left a clue behind – a wet sack cloth bearing the slogan *Mason, Derby Road, Liverpool* lying beneath the boy's remains.

A hand-written journal attributed to James Maybrick of Liverpool re-surfaced a century after its production. In it the author claims that he is 'Jack the Ripper.' Only a few days before Johnnie Gill's "unique" murder Maybrick confides to his diary that he is sick of his own children. He is looking forward to catching a train to Manchester – which happens to be on the same line as Bradford – immediately after Christmas Day so he can kill again...

Read about Haworth highwayman James Sutcliffe hanged for his nefarious crimes at York, the famed Haworth soothsayer and crystal gazer Jack Kay – a close neighbour and probable occult adviser to the Brontë family for many years together with numerous tales of ghoulish ghosts, religious fervour, early accounts of a Haworth UFO encounter and untimely deaths.

Check out old customs and superstitions, practised by the old wise ones and much, much more all gleaned from innumerable sources.

After reading *Strange World of the Brontës* one might ask was it the Brontës that made the village of Haworth famous or was it Haworth with all its peculiar eccentricities that helped shape the life and times of this famous literary family, of whom it has been said that they could: "no more refuse to obey the dictates of their minds than the nightingale could refuse to sing."

Acknowledgements

Quotations have been reproduced by the kind permission of: *Telegraph & Argus*; *The Keighley News; Yorkshire Evening Post; Yorkshire Post; Punch; TV Times, Times Newspapers* and Keighley Library.

Also, with grateful thanks to the following newspapers: *Bradford Observer, Iowa Weekly Republican, Craven Pioneer, Frazer's Magazine, The Microcosmos, Palladium, The Globe, The Building News, The Northern Star, Leeds Intelligencer, Leeds Mercury Supplement, Keighley Herald, St. George's Magazine, Gospel Magazine, Keighley Visitor, Keighley Investigator, Heckmondwick Herald, The Family Herald, Local Notes and Queries, Yorkshire Spiritual Telegraph, Yorkshire Briefs & Antiquarian Society, Bradford Star, Halifax Observer, Halifax Guardian, Halifax Courier, The Yorkshireman, The Bradfordian, Country Life, The Globe, The Christian Science Monitor, Boston, Gentleman's Magazine, Voice of Good Spirits, Quarterly Review, The Building News, Hartley Newspaper Scrapbook, Vol. 1, Daily News, Daily Telegraph, Yorkshire Observer, Manchester Guardian, Nelson's Leader, The Brontë Society Transactions, John O' London, The London Journal,*.

Local History Libraries and Records Offices were consulted in Keighley, Leeds, Bradford, Halifax, Colne, York, Liverpool and Hull. Thanks also to Susan Boone, Hale Family Papers; Sophia Smith Collection, Smith Collage, Northampton, Massachusetts; Bradford District Archives (BDA 51D81/1) notes in the Register for 1645-1727; The British Library. Special thanks to Keighley Reference Library and to staff members Mrs Pauline Barfield, Mrs Irene Mcnamara and Elaine Midgley for their valuable knowledge and assistance regarding my seemingly never-ending archive enquiries. And last but not least to Mrs Vera Jalil for all her help and support.

Marie Campbell

Contents

1 | *Dear Charlotte*

Charlotte's stone chair stands rooted at the foot of the Brontë Waterfall, rudely carved from a block of stone by unknown hands. No one knows how long the rock has existed at this site, but Brontë lore has it that Charlotte was fond of letting her thoughts run free here.

It was to this very place she walked with her new husband in the wild November grey of 1854. As the pair watched the flooding waters tumble down over rough boulders, it began to rain heavily. The consequences of this ill-advised outing, together with excessive morning sickness during the early stages of pregnancy helped push Charlotte into an early grave.

Brave to the End

Martha Brown cared for the ebbing Charlotte. She said afterwards that Charlotte had been a patient sufferer and was brave when death finally came into the same room from which her mother – who died at the same age – and her aunt had passed out of this world into the next. It was a room where dappled sunlight danced in the windows. Suffering had changed her face, Martha said, to that of a wizened old lady.

It was not long after this observation that the Passing-bell in the ancient grey tower of Haworth church sounded its doleful iron clang early on the morning of 31 March 1855, informing Worth Valley inhabitants that Charlotte Brontë was no more. In time-honoured tradition, Martha collected a great armful of evergreens and wild flowers; handing them to Charlotte's best friend Ellen Nussey to arrange about her friend's lifeless form, now lying in its coffin. There was no post-mortem.

Charlotte's funeral service took place at Haworth church after the coffin was carried through the parsonage ghost gate on 4 April. Silent villagers attended the customary bidding at a time when only a privileged few in the outside world knew of her passing. A blind girl living four miles distant from Haworth, to whom Charlotte had given money, longed so much to go to her funeral that she begged everyone she knew to take her. Finally, she got her wish and was led over the moors to the old church where Charlotte's body was laid to rest in the family crypt.

A homesick Charlotte had once written from Brussels, "Haworth seems such a lonely quiet spot buried away from the world." Now it was her turn 'to be "buried away from the world."

After Charlotte's lingering death there was no room left on the family's memorial stone to add her name so her husband caused a new memorial to be erected bearing the words:

Adjoining the Remains of
Charlotte Brontë wife
Of the
Revd Arthur Bell Nicholls, A.B. Incumbent.
And Daughter of the Revd P.B. Incumbent.
She died March 31st, 1855
In the 39th
Year of her Age.

In the *Daily News* in October 1888. the following appeared:

'The wind bloweth where it listenth, and there is no accounting by any scientific formula alone for the genius that enabled Charlotte Brontë to live so many lives in one'

And perhaps this poem from the *Keighley Visitor*, February 1859, might sum up best just how Nicholls felt at the time of her passing:

Yours Until Death

And art thou, dear one! Art thou dead?
The breath of life, like sun-beams fled?
That did ten thousand charms unfold,
For *ever* pale? – for *ever* cold?
For *ever* mute, for *ever* still?
Become ah, what! – must truth declare -
A nest for worms to gender there?
Then *Death* rejoice! The triumph's *thine*!
The Maid is *yours* – so lately *mine*.
Rejoice grim spoiler – seize your prey,
And revel o'er the putrid clay,
Yet *thine* she's *not* – nor ne'er shall be,
Her *love* still lives! – and *lives* with me!
With *me* in every thought and sigh!
With *me*, and but *with* me can *die*!

A Missed Opportunity

Miss Charlotte had hoped to secure a job as governess at Cottingley Old Hall, a post only a few miles distant from her Haworth home but was turned down because she was not musically talented. Had she been accepted, she would have taught Richard Thornton born on 5 April 1838, who grew up to be a talented geologist and geographer. He accompanied David Livingstone to Africa, sailing from Liverpool Docks to the Zambesi Basin on *The Pearl* a month before his twentieth birthday. Richard was one of the first Europeans to climb above the snow line in the mountains of equatorial Africa. Sadly, this promising young man died of malaria in 1863 and was buried in Central Africa on the right bank of the River Shire, where a tree marks his grave. Mrs Gaskell appears to reflect Richard's life as an explorer in her novel *Wives and Daughters*. His Cottingley home erected in 1659 was demolished in November 1872. Incidentally, the old road near here was used by John Nevison (*alias* Swift Nicks – not Turpin) the highwayman on his famous fifteen-hour journey on horseback from London to

York. The bridge that Nevison crossed over, situated on the Old Cottingley Road is still intact but has now become part of someone's private driveway.

Love and Tragedy

In her lifetime Charlotte was no stranger to tragedy or unhappy love affairs she once advised a local girl to marry someone more suited to her than the man to whom she had given her heart. The girl acted on her advice and wed another, which is just as well for her first choice turned out to be a cad, as Miss Brontë had predicted. Charlotte herself had received a strange proposal of marriage, by post, in 1839 from a man she had met only briefly! Within six months of receiving this offer, Revd David Bryce, the author of that letter, lay dead. He was buried in Christ Church Cemetery, Colne in January 1840.

At Ponden Kirk, situated on the crest of a ridge above Ponden Clough, there stands a natural holed stone. According to Horsfall Turner, this was often referred to as *Wuthering Heights*. Hopeful lovers visited the stone in order to pass through the stone gap. In Charlotte's time, a spinster wishing to acquire a husband within the year would squeeze through the hole to ensure she got one. Mind you, if her partner did not come up to expectations she could easily rid herself of him by repeating the process in reverse, thereby guaranteeing his death within the year!

Perilously ignoring superstition, Arthur Nicholls selected Thursday to be their wedding day, even though to wed on this day of the week was said to mean losses. Tragically, it was Charlotte who died within twelve months of her marriage.

Married At Last!

At the grand old age of thirty-eight Charlotte wed Irishman Arthur Bell Nicholls, a dark-complexioned man with black hair. It was very early on the morning of 29 June 1854 that John Brown told a young John Robinson to go to the brow of the hill and wait until he saw three men. On doing so, he was to run to the parsonage and tell whoever answered the door that three men were coming. "I went to my place and watched, and presently I saw in the distance Mr Nicholls, Mr Grant and Mr Snowden." On reaching the parsonage, John was instructed to run and fetch Joseph Redman the elderly parish clerk. John Robinson continues the tale, "I found him, and told him he had to come to the church as quickly as possible. He came immediately. On the way, he stopped and said, "I'd better lace up my boots," and he went to the wall and did so. We hurried to the church, and on the stroke of eight Charlotte entered with two of her woman friends. There were thus in the church, Charlotte, her two friends, the clerk, the sexton, and myself – nine persons in all. I don't think Mr Brontë was there. The ceremony was got through as quickly as possible". The wedding party went back to the parsonage for the wedding breakfast where her father was waiting.

Nicholls chose to take his Haworth bride to Hill House, Banagher, Co. Offaly in Ireland for their honeymoon. From its windows, the River Shannon and the Great Bog of Allen could be seen.

The Revd Sutcliffe Snowden, a dear friend of Arthur Nicholls performed the marriage ceremony. He was drowned on the wild storm-driven night of 8 August 1861, when he accidentally stumbled into the canal at Hebden Bridge. Snowden had been amongst the first to welcome the newly weds back from their Irish honeymoon. Mr and Mrs Nicholls secretly harboured thoughts of him and Ellen Nussey getting together but it was not to be. Nicholls read his friend's burial service on 13 August, as parishioners filed slowly past, dropping flowers onto the lid of the coffin as it was being lowered into the ground.

After their marriage, Mr and Mrs Nicholls planted two Scotch pine trees on either side of what is popularly known as 'the gate of the dead.' They may have been purchased from Keighley nurseryman John Carter who traded in Scotch pine, American and other forest saplings as well as assorted shrubs. In symbolic terms, the pine tree is recognised as a sign of immortality, fertility, growth and death leading to re-birth and is sacred to the Roman god Bacchus. To the Japanese, this tree symbolises vital energy and strength of character. In 1989, it was feared both trees might be "lost to the wind." Seeds were collected from their cones and several healthy saplings cultivated. One of which was sent to the "Land of the Rising Sun" together with some good Brontë earth and Haworth heather.

Following her death, Charlotte's wedding dress, stole and bonnet were wrapped and placed with other sentimental items in a box labelled *Rowntree's of Scarborough*. When Mr Nicholls died, Mary, his second wife passed the box, which also contained a pair of small single buttoned gloves and tiny sandals to his niece Charlotte Brontë Nicholls, instructing her that the dress must be destroyed by fire before she died. This was carried out to the letter in 1954 – a century after the wedding took place.

Fortunately, Charlotte Nicholls' niece, Margaret Ross had spied the bridal gown at her aunt's home and prior to her death a decade later, Margaret gave a detailed description of the dress to Jean Agnew who handmade a reproduction. When the gown first made its appearance at Haworth Parsonage, it was said, "at first glance … it appears like the image of some gentle wraith." Charlotte's original wedding veil *did* survive however, and was subsequently worn by Miss Shirley Stanton at her wedding in August 1951. A boudoir cap made from very fine lawn and crafted by her own hands, which Charlotte had given to Martha Brown, later became the possession of retired Bradford stone merchant Mr J.T. Reddiough, whose Haworth relatives had been friendly with Martha. Sadly, Margaret had not been able to catch so much as a glimpse of the bridal bonnet and thus its design and appearance could only be speculated.

The Reluctant Shadow

Patrick Brontë thought his new son-in-law to be a shallow fellow, only after his daughter's fortune. When questioned about the marriage, the Brontë servants Tabby and Martha Brown only *thought* that Charlotte was happy with Nicholls but on the other hand, *knew* he was happy with her. Later Ellen Nussey was to call him, "that wicked man who was the death of dear Charlotte."

John Lock writes in his book *Man of Sorrow,* that when questioned about Charlotte's husband and her father, William, the brother of sexton John Brown fame, intimated that although Nicholls and his ageing father-in-law resided together after all but they had gone, in reality they lived separate lives.

Nicholls was eventually ousted from Haworth church by a wealthy Methodist trustee's casting vote after Patrick's death. He chose to return to Hill House in Ireland with his sacred memories and mementoes of Charlotte. He shared the house with his second wife and cousin, Mary Bell Nicholls. Patrick's gun was propped behind the door, and Patrick's dog Plato and Martha Brown were by his side. Miss Frances Bell, Mr Nicholls niece, remembered being taken to the house by her father Revd Joseph Bell and savouring the tantalising smell of Miss Martha's Yorkshire sponge cake, made from an old Haworth recipe, as it wafted out to greet her.

Recipe For Yorkshire Sponge Cake
1lb Sugar
Eight eggs and the weight of eight eggs in flour.
Method – Blend eggs for ten minutes, add sugar, and blend for thirty minutes, add flour and fold in. Cook in even temperature oven until spongy.

It was just six years after Patrick's death that Nicholls had both Brontë memorials removed from the church and smashed to smithereens. The pieces were then buried in the parsonage garden to a depth of four feet, ensuring trophy hunters could not cart them away.

Around 1879, Nicholls promised that as soon as a new church was erected in place of the old St. Michael & All Angels, he would contribute to a new memorial – but in his wife's name only. It would be a splendid tomb, placed over the remains of his Charlotte and the rest of the Brontë family who lay beneath the foot of the pillar near the Chancel Arch. Put in place in 1882, this 'splendid' tribute, marking the exact place over the Brontë vault, turned out to be a rather insignificant, albeit pretty, brass plaque set into the stone floor of the church, recording nothing more than Emily and Charlotte's births and deaths. When it came down to it, after the demise of "Honest Grimshaw's" church, neither Nicholls, Wade (the new rector) nor George Smith of Smith Elder and Co. (Charlotte's publisher) was interested in raising an appropriate monument to this gifted family. Its existence is attributed solely to the efforts of one man, barrister Sydney Biddell of Stroud. Biddell begged Ellen Nussey for help, feeling he was up against it with both the new rector and Nicholls, who he called "a monster", saying "I do not have the courage to attempt more than a simple memorial cross or plate ... "

In 1963 when Sir Tresham Lever donated the money needed to construct a Brontë memorial chapel within the walls of Haworth church, it was mooted that Biddell's plaque should be ousted. Quite rightly, members of Haworth Parish Church voted to retain it.

Author Walter White visited Haworth in Patrick Brontë and Arthur Nicholls' day and after speaking to the hostess of the Black Bull felt the natives liked Charlotte's husband well enough. On the other hand, Charles Hale, a young American smitten by the famous family, found on his visit to Haworth in 1861 that Nicholls was exceedingly *un*popular with the villagers, commenting, "He certainly had a strange feeling, which one may understand but by no means justify about his wife's separate reputation. He hated that she should be remembered in any other relation than as his wife; as an author or as the chief personage of Haworth he could not bear to have her thought of." Because of this Hale said that, 'Mr Nicholls in going away took nearly everything of especial value or interest, which had belonged to his wife; but the remaining household effects were disposed of by public auction about three weeks ago (October 1861).' Whether liked or not, he returned to Haworth from Ireland only once after leaving the village.

When Arthur Nicholls died in 1906 the text of his funeral sermon included the words, *'Mark the perfect man, and behold the upright, for the end of that man is peace.'* His second wife continued to reside at Hill House surrounded by Brontë memorabilia until her death in February 1915, aged 102, and was the first person known to have died at Hill House. This property was sold in 1959 at a knock-down price of £1600 to the Select Vestry of the Church in Ireland for use as a rectory for St. Paul's Church. An auction here in the same year enabled the Brontë Society to purchase a first edition of *Villette* for £155. In 1992, Hill House was again offered for sale for a mere £180,000!

Under the Hammer

According to Charles Hale:

'The sale [of 1861] was considered a matter of no consequence; it was not widely advertised nor largely attended. I suppose the tray (this had belonged to Charlotte and was being used at the Black Bull) was obtained at the sale – the only other article I know of in particular is a copy of Goldsmith's History of England, four volumes in one, which all the Brontë family used, having MS notes by the father and Brown (the sexton) says by Charlotte also but I did not happen to see her turning over the pages. He knows he has seen her using the book and he bought it for eighteen pence. I would gladly have given as many shillings to be possessed of it – and many persons. I dare say, would have been willing to count the price in guineas ... Returning from my walk I went to the joiner's to see his treasures ... I saw the three pictures by Branwell ... and also the Goldsmith's History, which he got at the sale. He also had a pencil sketch by Emily Brontë of early date, of a girl and a dog, with her name in juvenile letters, and a sketch coloured by Charlotte Brontë of a goddess ... He would not part with these, for any consideration. He considers himself (and justly I think) the most familiar with the Brontës of any of the Haworth people – he is a jolly, frank, honest agreeable man. Next I went to Greenwood's the stationer. He is mentioned in *Life*, in a letter of Charlotte Brontë's to her publishers, describing him as a person who wrote an essay on *Jane Eyre* when it first appeared. He aspires to more culture than the rest: is a quiet gentlemanly person ... He has two nice India ink drawings by Charlotte Brontë; carefully preserved; one of them is marked in Mr Brontë's handwriting ... He said Charlotte was the best friend he had ever had. These things seen, I took the line of march back to Keighley. I had some freight to convey in rather bad shape – but I stuffed my coat pockets and wore my coat – strapped my bag across my shoulder and carried my shawl folded across my bag – carried in my right hand the parcels of glass (the actual sash window from Charlotte's bedroom) and photographs tied together, and could have carried the timber in my left hand; but Wood the joiner accompanied me and kindly relieved me of that ... This, by-the-way, is how I learned the weight in pounds of the glass. I had lifted one of the sashes before and found it very heavy ... I felt pretty tired and heavily-laden before I got to Keighley ... '

When Brown's Museum of Brontë Relics closed its doors, they had hoped to sell their museum treasures at the Chicago Exhibition, but it was not to be. A further attempt to auction one hundred and seven lots was made on Saturday 2 July 1898 at Sotheby's. Even this failed to attract many serious buyers. Amongst the effects that didn't receive a bid at all were J.H. Thompson's oil portrait of Charlotte and her doll's cradle. The Brontë Society spent just under £20 on the day, purchasing several Brontë mementoes. An unfinished counterpane worked by all three sisters was knocked down at £1. 2s. (£1.10), a signed watercolour of Anne's pet dog Flossy for £12, a lock of Charlotte's hair belonging to Martha Brown and taken after her death cost £1. 14s. (£1.70), while yet another fetched double that amount, a letter penned by Charlotte to Dear Nell on the eve of her wedding day and a lock of her hair given to Tabby Brown by Nicholls fetched £44 at auction in 1916. A small portion of Charlotte's hair was once in the possession of antiquarian Joseph Horsfall Turner.

The *Keighley News* reported on 23 June 1928 that letters from the library of the late Clement Shorter and written by Charlotte Brontë, separately describing the tragic events and deaths of her two sisters and Branwell, were acquired by a Mr John Symington of Newlay Wood, on behalf of the Brontë Society at Sotheby's auction for the sum of £1.15s.

Two Victorian dolls thought to have belonged to Charlotte and forming part of a bankrupt stock were sold at auction in 1930. Bidding began at 10s (50p) each, but was knocked down to 15s. (75p) for the two.

Three years later, two very old-fashioned simple wax dolls belonging to the Brontë girls were sold at Hodgson's London Auction Rooms, Chancery Lane, for just over £2 each. The attached ticket claimed that the dolls had come from the Brown family whom the Brontës visited. Had they no history they 'might have fetched 4d' (approx. 10p) 'at a jumble sale.'

Sothebys sold Emily's battered personal copy of Newby's 1847 edition of *Wuthering Heights* in 1964. Pencilled corrections inside the book were thought to have been made by Charlotte. This book together with two other volumes fetched £420 on the day of the sale.

In 1966, Hodgson's London Salesroom auctioned off more Brontë mementoes. A London correspondent described the depressing atmosphere of the auction room in which they were to be sold. He was shown Charlotte's well-used writing desk, inside which, upon lifting the lid he saw there were still a few of her personal trinkets, including a little bracelet worn by her and a lock of her brown hair. Prospective purchasers were informed that an anonymous collector who wished to keep his or her identity secret had owned the relics but was unwilling to disclose how the items came to be in their possession.

An anonymous American family sold a unique letter dubbed the *'Dreadful Dream,'* penned by Charlotte Brontë on 15 March 1849, describing the deaths of her sisters and brother, to the Brontë Society for the sum of £50,000. Ex-director of the museum Mr Mike Hill told the *Keighley News* on 18 April 1999, "This letter is the only one we know in which Charlotte brings together in a single account the story of the final weeks of her brother and two sisters." One Brontë Society member thought, "Charlotte would be smiling in heaven" now her letter had come back from America.

Memorabilia

Charlotte's favourite bible was a copy used in Haworth church since the time of the Commonwealth, printed by John Field of Cambridge in 1659. It has been said that Field was bribed to print this particular edition, noted for the alteration to *Acts 6 v. 3:* 'Wherefore, brethren, look ye out among you, you seven men of honest report, full of the Holy Ghost and wisdom, whom you may appoint over this business.' "We" in this edition was substituted for the word "ye." A book collector once offered the magnificent sum of £200 for this rarity but was turned down.

Mrs Gaskell's friend Charles Hale, writing from the Black Bull Inn on Saturday 9 November 1861, made the following interesting comments:

'The sexton came by appointment at about nine o'clock to conduct me to the places I wished to see. I first went to his house ... I then went to the church. I entered by the door by which Charlotte Brontë usually entered and walked round to her pew-sat a moment where she sat. She used to have a footstool necessarily under her feet, the seat was so high, and she so petite – this as well as the carpets, cushions and all fixtures of the pew, Mr Nicholls has carried away. Sexton ... showed me where the two dogs ... were buried in the garden ... I went next to the parsonage-here a great transformation is going on. The house is a hundred years old and is sadly out of repair, for Mr Brontë disliked to have mechanical work going on there. Only once, from absolute necessity, to keep out bad leakage, he allowed the roof to be mended. The new incumbent does not choose to go into a rotten old house, but they are doing very much more than making merely necessary repairs. They are putting in fireplaces and mantelpieces of marble, and windows of plate glass, a single pane filling the whole sash and weighing 30 pounds. The stone walls, stone floors of the passages and stone staircases will stand unchanged for another hundred years as they have the last ... In old Tabby's chamber for some reason, half the window had been walled up with a stone wall by Mr Brontë's direction: this erection has been pulled down. Mr Nicholls having neglected to bury these stones I might have brought one to America had they not been too heavy. I easily obtained however some very good memorials. I purchased of the proper person the whole lower sash of the window of the bedroom of Charlotte Brontë. This is the window she was most fond of sitting ... I have marked the window in the engraving. The panes of glass were cut out under my own eye. I also brought away myself plenty of the moulding or wood-work that went about the rooms, so I can frame photographs with wood and glaze them with glass from the place-we shall look at them through the same medium through which Charlotte Brontë saw the dreary landscape before her window and they will be surrounded by wood that was about her as she sat there. I also have the wire and crank of Mr Brontë's bell-pull, which he used daily for 41 years ... Such memorials I know will be valued by myself and my friends, besides the photographs which I was able to get of the sexton and of the stationer.'

In 1956, Charles King of Barlby discovered a red double photograph holder in a box of dusty old documents at Selby Abbey. There was a coloured picture of two Victorian ladies on the front cover and a small diamond-patterned shot-silk piece of fabric covered with glass. On the reverse side were written the words, 'this small portion of dress material is from a dress worn by Charlotte Brontë, the famous novelist. It was given to my sister Mrs Ickeringill, of Keighley, who was in the service of the family for a number of years. It has diminished very much in size since I first had it. The last piece went to the United States of America. J.M. Lee.' Just how did this Brontë relic find its way into Selby Abbey's scriptorium?

In 1963 Miss Catherine Alice Ripley late of Apperley Lane, Bradford left two wax dolls formerly belonging to Charlotte and Emily Brontë to the RSPCA.

On dipping into the late Mr J.H. Dixon's *Harrogate Folk-lore Catalogue*, I found many olde-world relics from Brontëland, including: a board for making haver bread; a 'sitting tree' (wooden stool); a peat spade from Far Withens; a sign announcing: 'My days are swifter than a weaver's shuttle' (*Job 7 v. 6*); the will of William Horsfall, dated 1 July 1536, leaving a "cowe" to his daughter; funeral cards belonging to the Brontë family and the Brontë piano which they had lent to J.B. Grant, vicar of Oxenhope. In addition, I discovered: Patrick Brontë's swordstick, given to Mr Hudson who repaired his boots; the bedposts from Charlotte's bed, which would have been destroyed by Nicholls if Martha Brown's nephew Robert Radcliffe hadn't salvaged them; Mr Brontë's blue six-piece toilet set; two separate Bibles, curiously sewn together and given to Martha Brown by Mr Nicholls; a lock of Charlotte's hair, cut by Elizabeth Brown and a collection of treen from Haworth old church. There were also the first and last verses of Emily's famous last poem entitled, *No Coward Soul is Mine*.

Fading Images?

A faded photograph in Claude Meeker's book, *Haworth Home of the Brontës,* featuring Haworth churchyard shows the distant figure of a woman dressed in a long dark dress and bonnet, silhouetted against the parsonage wall. In 1969, Brontë author Phyllis Bentley suggested that the figure might be that of Charlotte. If this is true then it is the image of Charlotte's ghost, as she had already been dead three years, according to the headstone placed over the open grave waiting to receive the body of Sarah Binns, wife of William Binns of Summerfield Villa, Oxenhope and dated 9 September 1858. George Feather thought this photograph had been taken by his father Edwin, delegated by the Brontës as their official photographer and the only person allowed to photo-graph either the family or the inside of the old Brontë church.

Mrs Mary Butterfield put forward a tentative theory in 1976 that another photograph taken in Haworth's old yard-of-the-dead had captured the images of the Brontë sisters, Branwell, Ellen Nussey and the sexton John Brown. The picture depicted 'Charlotte' standing on top of a tombstone – something she is unlikely to have done, for a friend once said that she turned "pale and faint" at Hartshead church when informed she was walking over graves. An anonymous Haworthian told the *Yorkshire Post* that she could identify the supposed 'Ellen Nussey' figure as her own great-great grandmother as she would have looked in

Haworth Parsonage and graveyard, as they are today *(Marie Campbell)*

1861 or 1862. Who was the anonymous Haworthian and who were the other figures posing in this photograph?

Doubt also surrounded the authenticity of a watercolour portrait, which had been purchased for the National Portrait Gallery by Lionel Cust and reproduced in the *Cornhill Magazine* in October 1906. There were several clues as to the supposed sitter's identity in an inscription on the back. The *Yorkshire Daily Observer* was quick to point out that the canvas bore Branwell's name but that it had been mis-spelled:

> The Wearin' of Green.
> First Since Emily's Death.
> CHARLOTTE BRONTË.
> This drawing is by Paul Heger *(sic)*
> Done from life in 1850.
> The pose was first suggested by her
> Brother
> By a sketch done by her brother Bramwell
> Many years prior.

Mr C. J. Holmes, director of the Gallery, was able to trace the words 'Portrait of Miss Mary Vicars', written in very faint lead pencil, when he scrutinised the portrait in 1913. Cust defended his purchase saying that he believed the "portrait was originally that of Miss Mary Vicars, but had been converted at some point into a portrait of Charlotte Brontë." Nevertheless the portrait was deemed a forgery and removed from the walls of the 'Where was Charlotte Brontë from 7 August to 17 October 1841?' exhibition.

There is a portrait in oils of Anne, Emily and Charlotte Brontë hanging in the National Portrait Gallery, which had spent over half a century collecting dust on top of Mr Nicholl's cupboard. When Miss Jean Nixon examined it more closely, she thought she could just make out another figure in the picture. The canvas was subjected to infrared photography in 1957 or 1958 when a fourth figure, that of a man thought to be Branwell, was revealed. Only the left eye and the framework of the head and shoulders could be made out. In the August 1897 edition of *The Woman at Home* the same painting appears under the heading *Supposed Portraits of Emily and Anne Brontë and their Aunt Branwell* (Charlotte would not have been amused!). On the same page appears another portrait, this time *A Supposed portrait of Emily Brontë* said by her brother-in-law to be unlike her. This was just one of several supposed drawings of Emily.

Fact or Fiction?

An undated letter in Charlotte's hand, but signed Currer Bell, written from the northern industrial town of Middlesborough somehow fell into the hands of Mr Symington. A facsimile of this letter describing Middlesborough as a 'very filthy place' eventually found its way into the pages of the summer edition of *The Microcosm* published at City Chambers, Leeds. Brontë author Clement Shorter insisted Charlotte had never set foot in the town and that the letter had to be false because he claimed the paper had been manufactured *after* the author's death. Symington, himself an expert in these matters, took the letter to one of the best authorities on manuscripts, Mr E. Zaehusdorf, director of Messrs. Zaehusdorf, London. After inspecting the document, Zaehusdorf declared, 'The writer has compared the Brontë letter addressed from Hartlepool to Miss Ingledew with other letters in the British Museum written within two years, that is to say, up to 1843, and finds that the paper used in these other letters is identical in texture with the Hartlepool letter, but the sizes all vary. There can, therefore, be little doubt that the paper *is* genuine.' Experts at the British Library also thought the letter genuine. Shorter, disgusted at the thought of Miss Brontë visiting the North-East, insisted a forger must have been at work!

Conflicting Opinions of Charlotte

Edward East, reporter for the *Daily News*, said of the mauve-stockinged Charlotte, 'I believe that she was too strong a nature to give way to grief. She faced the spectres of the mind, and laid them; and she had one resource, denied to others, in that she could pour out her passion upon paper.'

The *Keighley Herald* thought she was gloomy because, although she had more sunshine in herself, the harsh shadow of her surroundings showed in all except her last work.

Miss White of Bradford, who vividly remembered Charlotte when she was her governess, did not like her because she was 'shy, cold and prim. We especially hated the daily walk after lessons were done. She never said anything to interest children, and did not allow us to run about but held each of us by the hand.'

'All her life long' wrote *The Yorkshireman* in June 1879, Charlotte Brontë was 'haunted by a feeling of her own want of personal attractions. She was indeed of small stature. 'Stunted' was the word she always applied to herself ... her thick brown hair, and large expressive eyes, glowing as if some spiritual lamp illuminated them from within, caused the large nose and crooked mouth to be forgotten.'

In February 1899, Mr Ethelbert Binns told the *Leeds Mercury Supplement* that he knew of an old lady in Wilsden who owned several of the oldest portraits of Charlotte and her family known to be in existence. The old woman said she did not know of any likeness of Charlotte that was "hauf as nice as shoo wor ersen." Mr Binns agreed saying most of the drawings had 'too many hard lines, and make Charlotte appear a jealous, nagging creature, utterly devoid of that spirituelle countenance that one could best associate her character.'

R. Spence Hardy in his *Memorials of Jonas Sugden, 1858* wrote that Jonas was a great Methodist, dubbed by those who knew him as "The Walking Bible." Born in Haworth in 1767 in the house attached to Grimshaw's Methodist Chapel, he died in 1811. His last words were, "I shall soon be where the wicked cease from troubling." Spence Hardy did not feel the same way about Charlotte's character, however. Three years after her passing into the world of spirit he wrote, 'It is to be regretted, that with so much about the authoress of *Jane Eyre*, to excite our admiration and enforce our homage, she so resolutely shuts her eyes against all that is good and beautiful in evangelical religion. She seems to shrink from its approach, as if it would be to her dishonour, or as if it were something unwise and worthless; and as she sees it through a distorted medium, all her descriptions of it partake of this obliquity of vision. Her habitual reserve, partly the result of circumstances in which she was placed, prevented her from placing herself *en rapport* with the truths that would have changed entirely her intellectual being, if received in sincerity and power; and in consequence, though her descriptions of scenery are most truthful, through her pictures taken from the wild ways which still linger among families whose antique dwellings border on the moors are of thrilling interest, and there are evidences of a power of minute observance ... she is herself so sensitive, unyielding, and daring, and the world without is presented by her as so strange and wilful, that, as we close her works, we feel grateful that there is provided for man "a more excellent way," and would warn the young of the peril to which they expose themselves, when they give their minds more willingly to the fascinations of the shadowy that the discipline of the substantial.'

Things that went 'Bump' in the head

A poster printed in 1849 invited the Gentry and Public of Bingley and Neighbourhood to attend a meeting promoting the art of phrenology. 'The Factory Hands possess two hours each day, which they may turn to good account, and their highest and dearest interests should be to improve their minds – it is their duty to do so. They are not now killed with toil; they cannot say they are tired and want rest – so! Let the habit and custom of saying so cease, when the Ten-Hour Bill is Law.' Skull science is something Charlotte Brontë seems to have studied in great depth, for her writings point to it on many occasions, as we can see in *Jane Eyre*. An example of this is when Rochester 'pointed to the prominences which are said to indicate that faculty, and which, fortunately for him, were sufficiently conspicuous.' 'The *bony part* of the forehead, its form, its height, its arch, its proportion, its regularity or irregularity, mark the *disposition* and the *measure* of our *facilities*, our way of thinking and feeling.' Again, in *Shirley*, Charlotte speaks of 'two little of the organs of Benevolence and Ideality.'

The father of phrenology was Franze Joseph Gall, whom Emperor Francis of Vienna denounced as being a threat to God. Gall, after examining the heads of executed criminals and many others, believed that the brain was the organ of the mind. Interest in his work took hold in Edinburgh in 1815 where a society was formed and word spread to England and to Charlotte Brontë. Gall died in poverty in 1828.

Lectures on phreno-mesmerism were advertised as being a valuable source of information for teachers, governesses and unmarried persons. Indeed several such talks by Mr J.S. Butterworth took place at the Fleece Inn, Bingley in June 1849 – Charlotte having returned home only one week before from the east coast, after Anne's tragic death in May. Among subjects discussed were: how to choose a mate using the art of phrenology; the history of animal magnetism; suicide; the criminal mind and the history of clairvoyance. Members of the audience could volunteer either to have their heads examined phrenologically or be put into a hypnotic trace and made to perform wonderful and amazing acts on the day of the lecture. Those not wishing to attend in public could send a note to Butterworth for a private consultation at their home and for less than 10s. (50p), have a personal head chart drawn up also, accompanied by a full character reading. Booklets entitled *Phrenological and Mesmeric Chart, Miss Jenny Lind and Mesmerism, Poetic Phrenology, &c*, were available at all booksellers in the town.

In 1850, Charlotte's journalist friend Harriet Martineau persuaded her to take part in a mesmerism experiment. Martineau herself indulged in the art of Table-Rapping in the hope of receiving messages from the dead. The following item is taken from a supposed conversation overheard between two dead souls as printed in *The Voice of Good Spirits, Keighley, 1855*. "Have you ever heard of Table-Rapping?" And I said "Table Rapping! What do you mean by Table-Rapping?" And she said "Well friend, you must understand, that the good spirits go to a Table, where those in the flesh place their hands on the Table and the good Spirits move it for them, and then they can communicate with those in the flesh." And I said, Well friend, I should be very *glad*, if you could take me to a place where there is some Table-Rapping. And she said with a loud voice, "I will take thee to a place where thou can communicate with thy own sister!" And we flew away towards this dwelling … my little friend says, "You must take notice of how they do, and how they rap, and you must do the same." I then began to move the table: I soon found out that I could communicate with those in the flesh."

During the summer of 1851, a Mr and Mrs 'Fraser' were admitted to the London offices of Dr T.P. Browne (not to be confused with the London premises of Professor Fred Browne, a real hair wig specialist who invented an infallible method of measuring the head). The doctor immediately thought them both an oddly matched pair for the man was tall, young and attractive whilst the woman, was small, plain and much older. In reality, the 'couple' was none other than Charlotte Brontë and her publisher George Murray Smith (this was not the first time Charlotte had used an alias, for sometimes she called herself 'Charles Thunder' using part of her Christian name and the English form of her surname which means *thunder* in Greek).

The 'Frasers' had come to have their 'bumps' interpreted by the doctor who was a physiognomist and a phrenologist, practising the art of telling clients' fortunes by the lumps on their heads. After taking careful readings, Browne wrote two separate reports. Mrs Fraser's was entitled, *'A Phrenological Estimate of the Talents and Dispositions of a Lady'*. Amazingly, Dr Browne, by his art, correctly detected Charlotte's highly developed powers of the mind and what he termed her 'fine organ of language.'

Mystic, poet and physiognomist, John Casper Lavater, a Swiss pastor, was the first to publish a treatise of this nature – his friend Goethe even wrote one of the chapters – between the years of 1775 to 1798 (two original volumes can be found in Keighley Reference Library). He said 'Faces are as legible as books, only they are read in much less time, and are much less likely to deceive us.' His ideas were taken so seriously that a person writing to the *Gentleman's Magazine* in 1801 said that his works, even amongst religious persons were thought as necessary in every family as the Bible itself! A servant would scarcely have been hired at one time until the descriptions and engravings of Lavater had been consulted and careful comparisons made with the lines and features of the job seeker's countenance. Lavater explained that his idea of physiognomy was, 'in a restricted sense, the art of deciphering and interpretation of the human powers.' He strongly advised that the 'physiognomist respect the importance of the knowledge of the skull. The able, intelligent physiognomist ought to bend his whole attention to the form of the head. He ought to apply himself to observe ... Ye who adore the infinite wisdom which forms and disposes things, O, stop for a moment longer and contemplate with me the skulls of men!' Lavater died an early death; he was shot.

John Casper Lavater

One wonders what Charlotte might have of read in Branwell's classical profile. Did she carefully study the contour of his face, his large bumpy forehead; determine the small, deep, sunk ferret-like eyes, the prominent nose, the soft mouth and weak chin, in a bid to seek out his strengths and his weaknesses? Did she search in vain for a germ of innocence and goodness to find only drug-induced madness in its stead? Mind you, after reading *Villette*, Mrs Gaskell asked Charlotte if she had ever tried opium!

Just a step away from the Brontë abode a new religion called Modern Spiritualism sprang up in 1853 in the shape of The Society for Investigating the Phenomena of Spirit Intercourse. Thus, Keighley's little temple earned itself the title of *The Mother Church of Spiritualism.* Penny pamphlets were sold in Keighley Market where the purchaser would be, 'ENTERTAINED, THE SEEKER AFTER THE TRUTH, ENCOURAGED AND INSTRUCTED, AND THE SECTARIAN BIGOT TAUGHT THE PERILOUS POSITION IN WHICH HE STANDS.'

Seeking Inspiration

Charlotte is believed to have visited Norton Conyers with the Sidgwick family – an Elizabethan mansion some three miles from the town of Ripon – in the summer of 1839. It is generally thought that she used her memories of this visit in her novel *Jane Eyre* when describing the mad Mrs Rochester's attic room as being 'low and dark'. Jane Eyre asks Mrs Fairfax if there are any ghosts or legends connected to the attics here. The housekeeper says not, although there is a story about a mad woman whose name has been long forgotten, being imprisoned in the garret sometime during the eighteenth century.

Was this the house that fired Charlotte's vivid imagination with its long gallery, high-latticed windows, dark oak panelling and family portraits of bygone generations? And *was* Hay church modelled on nearby Wath church where Jane and Edward Rochester were about to marry before their wedding service was so cruelly interrupted? Jane then runs from the pain and humiliation Rochester has subjected her to and eventually finds herself in the fictional village of Morton.

In 1833, Ellen Nussey's brother Henry proposed marriage to Charlotte after being turned down by Mary Lutheridge and was rejected a second time. In the summer of 1845, Charlotte visited Ellen at Hathersage, Derbyshire, while Henry was away on honeymoon with his bride, the wealthy Emily Prescott. Charlotte occupied a little room in the vicarage overlooking the graveyard and found time to explore the area.

Clues can be gleaned as to how she may have used these surroundings in her novel *Jane Eyre*. For example, the name *Morton* appears on the Parish Church charity board and there is a tomb containing the dusty bones of Robert *Eyre*, knight errant, his wife Joan and their numerous offspring.

The Revd J.H. Brooksbank of Hathersage thought Charlotte took the name of her book not from these Eyres but from another Eyre clan in the area that had several Janes in the family. Alternatively, perhaps Jane was taken from Emily *Jane*? Anyway, the Eyre family erected several properties around Hathersage, including Moorseats (the fictional Rivers home Moor House?), standing beneath Stanage Edge.

Another Hathersage Eyre property – identified by the family crest in what was once the master's study – is battlemented North Lees Hall, a house of sinister aspect. Charlotte's description of Thornfield could so easily have had this particular building in mind – it being, 'three stories high, of proportions not vast, though considerable; a gentleman's manor house ... battlements round the top give it a picturesque look ... '

In a recent conversation between the author and an American Brontë enthusiast, Bud Snyder (met by chance on the track leading to Top Withens), Mr Synder said he had just come from visiting North Lees Hall where he was shown round by a chambermaid he had befriended and, for his money, *this* was Mrs Rochester's attic prison.

Charlotte describes exactly the Apostles cupboard 'in grim design' owned by the Eyre family. It was housed at North Lees until 1880 before being removed to Fox House. Was the '*dark and low*' beamed cell beyond a heavy door at the top of North Lees' once ruined square grey tower, approached by a narrow oak spiral staircase leading directly to the *third* floor, the mad woman's secret prison? It certainly fits the description given in *Jane Eyre:* 'All these relics gave to the third story of Thornfield Hall the aspect of a home of the past – a shrine of memory.' In another part of the house, below the cellar, a secret underground tunnel ran for about 400yds, having been used in the days when Roman Catholics faced persecution, ending beside a small ruined *church.* Was *this* Hay church?

Furthermore, the original whitewashed stone signpost or pillar Moscar Cross at Moscar Top might have been the place where Jane says *four roads met.* The marker, buried during the Second World War, was re-instated some twenty years later but seems to have disappeared now, as has the old coaching road of Charlotte's day. Was this place Whitecross where Jane left the stagecoach when fleeing from the horrors of Thornfield Hall?

At Coggers Lane, a *one-roomed schoolroom* erected in the early part of the eighteenth century and known as Eyre's school, could have been the school run by the fictional St. John Eyre Rivers. The Hathersage Eyre family kept a treasured rare first edition of *Jane Eyre* in pristine condition for almost one hundred years until it was auctioned off after the death of Mrs H. Eyre Williams in 1940.

Another possible clue to the mad Mrs Rochester's identity comes from a house named Springhead that stands between Oakworth and Haworth. Halliwell Sutcliffe thought it best seen in November under a dark and brooding sky when: 'the firs that stand on either side the garden walk are sober green, and moan disconsolate; the trees, sloping southward in memory of many a dead north wind, rustle in their nakedness, and are afraid; the bare house-front looks sadly out upon it all, and grieves without complaining.' Apparently, Oakworth curate James C. Bradley (alias David Sweeting of *Shirley*) told Charlotte the story of an insane wife suffering from severe delusions of the mind being imprisoned in the attic of Springhead by her husband.

In Frederic Montagu's *Gleanings of Craven* published in 1838, there was an interesting sketch, set at the Commercial Inn, Ambleside, which has been compared to the story of Rochester's mad wife. The passage begins, 'Midnight had scarcely fallen when I heard voices in the room below, and by a light which grew stronger every moment, I felt certain that some person was about to ascend the ladder. At this moment, every murder committed which I had read or heard of, crowded upon my brain, and I instantly determined to make the best fight I could; so, taking my pistols into bed, I kept my fingers on the triggers, and with my partially closed eyes turned towards the trapdoor. I had only just time to make my arrangements, when, clad in a white gown fastened close up to her neck, with her black hair matted by carelessness hanging over her collar, and as pale as death, ascended my hostess. I shall never forget her dreadfully hideous expression; she came up to the bed-side, and looked at me for a full minute, and after passing a candle carefully before my eyes, left me ... in a sort of frenzy she seized the bedclothes.'

I have found no evidence to connect any of the Brontës with this work.

Jane, in her frantic search for Rochester, says "I beheld a railing, then the house-scarce, by this dim light, distinguishable from the trees, so dank and green were its decaying walls." It is easy to see why Charlotte picked the secluded ruin of Wycoller Hall near Laneshaw Bridge as the setting for Fearndene Manor, home of the blinded Mr Rochester after his deranged wife burns down Thornfield Hall. Wycoller Hall 'buried deep in a wood' was first erected in about 1596 and became the home of the Cuncliffe family for several generations.

This property has always been tenanted by both the living and the dead. There have been numerous sightings here of several terrifying ghosts directly linked to previous occupants. Stories abound of gypsy curses, gruesome murders and the ghost of a white horse and rider galloping wildly across the double-arched packhorse bridge close by the hall. Wycoller, now in a ruinous condition, was more intact in the Brontës' day, for the haunted upstairs chambers still existed, but by 1948 farmers' pigs wallowed happily in thick mud inside the forlorn old hall which had become overgrown by tangled weeds. Only tumbled down piles of stone traced the ancient walls although the great fireplace, partly defaced by graffiti and pockmarks made by gunshot, still stood. Villagers living here in the early 1900s were very poor and often had

"Miss Brontë, I loves 'oo!" – Charlotte seated at the table with the Reed family *(St George's magazine)*

only flour porridge to eat and candles for light. There were no toilets, electricity, gas or running water inside the cottages. The ghost hamlet of Wycoller fell rapidly into ruin in the twentieth century and lay abandoned for many years. It is a curious fact that when the first illustrated edition of *Jane Eyre* appeared in 1872, a drawing of Fearndean Manor by E.M. Wimperis was based on Kirklees Hall, near Huddersfield not Wycoller.

Charlotte thought her employer Mrs John Benson Sidgwick treated her no better than a common servant. She depicted her employer – whose remains lie in a quiet little graveyard at Riddlesden, Keighley – as the awful Mrs Reed turning her home at Stonegappe, Lothersdale (*alias* Beggars' Valley – possibly meaning 'a place for refugees') into the fictitious Gateshead Hall featured in *Jane Eyre*. Stories told by Charlotte about Mrs Sidgwick were said by a friend of the family to be "absurd." Sarah Sidgwick had indicated that her nursery governess often spent all day lying in bed, leaving her to cope with the children. Charlotte, she said, possessed a "most unhappy difficult temper, and that she took offence where no offence was meant."

What The Papers Said

Lady Eastbank wrote a cruel appraisal of *Jane Eyre* after publication, which appeared in the 1847 edition of the *Quarterly Review*,

> '*Jane Eyre*, as a work, and one of equal popularity, is, in almost every respect, a total contrast to '*Vanity Fair*.' The characters and events, though some of them masterly in conception, are coined expressly, for the purpose of bringing out great effects. The hero and heroine are beings both singularly unattractive that the reader feels they can have no vocation in the novel but to be brought together; and they do things which, though not impossible lie utterly beyond the bounds of possibility ... it is stamped with a coarseness of language and laxity of tone which have certainly no excuse in ours. It is a very remarkable book: we have no remembrance of another combining such genuine power with such horrid taste.'

Two years later, on 7 December 1849 *The Times* reviewed *Shirley* just as Charlotte was visiting her publisher in London. It seems that the paper was hidden from Charlotte's gaze until she guessed the real reason for its sudden disappearance, after which George Smith's mother produced it. Lifting the paper close to her short-sighted eyes, she read these words:

> 'SHIRLEY – By the Author of JANE EYRE
> With all its faults, 'Jane Eyre ' was a remarkable production. The volumes were disfigured by coarseness; in the final development of the plot the craft of the bookmaker was more commendable that the subtle and fine working of the master; after the story had been told, pages and pages of unnecessary matter were forced upon the reader to complete three imperfect volumes, and to spoil two which could hardly be improved; yet, in spite of these ... the early scenes of 'Jane Eyre' are not to be surpassed ... '

As to *Shirley*, the journalist wrote:

> 'Personages ... come and go without exciting anything more satisfactory than a sigh or a yawn ... indeed the whole structure seems erected for the simple

purpose of enabling these creatures of the author's brain-certainly not of our everyday world- to do nothing, but to talk in the manner of such purely intellectual companions. And it would be unjust to the fair authoress ... if we did not allow that at times the talk is worthy of her genius and that gems of rare thought and glorious passion shine here and there throughout her volumes. But the infrequent brilliancy seems but to make more evident and unsightly the surrounding gloom. *"Shirley"* is not a real picture of real life ... It is a mental exercise that can bring its author no profit ... *"Shirley"* is at once the most high flown and stalest of fictions.'

The poor girl wept tears after reading this hurtful article, coming as it did so soon after the tragic loss of her siblings. She must have felt the all world was against her. Little did those unjust anonymous critics dream of the fame that would follow Charlotte beyond the grave. Indeed, during the spring of 1850 she informed a friend that Haworth folk were actually fighting over who should read the new copies of *Shirley* first! In the end members of the Mechanics' Institute cast lots to decide who should get the three volumes, which the winner was only allowed to keep for two days or risk being fined a whole shilling (5p). At the same time, the authoress included a cutting from an American newspaper written by a poor emigrant known to her from Haworth on the subject of *Jane Eyre*. Charlotte judged the contents to be a "curious mixture of both truth and inaccuracy".

In and out of Fashion

Brontë admirer, Methodist preacher and blacksmith, Robert Collyer was born in Keighley. His father, a Nelson man, fell at the Battle of Trafalgar. Robert became a 'missionary at large', leaving the relative safety of Ilkley, where he had lived for many years, for the shores of the New World (America) in 1850, to call heathens to God. One day, when browsing in a market his homesick eyes joyfully alighted upon a copy of *Jane Eyre* lying on a bookstall, which he purchased for twenty-five cents. Taking it home, he sat down and read on until the last page was finished. Afterwards he recorded, 'I felt I was being borne away on invisible wings right into the old nest. I saw the hills and the moors again, standing out against the northern skies, heard the old tongue again, and was folded back into the old life, could hear the bells ringing in the steeples and the voices singing in the churches, and watched the light play on the faces at the old fireside.'

In 1877, Sir T. Wemyss Reid wrote in the *Heckmondwick Herald* of Charlotte's dwindling celebrity status, 'The fashion which exalted her to such a pinnacle of fame, like many another fashions, has lost its vogue, and the present generation wrapped in admiration of another school of fiction. Has consigned the works of Currer Bell to a premature sepulchre. But her friends need not despair, for, from that dreary tomb of neglect an hour of resurrection must come, and the woman who has given us three of the most masterful books of the century, will again assert her true position in the literature of her country,' That prophecy was more than fulfilled.

Still In Fashion

Famous Huddersfield actor, the late James Mason, an ardent fan of the Brontës, visited the Parsonage Museum in June 1969, accompanied by his daughter

Portland, having just completed the film *Spring and Port Wine*. He said that he wanted to fulfil a life-long ambition of both acting in and directing a re-make of *Jane Eyre* the following year. Mason, then living in America, had approached Fox Studios with his ambitious project but was turned down because they said he wasn't famous enough to support a leading role in the USA unless he could attract a big name American actress to play the part of Jane. To this end, James approached Joanna Woodward, and also sent a script to Audrey Hepburn's agent but since neither was interested, he settled for a "very enthusiastic" British actress Rita Tushingham to play the part of Jane. James interviewed several writers before settling on John Byrne who wrote the classic *Room at the Top*, filmed in Keighley. Filming was to take place in Ireland because "There are buildings there, which are equivalent to the ones in the story and we could easily find a suitable house for Rochester's 'pad'."

Sadly, nothing ever came of the actor's dream, for American star George C. Scott, who was able to get studio backing took up the idea to re-create a film version of *Jane Eyre*. Pipped at the post once before when he wanted to make a film of the Brontës' life, one can only imagine how James Mason felt on receiving this news.

Goodbye Dear Ellen

On the day of the burial of Charlotte's best friend, Ellen, torrential rain fell as the cortege moved slowly down Moor Lane, Gomersal in November 1897. It was a perfect day for a funeral: a small gathering of mourners clad in black stood around the open grave beneath an equally black thunderous sky at Birstall churchyard in front of the curious Gothic church.

During her lifetime, Ellen had been a true and faithful friend to Charlotte and, in return, Ellen was to be remembered as Caroline Helstone in *Shirley*. On 27 June 1952, a Mrs Brooke told *The Yorkshire Observer* that Ellen Nussey once showed her a gold-clasped bracelet made out of braided hair from Charlotte's head, which Ellen wore as a reminder of their old friendship. (Did Charlotte have any hair left when she went to her grave?)

Religion ruled Ellen's existence, for the church was her favourite theme. She gave every tram conductor in Birstall a Testament at the time of Queen Victoria's Diamond Jubilee. Lawyers warned her friend Mrs Brooke not to remove anything from the house after her death, otherwise she would be arrested! The thought had never entered poor Mrs Brooke's head. We would have known so much more about the history of Ellen's precious Brontë possessions if only someone had bothered to ask this lady what Miss Nussey had told her ...

Remembering Charlotte

Remembering Charlotte

Each little relic of thy sojourn here,
Each deed of love and kindness thou hast done,
Thy name in Yorkshire hearts will aye endear.

Elsie M. Lush, Bradford

2 | The Brontë Family

Born on St. Patrick's Day, Patrick Brontë was named in honour of the Saint who drove out snakes and preached the Gospel to Irish pagans. Patrick Brontë (who took both sugar *and* salt in his tea) and his wife Maria (the latter dying of cancer in September 1821) were responsible for the beginning of the Brontë cult. Nicknamed "Old Staff", due to his habit of carrying a shillelagh or stick everywhere with him, he caused Haworth poet Joseph Hardacre to pen these lines:

> The neat shillelah, (sillelagh) strong and stout
> That scorns to break or bend to ought,
> But lately from Hibernia brought,

Contrary to adverse reports about Patrick, he was known for his acts of unlimited kindness during the forty-one years he spent ministering in Haworth – a far cry from those early days in the village, when hostile rustics cried, "Here comes a Paddy!" According to the *Keighley Herald* he was, "Friend and patron to every agency that came to the village." Martha Brown reinforced this statement when she said, "A kinder man could not be, although he was sometimes queer and reserved before strangers."

There are those who have hinted that Patrick was an inconsiderate father to his motherless children. However, I am certain that he did the best he could for his family. Other children of the day were not so privileged, however, and some as young as five were forced to slave underground in Wilsden and Bradford. The little mites were constantly cold, filthy and wet and, until the 1842 Children's Employment Act, these poor children only saw the light of day on a Sunday. During the course of their long and miserable working day, young girls were harnessed with chains about the waist and between their legs before being hooked up to a cartload of coal that had to be dragged from the bottom of the mineshaft to the surface.

One inhabitant said of him "he'd ha' gi'en you owt nearly." This sentiment might be echoed when, at a Vestry meeting held on 17 June 1829, Patrick suggested that rather than erect a purpose built workhouse to accommodate the poor of Haworth, the committee should buy two or three cottages in the best situation they could find. Joseph Craven stated there was a field known as the "Workhouse Field", a little past Robinson's Mill on the old packhorse route from Stanbury to Haworth Moor. However, it appears that Patrick's idea was never followed up, for the poor and destitute were packed off to a dilapidated farmhouse-cum-workhouse at Exley Head near Oakworth, instead.

Charles Hale wrote the following illuminating tale about Patrick's character when he visited Haworth soon after the old man's death in 1861:

'The sexton has his own portrait painted by Branwell – and the joiner has three pictures of his, which the following singular and interesting story attaches: – 'One time Charlotte had set her heart on something in his (joiner's) shop which she desired for the better furnishing of the house: I thought Brown said a mirror, but this seems hardly characteristic. After a while, Mr Brontë consented to the purchase and the article was sent for and delivered. The price was five guineas. Now Branwell had been sent to study, (or "apprenticed" as they said here) with an artist in Leeds named Bradley; and under the eye and with the assistance of his master he had executed three oil paintings: one representing Jacob's Dream, and two others. These his father had purchased of the master for ten guineas. Accordingly when the joiner went to the parsonage to get his money (or "brass" as they say here) he found Mr Brontë and Charlotte sitting by the new piece of furniture and the father told him he would give him these three pictures which had cost ten guineas, in payment for his bill of five. Our simple joiner of course was somewhat disconcerted at this proposition, which would pay him with something that he could not but regard as nearly worthless to him; and would have refused point blank but Charlotte ("Char-lotty" he always said: three syllables) looked at him so pleadingly that he held his peace; until presently Mr Brontë went out of the room saying, "Well you may do just as you please; you may take away your Mirror (or whatever it was) or you may take away Branwell's three paintings. Suit yourself, I have nothing more to say." Then Char-lotty said, "Now William, please take the pictures and I will make it up to you some time." So his heart softened and he went away with the pictures; 'though I felt like a fool" said he "as I came down the lane, to come back with three pictures not worth a sixpence instead of the brass that I expected." But Charlotte did make it up to him – for when she became famous and rich she gave him an order to renew the furniture of the house from top to bottom throughout with his own make. And since her death and Branwell's he has been offered a very large sum of money (I think 50 guineas) for the paintings; but he will not sell them at that price.' He told me with some pride parenthetically that the Rocking Chair, which he made for Mr Brontë as part of this refitting of the house, was so good it sold at the sale for three times its first cost to the Brontës.'

A rival minister once taunted him by saying he could not pray without a prayer book. He was made to eat those words when, after the minister took ill, Patrick Brontë went into this fellow clergyman's home and prayed fervently with him, handing him a gold sovereign in order to purchase food and medicine.

One grateful parishioner, knowing that Auld Lang Syne was Patrick's favourite Scottish tune, stood in the parsonage garden, just after the church clock struck the hour of nine one evening and played the chords to it on a portable musical instrument. At once, Pat threw open his bedroom window so that he would not miss one single musical note.

Patrick's poetry, we are told in *Local Notes and Queries*, was the 'merest jingling, rackety rhyme, and his prose nothing above the mediocre line', quite unlike his father Hugh, who concocted the most wonderful poetry and, being possessed of a wild and vivid imagination, told thrilling tales of devils, banshees and ghosts. Patrick did possess a sense of humour however, for when the church needed a new peel of bells, he suggested that anyone giving money for a new large tenor-bell could have their name inscribed and "thus have his praises sung for all time!" Patrick had his name and that of both churchwardens George Feather and a Mr Lambert inscribed upon the bell, thus having *their* praises rung for all time! Incidentally, these bells, originally installed in the 1840s and restored in 1988, rang out at both Charlotte's wedding and funeral.

Mrs Briggs told the *Methodist Recorder* in March 1900 how she and her beau waited three hours for the blind Patrick Brontë to rise from his sick bed to make them man and wife. They were the last couple to be married by him. Kneeling on the floor he prayed: 'God bless you, and may the blessing of Him who dwelt in the bush follow you both wherever your lot be cast.'

An Eccentric Hobby

Pockmarks seen on the old church tower facing the parsonage were supposedly made by Patrick discharging his loaded pistol from his bedroom window. Martha Brown swore she never saw her master shoot in passion. She may have been right since Patrick appears to have had a scientific reason for his seemingly eccentric actions. He is now known to have contacted the Ordnance Office regarding his new but alas old-fashioned firearms inventions. Village gossips at the time whispered that the parson discharged his pistol in order to quieten his children or ward off would-be burglars! He taught his daughter Emily to shoot. During the 1960s, Patrick's gun and watch were stolen, even though the whole parsonage was wired up to Haworth Police Station! These thefts amused the locals no end.

Loved and Lost

A slanderous story circulating in America during the twentieth century told of Patrick being infatuated with a girl not yet in her teens. This tale was, of course, untrue, though he *did* offer to wed his old love Mary Mildred Davy Burder when his wife Maria Brontë died, but she refused him. The following narrative, by the daughter of Mary Burder was published in the *Keighley News, March 1926*:

'In the year 1806 Patrick Brontë took his Bachelor's Degree at Cambridge, and in October of the same year appeared in the village of Wethersfield, in Essex, as the new curate. His first writing in the parish church register is a baptism on October 12, 1806. Mr Brontë found a home in Wethersfield with an elderly maiden lady, named Mildred Davy, who was a cripple. She was a well-educated woman of good repute. Her sister had married Mr John Burder, a farmer in very good circumstances, living at a farm called 'The Broad,' three miles from Wethersfield. He was loved and respected by all who knew him. Shortly before Mr Brontë's arrival, the Burder family did not attend the parish church; they were dissenters and worshipped at the village meetinghouse. The story goes that Mary Burder was sent one day to her aunt, Miss Davy, at Wethersfield with a present of game from her mother. Mary stayed and helped her aunt prepare it for the dinner and spent the day there. That was the first meeting of Mary Burder (aged eighteen) and the Revd Patrick Brontë. Henceforth, Mary's visits to Auntie Mildred were frequent, and of course, Patrick took the young lady home at night. To all intents and purposes they were mutually agreed and happy, and on the road to an "engagement." But true love never did run smooth, as the old adage has it. Fate stepped in, in the person of Mary's uncle, her father's brother, who lived at Yeldham, and was her father's executor and Mary's guardian. It is said that the uncle was a cold, heartless, stern man, and on hearing of the attachment that had sprung up between his niece and a curate, who was also an Irishman, he wanted to know all about it. He did not get to know all he wanted, but said the affair must stop at once. But go on it did, until later on he invited Mary to his house at Yeldham, and kept her there, virtually a prisoner, waiting for love letters that never came. This was not Patrick's fault, as his letters were intercepted. When she returned to Wethersfield, Patrick Brontë had gone to another curacy at Wellington, in Shropshire, but no one knew where he had gone. Mary's letters to him had been demanded from him, and he returned them. When Mary opened them there was her lover's face in profile on a small card, and under it were the words: 'Mary, you have torn my heart. Spare the face.' I think they never met again.'

Miss Burder eventually became the wife of Revd Peter Sibree. She died in 1866 at the age of seventy-seven.

And so To Rest

Patrick, living beyond the 'allotted span' of the Psalmist drew his last breath on Friday 7 June 1861. After the funeral service, a village plasterer whitewashed over the top of Patrick's final resting-place where "he laid a corpse."

AT HAWORTH CHURCH
As Memory evokes his long-lost dears,
Children of Genius, that sleeps below.
Poor lonely Patriarch! If weak and slow
They faltering step, what matter? If it nears
Their time and sound wax fainter, clearer glow
The things unknown to mortal eyes and ears
They, let me learn thy wisdom ere I leave!

> *Flowers from the Glen, The Poetical Remains of James Waddington, Saltaire 1862*

The Brontë Brood

First To Come and First To Go

The first born and prettiest child, Maria, who her father thought the most gifted and intelligent of all his brood, possessed "a heart under Divine Influence." As her parents were married on 29 December 1812, it is probable that Maria arrived during the last quarter of 1813. Born at Clough Lane, Hightown, Spen Valley and baptised in April 1814 at Hartshead church, her baptism entry in the register is the only one containing the mother's name. After the death of her mother, little Maria naturally became a guardian to her younger brother and sisters, until God called her home.

Maria's stark obituary appeared in the *Leeds Intelligencer* on 12 May 1825, 'On Friday last ... of consumption, in the twelfth year of her age, Miss Brontë, eldest daughter of the Revd P. Brontë, incumbent of Haworth, near Keighley.'

Appearing in the same death column was another child's more touching obituary, 'To the inexplicable grief of her parents and friends, Jane Elizabeth Cross, only daughter of Mr John Cross, of this place (Leeds): a child of affectionate and most endearing disposition, and of a peculiar precocity of intellect.'

Maria was to be immortalised forever in *Jane Eyre* in the personage of Helen Burns, when Charlotte writes, "And shall I see you again, Helen when you die?" Helen assured her she would, but Jane questions her further, "Where is that region? Does it exist?" The two fall asleep in each other's arms but only Jane awakes from her slumbers.

'The Master called out Elizabeth.' On 18 June 1825, four weeks after Maria's death, her sister Elizabeth (meaning consecrated to God), also born at the house in Hightown, gave way to the same illness. Charlotte was to immortalise Elizabeth too, in her novel *Jane Eyre*, as Julia Severn. Mrs Gaskell claimed on page ten of the Haworth edition of Charlotte's *Life* that Elizabeth was born at Hartshead on 27 July 1814 (according to author Isabel C. Clarke she arrived sometime in February 1815) and was christened at Thornton sometime during August 1815. Both Maria and Elizabeth died at Haworth.

Emily – The Loner

In the words of Charles Simpson, 'Seldom has a phantom so vast and so shadowy been raised above a personality so elusive as this real Emily.' She was born at a time when old traditions and moorland legends gripped many, but with a waning power. Her illness had begun with a slight fever – worse at night: flying stitches, a flushed face, a sharp pain to her side and salty spit. After a time, the dry cough she had acquired became worse and she began to vomit after eating.

Virginia Moore believed Emily Jane actually wanted to die and that that the facts of Emily's death were 'almost as if she had drunk of a deadly poison.' The girl refused to take any of the medicine (except *Lowcock's Cough Wafers*) that Charlotte or doctors tried to administer. Perhaps she was afraid they were intent on harming her in some way. Was this the reason for Charlotte saying Emily that was reluctant to leave life? Charlotte thought her sister possessed 'a secret power and fire' within, but had 'no worldly wisdom' to match, that her will was 'not very flexible' and her spirit 'altogether unbending.' Emily's triumphant last lines were, *'No coward soul is mine.'*

Death came to Emily Jane Brontë at two o'clock on a Tuesday mid-winter afternoon, as she lay exhausted on the sitting room sofa at Haworth Rectory. Only three hours after rising she finally succumbed to the deadly white death (tuberculosis) that had invaded her frail body, causing her to cough up blood, turning her joints white and dragging her slowly and painfully into an early grave. Her slender coffin was five feet seven inches long by sixteen inches deep.

Death of a Genius

Fly then
To thy coffin Emily
If thou must
To lie in death
And turn to dust.

– Marie Campbell, 1999

Charlotte said that Emily "died in a time of promise": for she was never to know that she and her family were destined to become famous for all time.

Emily Remembered

Emily preferred to stay at home and write her poetry, work on her manuscripts or play the pieces of Mozart she had learned from her music teacher, Abraham Sunderland, on a cheap cottage piano in the parlour, provided by her father. Her favourite pastime of all, however, was to wander the beloved moors she understood so well.

"I remember Emily Brontë walking in Haworth, a quiet unassuming lass, with simple long clothes" said Joshua Baldwin.

Emily's friend Mary Robinson described her as being 'a tall long-armed girl, elastic as to tread, with a slight figure that looked queenly in her best dresses, but loose and boyish when she slouched over the moors, whistling the dogs and taking long strides over the *rough* earth.'

According to a report in the *Bradford Observer* dated 17 February 1894, "Emily was wont to sit bolt upright in the corner of the pew, as motionless as a statue. Her compressed mouth and drooping eyelids and indeed her whole demeanour appeared to indicate strong innate power. A large protruding tooth added to her peculiar aspect." Mrs Gaskell thought, "Emily must have been a remnant of the Titans" because her expression was mostly a stern one. Mildred A. Dobson believed that Emily whom she christened the "dark sphinx" in spite of her Christian background was predominantly pagan and Princess Amelie Troubetzkoy said of her, "Emily Brontë has always seemed to me a white flame and a dark flame rolling upward – but, mind you, no evil in the darkness." While Sir Clifford Allbutt complained publicly, that nobody could get along with the girl.

In the 1920s, Brontë enthusiast and author Mrs Clarke declared that Emily practised 'Roman mysticism' after discovering a 'queer' book in M. Heger's library on the subject of ecstatic nuns entitled *The Spiritual Espousal*. This little volume, she says, encouraged Emily to write *Wuthering Heights* and some of her best poetry, including *No Coward Soul is Mine*.

Friends and Influences

The following passage, taken from the pages of *Eugene Aram* published in 1832, evokes Emily Brontë's persona for me, conjuring up her innermost thoughts. 'These herbs at your feet, I know their secrets – I watch the mechanism of their life, the winds – they have taught me their language.' (Emily, on the other hand, said "The wind I hear it sighing"). 'The stars – I have unravelled their mysteries; and these, the creatures and ministers of God – these I offend not my mood – to them I utter my thoughts and break forth into my dreams, without reserve and without fear. But men disturb me – I have nothing to confide in them; they cripple the wild liberty which has become to me a second nature. What its shell is to the tortoise, solitude has become to me – my protection, nay, my life.' It has been said that an "interpreter ought always to have stood between her (Emily) and the world."

Emily had much in common with the occultist Edward Bulwer-Lytton; among other things, they were both great mystics. He was particularly interested in the power of clairvoyance and the mysteries of dreams, which he described as "spectral phenomena ... turned inside out".

Bulwer-Lytton, Grandmaster of the Scottish Rite of Freemasonry, was born on 25 May 1803 at 31 Baker Street, London. He produced *The Haunters and the Haunted* based on the mystery and supernatural horrors of 50 Berkeley Square, Mayfair, London. This tale is considered one of the most terrifying ghost stories ever to have been written. He was a good friend of Benjamin Disraeli, who visited the Aire valley, composing part of *Sybil* while sitting by the Druids' Altar above Bingley. Disraeli was also acquainted with John Nicholson, the ill-starred Airedale poet. Others included in his circle of friends were the poet Matthew Arnold and economist Harriet Martineau both of whom knew Charlotte Brontë. In fact, a book written by Miss Martineau and inscribed to Miss C. Brontë, entitled *Eastern Life, Past and Present*, is held at Keighley Reference Library. Both Martineau and Bulwer-Lytton were converts to mesmerism

Mystic Lord Lytton, author of *Eugene Aram (The Life, Letters ... of Edward Bulwer, Lord Lytton, by his son, 1882)*

and believed in spirit manifestation. Martineau attempted to practice the art of mesmerism on Charlotte Brontë at her Ambleside home but for some unknown reason stopped the experiment. Bulwer-Lytton spent an autumn at Harrogate taking the famous Yorkshire health-giving spa waters in 1854. When Bulwer-Lytton died in 1873, he was buried on the south side of St. Edmund's Chapel in Westminster Abbey.

Miss Romer Wilson, who wrote *All Alone*, said that Aunt Branwell shut little Emily up in the room where her mother had just died. This cruel action caused the child to fall into a strange trance-like state after which she began to experience weird terrifying devilish dreams. Wilson also claimed that Emily was really a male locked inside in a woman's body. Writer Charles Simpson described her as being "happy as a boy – a wayward, friendly boy ... and gallant."

Theories about Emily's sexuality

American writer, Virginia Moore, claimed in her book *The Life and Eager Death of Emily Brontë* that Emily turned down four marriage proposals. Miss Moore raises the theory that Emily was in fact a lesbian. This idea seems to have been based on Charlotte having said that Emily was "stronger than a man," and M. Heger passing comment that she *should* have been a man. Haworth village folk agreed that she seemed more like Branwell's brother than sister and of course, there was her supposed aversion to (or just plain shyness of) men. It has long been thought, though never proved, that Emily had a secret lover. Perhaps, during her time at Law Hill, she secretly found a close female companion. Did she offer her heart to an unknown female living at Halifax? A painful and unrequited love causing her to write the lines:

> And yet for all her hate, each parting glance would tell
> A stronger passion breathed, burned in this last farewell.

George Henry Lewes had a very effeminate look about him, combined with a boyish expression. He was considered by many to be an ugly, effeminate type of man. Mrs Gaskell told Ellen Nussey that Charlotte was almost moved to tears when meeting Lewes for the first time because his features were so like Emily's – an identical slightly aquiline nose, beautiful hazel eyes, brown hair and that prominent mouth of hers. Charlotte thought a pencil drawing of G.H. Lewes sketched by Anne Gliddon in 1840 (holding what appears to be an opium pipe) also looked uncannily like Emily. Did Emily lead a double life and was Heathcliff actually the male side of her hidden persona?

Having advanced her theories of lesbianism, Virginia Moore turned her attention to a manuscript of poetry which had been in the hands of Emily's brother-in-law until his death in 1906 and sold at auction to George Smith's widow the following year, before being passed to the British Museum in 1933. We are informed by Miss Moore that, on microscopic inspection of this particular document, dated 17 October 1838, she found the name 'Louis Parensell' which appeared above the line *"I knew not 'twas so dire a crime"*. This melancholy poem describes the pain and hurt ascribed to the sorrowful farewell of a loved one. She believed it was written at the time when Emily fell deeply in love with the mysterious Louis; she also thought that Charlotte had pencilled in the name of Emily's 'lover' after her sister's death.

Extensive enquiries were made in Haworth, Halifax and elsewhere by the author, but information about the elusive Louis continued to evade her. Finally, further scrutiny of the paper by representatives of the *Telegraph and Argus* revealed that the words Louis Parensell were actually *Love's Farewell* and Miss Moore was forced to admit that she had made a terrible mistake in deciphering the poem's title when examining Emily's little red book.

Emily liked to visit Ponden Hall. Relatives claimed she was besotted with Robert Heaton and he with her. Robert was supposed to have planted a pear tree in his garden in honour of Emily Brontë. Edith Heaton told the *T.V. Times* in 1979 that, 'It was always accepted that there was something between Robert and Emily' but family differences on both sides forbade a union between the two. It would be nice to think Emily found love before going to her maker. As for Robert he died a bachelor on the 3 March 1898 aged seventy-six, grieving for his brother and close companion, Thomas Midgley Heaton who had passed away only weeks before.

Emily's Verses

After Emily's death, her sister Charlotte chose to publish a small selection of Emily's unpublished poetry. Long after Charlotte's time, Arthur Bell Nicholls lent "in what was certainly an evil hour" a manuscript containing more unpublished poetry written in the hand of his late wife's sister, to Clement Shorter, who had them published privately (*Dodd, Mead & Co. 1902*). It transpired that there was an amount of poetry attributed to Emily, which was not of her making and in 1911, this newspaper article appeared,

The Brontë Sisters' Secret.
Emily's poems altered by Charlotte.
New Manuscript found
This is the question raised by Mr Davidson Cook. Within the last few years justice has been done to the memory of Emily Brontë, many critics now believe that her novel *Wuthering Heights* far excels in merit any of the Brontë novels ... The question of the real authorship of the poems which have appeared under the name of Emily Brontë is of peculiar interest. Mr Cook has had access to a manuscript volume of poems, in the handwriting of Emily Brontë, which is in the possession of Mr A.J. Law. This volume contains thirty one poems, dated 1838 to 1846, and the comparison has been made between the poems which Emily wrote and those which appeared in print under the revision of her sister Charlotte shows some amazing discrepancies.' 'The publication increases our admiration for the selective ability of Charlotte Brontë' wrote the *Keighley Herald* on 5 November. But 'the poems printed add nothing to, if they do not subtract from the high estimation placed upon Emily Brontë's ... works and that sometimes the more you add, the more you take away. It is something like an insult to the memory of these talented sisters to publish now, what had been deliberately culled out as unworthy of her matured talents.'
'The differences between Emily's written lines and Charlotte's printed version must be accounted the work of the editor, and the author of *Jane Eyre* cannot be freed from the onus of tampering with her sister's poems and vitiating (corrupting) the text by a tinkering process of alteration, addition and suppression, of which no hint in presenting the poems to the public.'

'The plain truth is that Charlotte was inferior to Emily as a poet' wrote a correspondent for the *Telegraph & Argus*. Nevertheless, Clement Shorter, having managed to obtain the copyright in all the Brontë writings that were still protected by law, encouraged C.W. Hatfield to publish two further volumes of Brontë poems in 1926.

Was There More?

Unanswered questions remain today about the elusive Emily. Did she really write a sequel to *Wuthering Heights*? When she finished *Wuthering Heights*, she would have had almost two years in which to bequeath the world another masterpiece. A letter, dated February 1848 was recovered from her writing desk in an envelope addressed in the same hand. It was to Ellis Bell, Esq., from her London publisher Newby and seems to indicate that there really was an unpublished manuscript in existence. Within the text of this correspondence, Newby promises to make arrangements for her next novel to be published.

Just weeks before Emily's death Charlotte hoped her sister would refuse Newby her new manuscript for publication because of his past incompetence. If there really was a second manuscript, it has yet to surface. What was the real reason behind Charlotte's seeming total lack of sentiment when destroying her dead sister's personal effects so soon after her death? Was it because they held the key to Emily's secret, innermost thoughts, needs and desires for love, some side of the outwardly cranky sister that Charlotte was unable to comprehend or perhaps a more sinister reason?

As we know, Emily was a very private soul, who guarded her secrets well. She appeared to shun most human contact, preferring instead the company of animals and the freedom of her storm-driven moors. She left us no real clues as to her personal dreams, unless of course Charlotte did burn her confidential diary papers and perhaps even a second novel. After all, if Emily kept her first work hidden then she probably did the same with its sequel.

A Few Last Words ...

Writer Halliwell Sutcliffe, reported the *Keighley News* on 11 March 1922, had

'wandered on many moors in his time, but there was one, Haworth Moor, on which he was born, on which he was bred, and which he understood. He had walked along Haworth Moor at pretty well at all times of the day and night, and in all seasons, and there was something about that moor a something that no other had. He had been privileged to feel it. It had not one magic only, nor one call only. It had a charm he could not describe. He remembered once, it was broad sunlight in the middle of winter. He was alone, and he came to a place away at the back of Haworth Moor, a place he had never been in before – a place he knew nothing about then – but if he had dared to be such a coward he would have cut and run. The place was appalling in its terror. "I do not know what black tragedy might have been there in times gone by. I can only say the mystery was absolutely unmistakable. Mr Sutcliffe said he wished to make a public confession of faith of the inspiration and the joy that Emily Brontë had been to him personally. Not only Emily as a writer, though that was great, but Emily the liver of life; her clean and marvellous courage – courage against what seemed to him almost insurmountable hardship. It was her example of living and the wonder of her writing that had made Emily Brontë to him what Joan of Arc was to the soldiers of France.'

These few words by Mr Sutcliffe sum up Emily best: 'It is Emily whose presence seems at times to overshadow Haworth ... we see her climb up, until her figure slight against the sunset red, dips over the moor-crest and is lost. The wilderness has found its mate.'

'When such wonderful creatures as Charlotte and Emily have passed away, it is quite understandable – although a bootless quest – that we, the leather and prunella of this world, make comparisons of one with the other; and ... there have been people who profess to believe, or genuinely believe, Emily to have been the greater. Of such opinions I have nothing to say more than this, that, if Emily surpassed the author of *Jane Eyre, Shirley, Villette*, and that little gem

PRIVATE VIEW

Script writing with the Brontës (Punch, September 1957)

without a flaw, *The Professor,* then that lady must reign as the greatest English woman writer of fiction the world has yet known'.
– *Henry Williams, 16 April 1924.*

Branwell – The Only Son

Red-haired Branwell was born a 'naturally brilliant' boy, but if we are to believe his critics, he grew into a self-indulgent and dissolute man, mostly preferring to pass his time in the company of innkeepers and village rustics. Using his gift of words to 'set the table in a roar.'

Social (and otherwise) Habits

Branwell, the dutiful schoolmaster would take his pupils over to the church, where his favourite trick was to retire into a corner near one of the windows and close his mind to all but the book he was reading, which of course was *not* a prayer book!

After attending the funeral service for his aunt, Branwell never again set foot inside Haworth church until his own corpse was laid to rest close by the square family pew with its worn hassocks and green baize seats.

Had it not been for John Brown (who Branwell dubbed the Knave of Trumps), the village sexton and stonemason who joined the Freemasons in September 1830, freemasonry might have been lost to Haworth. The Order moved to Newell Hill (now Lodge Street) in the autumn of 1833, where they rented a room in a property belonging to Mr William Eccles; they continued to meet there until moving to larger premises in 1907. Traces of Masonic decorations in the old lodge rooms were still visible in recent years. Brown remained an active member of the lodge until his death in 1855. His friend Branwell was accepted into the circle on 29 February 1836 at the tender age of nineteen – even though he was two years below the minimum accepted age. According to *The History of the Three Graces Lodge No. 408, Haworth 1792-1931,* he quickly advanced to the degree of master mason. The last meeting Branwell attended was on Boxing Day 1842. Is the yellow silk square, edged with occult symbols connected to Freemasonry, and reputedly belonging to Branwell Brontë, in anonymous private hands?

Stanbury lad, John Robinson, remembered Branwell as being different from the rest of his family, saying that he was 'of a more gay disposition' particularly when he was holding court in his favourite seat amidst the rickety furniture of the small parlour at the Black Bull. The original three-cornered chair belonging to William Sugden, landlord of the Black Bull Inn, which Branwell claimed as his, is now housed in the Brontë Museum. A replica of the chair is kept at the turn of the stairs at the Black Bull in memory of the gin drinking Branwell, who also had a favourite chair at the Lord Nelson. We know the mercurial Branwell was something of a wizard in the field of entertainment. One of his many party tricks was to take a pen in each hand, writing with each pen at the *same* time on two completely separate subjects whilst discussing a third!

Among Branwell's other favourite haunts, was the George, on Market Street, Bradford which really ought to have been named The Bohemian, for it was here that notable painters, writers and artists rendezvoused – Charles Dickens stayed here for one night in 1854. Branwell was often seen in the Talbot Hotel, Bradford: the Conservatives' headquarters. I wonder if he ever frequented Laycock's dram shop nicknamed 'Hell's Kitchen'? The Cock, in Halifax was another, as well as the Lord Nelson at Luddenden, situated in the quaintest part of the village. This hostelry became a haven to Branwell and his Halifax cronies who visited the library here, founded in 1776 and housed in an upper chamber. For many years, the inn, dating back to the time of Charles I, had close connections with religious organisations. During a restoration project in the 1920s, a number of old gravestones were discovered in its chimneys. Above one of the mullioned windows is a long-tailed arrow symbol very much like the one that is carved above a window at Pierce Close Farm, Cross Roads, near Haworth pointing towards the Druids' Altar, Bingley. One wonders what the significance of this curious symbol might be or is it just plain drip mouldings?

No one knows exactly where the Shake Hands beerhouse was, other than being located somewhere between Exley Head and Oakworth near Keighley, but it was here each Sunday that Branwell sent a boy to collect his eagerly awaited newspaper – a vital link to the outside world. John Clayton, licensee of the Shake Hands had his beer certificate refused in October 1868, on the grounds that the house was not rated high enough.

Was Branwell Brontë a regular patron of the taverns of Wakefield? In 1979, Mr Joshua Schofield of Horbury contacted the *Yorkshire Evening Post* convinced that an edition of *Jane Eyre* printed at the Albion Works of W. Nicholson and Sons in Wakefield – a copy of this edition being lodged in the Brontë Society archives – was of Branwell's making. Mr Schofield maintained that Branwell had stolen his sister's manuscript in order to sell it and thereby obtain drink and opium. His ill-gotten gains enabled him to frequent Wakefield gin-palaces and dens of low repute, selling adulterated, mixed and sometimes even drugged beer. Mr Schofield called for a plaque to be erected at the site of the now defunct printing works in order to commemorate the Branwell/Wakefield connection.

By the age of twenty, Branwell had acquired a considerable thirst for alcohol. At one stage, he signed a pledge – which he failed to honour, promising to abstain from 'ardent spirits' and for a limited time, was secretary of the local Temperance Society, of which his father was President. Whisht or Silent shops (illegal drinking houses) were so common in the village at one time that Patrick became worried about the moral and spiritual effect on his flock from frequenting such places. During a meeting held at the Keighley Temperance Hall in 1887, the speaker, eccentric 'Pie' Leach (he kept his coffin behind the door in his kitchen), warming to the topic of Patrick Brontë's family, asked of his captive audience, "What did they call his son?" Bill o' Hoylus End, Keighley's working man's poet, who was fond of imbibing hard liquor himself, replied, "Branwell, Mr Leach." To which Mr Leach chuckled, "Ay, he braided o' thee; he wor a drucken beggar" for it was a well-known fact that Branwell had been barred from a number of beer houses because of overindulgence.

A man named John Rushworth frequently saw Branwell at 8.30am "looking as fresh as a bobbin." Yet Elizabeth Gaskell claimed the highly-strung Branwell was not much more than a 'depraved drunkard', capable of murdering his own father! Those who knew Branwell claimed Gaskell had "told a pack o' lies" about him in her biography of Charlotte Brontë.

Just a step away from the parsonage was Bessie and Joseph Hardakers' druggist's shop on Main Street, which supplied Branwell with opium-laced laudanum – medics at the time recommended this as both a sleeping draught and a painkiller (was Branwell a hypochondriac?) Laudanum mixed with camphor and chloroform was a popular remedy for toothache. It was also taken to ward off cholera. The opium to which Branwell was also addicted was promoted in those days as giving a sort of health to the system. Constant misuse of these loathsome narcotics gave him the characteristic pallid appearance of an opium addict and caused his hands to shake.

Faithful Emily always remained devoted to her brother, often staying up late to let him into the parsonage long after the others had retired to their beds. She would leave a small lamp shining in the window to help guide her drunken, drug sodden brother home in the darkness of the night. Poor Branwell forgot that "Drunkards shall not enter the Kingdom of God." *(1.Cor. v.10)*.

Wasted Talents

The *Keighley Herald* said of him in April 1879, 'With all his talents he was not fit for association with respectable sons of the clergy.' Nevertheless, Branwell possessed a natural gift for writing and art, which came to nothing in the end, except for a quantity of poems, some of which,

The artist at work *(William Hone's Everyday Book)*

according to the *Yorkshire Post* of 31 May 1915, it 'would have been better to leave … in merciful obscurity where Charlotte was content they should remain.'

Within the musty pages of Thornton's 'Old Bell Chapel's Burial Register', spanning the years between 1807 to 1822 lies a hitherto unsolved mystery in the shape of the following four lines:

When I can see my title clear
To mansion in the skies
I'll bid farewell to every Fear
And wipe my weeping eyes.

The crabbed handwriting is said to have belonged to Patrick Brontë's forerunner, Revd Thomas Atkinson. Branwell included these lines as part of a longer poem when he wrote to William Wordsworth in January 1837; by altering just a few words, he claimed the verse as his own. How and where Branwell found these lines is the great mystery; he was not old enough to read when he left Thornton. Could his father have made a copy of the poem, which, in due course was discovered and adopted by his son?

No Coward, He

This curate's son was no coward however, for when Liberal Lord Morpeth arrived in Haworth in order to further his political career by gaining voters, Branwell and his father, both Tories, stood square against him on the 'Blue' platform placed near the Black Bull Inn. As Patrick endeavoured to put his part to Morpeth, a rented mob roared against his words, causing Branwell to rush to the fore, yelling that if they would not allow his father to have *his* say, then *they* wouldn't have one either.

Afterwards, Branwell was forced to duck into the nearest shop when the opposition marched up Main Street carrying a stuffed effigy of him, with a herring in one hand and potato in the other – symbolising the Brontë family's Irish origins – before setting it alight.

Affairs of The Heart

In July 1840, just two years after Branwell had returned from his lodgings in Bradford, a red-haired child named Mary Ann came into the world and was christened by the Revd Patrick Brontë. Whispering gossips said the child was the product of an illicit assignation between Martha Judson (nee Feather) and Branwell Brontë. True or false, within weeks of the birth, Branwell departed the village for pastures new. In a letter to a friend, Branwell refers to a 'beastly-hearted fellow' who could do him harm. Was this person Martha's legal spouse James Judson?

More shocking without doubt, is Miss Kilnsley's assertion in her book *A Pattern of Genius* that Branwell and Emily were incestuous lovers.

> For I, as usual was wrong,
> *She* was his sister, *he* a long
> Lost, loved brother.
>
> W.F. Yorkshireman

Branwell suffered the consequences of unrequited love – perhaps even dying of a broken heart, after falling in love with the wrong woman: Lydia Robinson of Thorp Green Hall, near York. She chose to elope to Gretna Green with a Scarborough actor of little or no account, according to one story. Some claimed Lydia's mother, who was seventeen years older than Branwell, seduced and tormented him. When her invalid husband died, Branwell harboured high hopes that Mrs Robinson would consent to be his wife. Dreams of married bliss were dashed when he received word via a trustee that the late Mr Robinson had stated in his will that his wife would be cut off without a penny piece if Branwell so much as tried to contact her. This was actually a lie conjured up by the widow in order to oust Branwell in favour of the elderly, but wealthy, Sir Edward Scott, whom Mrs Robinson married soon after.

However, the truth may never be known, as the Robinson family did all within its power to conceal the facts concerning the Branwell affair. Grief stricken Branwell was utterly inconsolable when the news of the marriage reached him and Patrick Brontë, fearing his only son might endeavour to kill himself, monitored his actions closely. In spite of this, the Great Architect decreed that he should die, regardless of his father's fervent prayers and on the 24 September 1848, in the third decade of his life, Branwell closed his eyes forever.

Another Brontë Lost

Dr John Bateman Wheelhouse (who Branwell dubbed *Holy Wheelhouse*) registered the cause of Branwell's death as being, 'chronic bronchitis: marasmus.' Nowadays, doctors would ascribe his demise to tuberculosis. How much more romantic if the diagnosis could have been 'died of love sickness', instead.

Branwell's poor wasted body was laid to rest in the family crypt, in the Chancel of old Haworth church. His memorial card was heavily outlined in black and decorated with an urn containing wilted flowers and folded drapery. *Note:* Black symbolises winter, mourning and justice and is dedicated to the planet Saturn the great ruler of the underworld.

For reasons that can only be speculated, Branwell disliked Dr Wheelhouse, penning a vitriolic poem about him entitled, *Holy Wheelhouse*. Here he writes amongst other things that Wheelhouse's guts 'are all his riches' and his 'temper is the Devil' and that 'his tongue no more to curse his fate'. Branwell's poem, I think, is reminiscent of two far older poems, the first penned by the Revd Miles Gale of Keighley Parish Church written around 1714 to the Archbishop of York. His scathing verses were directed against Robert Hall – a man Gale hated with a passion – and his son William Hall, of Newsholme near Oakworth.

> Unto his son he leaves his brain,
> William mostly was employ'd in Wht was vain.
> Unto 3d he gives his lying Tonge,
> After 10 days in pickle to be hung.
> In boiling he must take of all ye skin,
> To let the venum out, that is within.
> The broth will poison either dog or cat,
> And is good for rats ...

The second example is a poem entitled, *The Grave* written in 1818 by Robert Blair. A copy of this was available to Branwell and his sisters at Ponden Hall's well-stocked library and has been linked to Emily's *Wuthering Heights* when Heathcliff endeavours to dig up his dead true love.

> Of temper so transcendently malign,
> That toads and serpents, of most deadly kind,
> Comparar'd to thee, are harmless – Sickness
> Of every size and symptom, racking pains,
> And bluest plagues are thine – See how fiend
> O great man-eater!
> Whose ev'ry day is carnival, not sated yet!
> Unheard of epicure! Without a fellow
> The veriest gluttons do not always cram

And thousands that each hour thou gobblest up,
This, less than this, might gorge thee to the full
As if diseases, massacres, and poison

The words 'Well, some may hate and some may scorn' had been read as Branwell's eulogy, until someone noticed they were penned nine years *before* his death. Perhaps this little offering might have been more acceptable to remember him by:

The Dying Musician or The Wolf is at the Door

Death's dark shadows o'er me stealing,
Gloom and sadness round me shed -
None are watching, none are weeping
By this lonely dying bed.
World of life and light I leave thee,
Fading slowly from mine eye,
Yet one harmony bequeath thee,
One last effort ere I die.
No, ah, no! – the sigh of sorrow
Shall not echo to my strain;
Gentle hearts shall from it borrow
Solace to their grief and pain.
Earthly cares no longer grieve me,
Earthly joys no more control;
Heavenly harmonies sustain me,
Heavenly visions fill my soul.

H. *The Family Herald, 19 February 1853*

To Be Remembered By ...

In 1949, B. H. Fawthorpe of Hertfordshire sent a copy of a miniature watercolour portrait to *Country Life*, which he hoped readers might be able to identify. Mr Fawthorpe's father had purchased the painting some fifty years before, when visiting the Haworth area. The seller had said it might be a self-portrait of Branwell. There was illegible writing, written in two separate hands on the back but only the name 'Patrick' could be discerned.

While working on the new museum extension in the late 1950s (built from reclaimed stone taken from St. Mary's Church, Keighley), Jack Wood, the proprietor of Worth Valley Builders came across a dagger in one of the walls. Could this have been the carving knife, which according to his friend Francis Grundy, Branwell had pulled out from his coat sleeve at their last meeting and admitted having "long secreted"? Did the parson's deluded son replace this knife in its hiding place in the wall, before returning home that same night? Around the time of his discovery, Mr Wood's employees complained to him of experiencing an unpleasant atmosphere every time they passed through Branwell's study ...

Posthumous Celebrations

An unusual meeting of Ancient, Free and Accepted Masons was held at The Lodge of the Three Graces (Faith, Hope and Charity), Haworth, in order to celebrate the centenary of Branwell's rising to the degree of Master Mason. Former member Ira Sugden presented a rose bowl that had once belonged to

Patrick Brontë to the Lodge. At some stage, Patrick had given this Brontë relic to his next-door neighbours, named Leach who then gave it to Mr Sugden in return for certain services rendered. On presenting the bowl, Sugden said, "It is our duty to be connecting links between past and future, and so prevent the memories of one who was a member of a family of world-wide celebrity from fading into oblivion. To ensure this, may I suggest that the lodge meeting every April be recognised as Brontë night?"

Nobody bothered to celebrate Branwell's actual centenary day, which fell during the First World War, and thus it was that 'the Vicar's Patrick' was passed over again.

Had Branwell been alive he would have been most gratified to witness the sight of a new postage stamp issued in his honour by the Keighley & Worth Valley Railway, until spotting a monumental blunder, for his name was mis-spelt as Patrick Bramwell Brontë. An eagle-eyed journalist at the *Evening Post* was sent an advance copy. Just one glance inspired him to telephone the Brontë Museum who agreed that the 'm' should in fact be an 'n'. Reprints were hurriedly made and railway postmaster Ron Hunter was given the job of stoking the steam train engine with the faulty stamps on Wednesday 9 July 1980 en route from Keighley to Haworth at 12.31pm. Collectors should be aware that a few stamps escaped destruction and are very valuable today.

The Keighley & Worth Valley Railway was not the first culprit to spell his name incorrectly. It has been mis-spelled time and again. John Elliot an Irish visitor to the Brontë shrine in 1858 even called him Bramwill!

Epitaph To Branwell

Perhaps the best and most fitting epitaph to Branwell was Francis Grundy's view of him, 'Patrick Branwell Brontë was no domestic demon – he was just a man moving in a mist, who lost his way. More sinned against mayhap than sinning, at least he proved the reality of his sorrows. They killed him ... '

Wuthering Heights: Charlotte, Branwell or Emily?

As to Emily's imaginative work, "They would explain the atmosphere of *Wuthering Heights* when they could explain the mysteries of human personality" was the opinion of Revd W. Thompson Elliott. *The Times*, always keen to review new books, amazingly ignored *Wuthering Heights*. However, there has been continuing interest in the authorship of this book.

At the turn of the 20th century, John Malham-Dembleby, of Scarr Hill, Bradford, stood accused by Brontë lovers of deliberately setting out to prove in his book *The Lifting of the Brontë Veil* and other works, that it was Charlotte and not Emily who had penned *Wuthering Heights*. Furthermore, the author asserted that the plots of both *Wuthering Heights* and *Jane Eyre* came about because of one obscure publication published in 1838 and printed in Leeds by A. Pichard, entitled *Gleanings in Craven*. This was a sort of tourist diary of rambles and ghostly goings-on in Yorkshire written by Frederic Montague (a relative of the fourth Earl of Sandwich) but there is no proof that any of the Brontës actually read this little tome.

On 22 February 1911, *The Yorkshire Post* reviewing *The Key to The Brontë Works*, wrote, 'Mr Malham-Dembleby ... has made a discovery which is a real contribution to Brontëana (namely, Montague's book). We have not the space for showing how the little book can be associated with the Brontë novels, but the discoveries are very remarkable, amongst them being the likelihood that from it Charlotte took her pen-name Currer Bell.' Malham-Dembleby thought her pen name came from the famous book collector mentioned in *Gleanings*, a Miss Mary Richardson *Currer* (1785 to1861) of Bradford and of Eshton Hall. It transpired that Miss Currer also happened to be a member of Keighley Mechanics' Library at the same time as the Brontës and that other members of this same library were a Mr William *Ellis* (Emily's chosen pseudonym) and three of his sons from Castlefields near Bingley. As soon as Malham-Dembleby stumbled across *Gleanings*, he was convinced that the idea of Heathcliff being a foundling came from page 49:

> 'It was on top of this mountain (near Simon's Seat, close to Bolton Priory) that an infant was found by a shepherd, who took it to his home ... he was unable to maintain the foundling ... it was ultimately agreed to by the shepherds, that the child should be kept "amang 'em" and so boy became known as Simon Amanghem.'

Malham-Dembleby even claimed that Charlotte was forced to deny that *she* had written *The Heights* because it, 'was issued under the condition that the next book by its author went to the same publisher, a Mr Newby, which, of course, made impossible thereafter for Charlotte Brontë's acknowledging her author-ship of this work, as the next book by the author of *Wuthering Heights*, her *Jane Eyre* was published by another house ... she was very much afraid of this Mr Newby, (whom she described as a 'shuffling scamp').' Newby also firmly believed Charlotte was the author of *Wuthering Heights*, and that she gave to Emily the 'passionate record of her soul's tragedy, written in agony of mind, with tears of blood.' Did Charlotte lie then, Malham-Dembleby asked, merely to escape a contractual agreement made between her and the slipshod Thomas Newby, who cared only for the sound of money jingling in his pockets?

In 1924, author Miss Alice Law claimed Branwell was the true author of *The Heights*, in her book *Patrick Branwell Brontë*. Simply because she believed a woman could not have written it. In her opinion, Emily, a Victorian Miss, could never have dreamed up, let alone written a plot like *The Heights*; it just wasn't done in those days.

What *is* known is that in 1845 Branwell wrote to Francis, the brother of Joseph Leyland, saying 'My novel is the result of years of thought, and it gives a vivid picture of human feelings for good and evil-veiled by that cloak of deceit ...'. In his book *Pictures of the Past,* Branwell's friend Grundy stoutly defends *him* as the author, writing 'One very important statement which he (Patrick Branwell Brontë) made to me throws some light upon a question which has long vexed the critics; that is, the authorship of *Wuthering Heights*. It is well-nigh incredible that a book so marvellous in its strength, and in its dissec-tion of the most morbid passions of diseased minds, could have been written by a young girl like Emily Brontë, who never saw much of the world.'

Emily though, was not a mere mortal in the ordinary sense, for she was one of life's great mystics and a loner with a brilliant sense of dramatic words and moods. An example of this can be found in the title: the word *Wuther* means a sobbing sound created by the wind dashing against a building thus *Wuthering Heights* becomes *Sobbing Heights*.

An article, which appeared in the *Halifax Guardian* of June 1867 described the time the writer, a Keighley schoolmaster named William Dearden, Branwell and Francis Leyland met up at the Crossroads Inn, near Keighley in 1838 or 1842 (where one can still purchase alcohol). All three were to read out various pieces of poetry they had composed themselves. When Branwell's turn came he searched his stove pipe hat for a piece of paper containing his verses entitled *Azreal* or *The Eve of Destruction* only to discover he had inadvertently brought some notes on a nameless novel he had begun to write. His friends encouraged him to read it to them and he did so, giving the real names of his characters as he went along. This raw material, his friends vowed, was none other than the plot and characters of *Wuthering Heights*. Dearden wrote a long poem about the Cross Roads incident entitled:

A Retrospect

The moon was on the wane, when I
Met at Cross Roads my Brontë challenger,
Brontë drew from his hat
A manuscript, which, when his eyes beheld,
He stood aghast: and, turning rapidly
The quivering leaves, he said, "O, friends, I've made
A strange mistake! This is a novel on which,
Some time ago I tried my prentice-hand,
And which in my hot haste, I must have snatched
Instead of Azrael, from my private drawer.
"I swear," cried Brontë, " by the scared Nine,
The first fytte of my poem lives in lines
Legibly written by this very hand:
And if you'll grant me forty minutes' space
To seek the parsonage, and these return,
Your eyes shall vouch the truth of what I say
Instead of reading his verse Branwell Brontë read,
For one hour long, long chapters of a tale,
To which the monstrous figment, *"Wuthering Heights."*
(The credulous world receives as Ellis Bell's)
Bears, in its characters and incidents,
Too strong resemblance ever to be deemed
Entirely accidental
A prototype in man or Demon-such
As the foul Caliban of "Wuthering Heights."
Before the world had Heathcliff loathed in print,
He shocked our hearts in Branwell's manuscript.

In 1929, Charles Simpson insisted in an article in *Country Life* that there could not be the slightest doubt that Emily alone wrote *The Heights*. Exactly how she managed to achieve this masterpiece, or on what it was really based, he believed

The Crossroads Inn, where Branwell met with his literary friends and read out a passage from *Wuthering Heights (courtesy of Brian Moorehouse)*

no one would ever know. He thought, however, that Branwell *did* have a hand in it.

Martha Brown always maintained that Patrick Brontë was most indignant after hearing that *Wuthering Heights* had been written by both Emily and Branwell. Patrick insisted his son had played no part in the production of the book, saying Emily kept her work a "profound secret."

Background Sources

It has been suggested that Emily took the exterior of *Wuthering Heights* from the gateway of High Sunderland, the interior from Ponden Hall and the actual site from Top Withens. Historian Mrs Butterfield believes that the setting for Wuthering Heights was not Top Withens at all, but Ponden Old House and that Ponden Hall itself was the original Trushcross Grange.

After reading *The Sources of Wuthering Heights* by Mrs F.S. Day, an anonymous book reviewer for the *Yorkshire Post* commented on 11 November 1937: 'It is an extremely ingenious little book which points out a number of exact parallels between *Wuthering Heights* and *The Black Dwarf* by Walter Scott ... There are similarities in the plot, in the names and even the words. One might say that the author had made out her case were it not for the fact that Mrs G. Elsie Harrison has made out one equally as strong tracing *Wuthering Heights* back to stories of William Grimshaw, parson at Haworth ... And in addition to this it has been most satisfactorily proved that the book *Wuthering Heights* is an extract from the family history of the Heatons of Ponden Hall.' Scott's *Black Dwarf* was available to the Brontës as it appeared in the 1841 inventory of books held at Keighley Mechanics' Institute, of which their father was a member.

Could it be that the novel *Eugene Aram* inspired at least some sequences of events in Emily's *Wuthering Heights*? Edward Bulwer-Lytton felt that this work ranked among the best of his novels. A copy of this is also listed in the records of the Keighley Mechanics' Institute's library. Branwell Brontë read aloud some of the passages from *Eugene Aram* at the parsonage and Emily recorded the fact in her diary paper of 26 June 1837, when she says that she could hear Branwell reading *Eugene Aram* to her aunt.

Both *Aram* and *The Heights* contain a somewhat unconventional structure within their text and usage of chronological framework. Although Heathcliff and Eugene are exact opposites in character, they both disappear for some years and acquire money. Additionally, the narrators in both stories are drawn to a churchyard to visit the dead. While Bulwer-Lytton wrote:

'He passed over the rude mounds of earth that covered the deceased poor, paused at a tomb higher, though of simple pretensions; it was not yet discoloured by the dews and seasons, and the short inscription traced upon it was strikingly legible in comparison with those around.' Blessed Are They That Mourn, For They Shall Be Comforted.'

Emily's version was:

'I sought and soon discovered, the three headstones on the slope next to the moor ... Heathcliff's still bare ... I lingered round them ... and wondered how any one could ever imagine unquiet slumbers for sleepers in that quiet earth.'

The outcome of each man's life was similar – violence and death.

In March 1985, after many years research, Kim Lyon, backed by English lecturer Christopher Heywood of Sheffield University, alleged that Emily had based Heathcliff on a man named Richard Sutton (1782 to 1851), who lived near Sedbergh, in the village of Dent. In addititon, Mrs Lyon stated his farmhouse home at Rigg End was in fact the true Wuthering Heights homestead – this building had once been the abode of the slave owning Sill family, about whom Emily may have read, leading to her keen interest in anti-slavery laws.

The story goes that Edmund and Elizabeth Sill already had one natural daughter, Ann and three sons, before adopting Richard Sutton as a youngster. By 1807, both parents were dead. When Ann died in 1835, she bequeathed her entire estate to Richard, rather than leave her wealth to her brothers. Mrs Lyon believed Hindley Earnshaw was modelled on all three Sill boys, who were known throughout the district as drunkards and wastrels.

Another idea put forward over the years, is that Heathcliff was modelled on Jack Straw, previous owner of Miss Patchett's Law Hill School, where Emily taught. Jack Straw, another adoptee, built Law Hill around the early 1700s. Jack, by some devious plan, managed to acquire his patron's lands and property at Walterclough Hall (note the initials WH) out of revenge, just as Heathcliff did when he purchased Wuthering Heights. Incidentally, a woman servant named Earnshaw earned her keep in this fourteen-roomed house.

Halifax solicitor, Robert Parker has also been likened to Emily Brontë's Heathcliff, for he too rose from obscurity and married a wealthy woman almost twenty years his senior. His wife was Ann Prescott and after their marriage in 1754, Parker went into partnership with her kinsman John Baldwin, a lawyer.

Parker quickly rose to become a prominent figure in Halifax. He lent money to Baldwin who defaulted on the debt. Parker took Calico Hall, his debtor's family home in lieu of payment. Robert died a wealthy man but his son Robert Jnr. was a bitter disappointment to him for he was a weakling just as Heathcliff and Isabella's son Linton was. Emily may have heard Parker's story when she was at Law House.

Joseph Hardacre, a Haworth man of many parts, published *Poems Lyrical and Moral on Various Subjects* in September 1822, just a year after the Brontë family's arrival in the village. In one of his poems entitled *The Foundling*, we can see some of the elements of Heathcliff and Cathy.

(Heathcliff)

> Who comes uncall'd for on stage of life,
> A helpless, poor, unwelcome, child of man
> His country's laws no sanction give his birth
> He is in the world merely to live
> A wand'ring outcast, indigent, and poor:
> He on bounty of benevolence,
> Of soft compassion never bursts o'er him
> Sometimes the foundling finds a rougher way
> No! no! a harder destiny his:
> His morals watch'd with scrutinising eye,
> Shakes hands with charity, and in the world
> Tries for himself, and seeks his fortune there;
> Still! Still! Full oft his destiny is hard.
> He sighs, and silent this reflection makes: -
> No loving brother, no fond sister, e'er
> Stand at the door, and welcom'd my return;
> Whilst I, less favour'd, here abandon'd live,
> A brother spurn'd, an unacknowledg'd son,
> Cast on the wild waste of this weary world.
> To be base-born, is it to be cast off?
> Teach me, O Heav'n! submission to my fate,

(Cathy)

> When strech'd or struggling on her dying bed,
> Beneath the cold, the iron grasp of death?
> When her wild eyes in dreadful phrenzy start,
> When recollection on its hinges turns,
> Grates on her soul, unravels all her schemes,
> Displays her guilt in all its dread array?
> For conscience softens at the approach of death:
> For deep contrition, what field is here!
> For him no less, the accomplice of her guilt!
> Tis all recorded in a great black book.

Cursed?

For a time it was felt that productions of *Wuthering Heights* were hexed. During a 1940s Leeds production, a principal character broke his arm and when thespians enacted the fight between Earnshaw and Heathcliff at Keighley Hippodrome, it ended rather abruptly when one of the actors was carted off the stage unconscious! The Keighley Little Theatre also suffered its fair share of jinxes. The drama's accident prone Heathcliff (Fred Pye) first slipped down a flight of steps and lost consciousness, then put his foot through a wooden chest, being tossed heavily to the ground and lastly, a brandy glass mysteriously exploded in his hand cutting him quite badly.

Up to Date

In 1988, Japanese film makers made a bloody and violent Samurai version of *Wuthering Heights* entitled *Onimaru* meaning Demon Child, which was shown at Cannes. The film's director Kiju Yoshida said in an interview with the *Telegraph and Argus* in May of that year: 'Emily Brontë was a kind of witch with extraordinary occult power and it is the contrast in *Wuthering Heights* between the supernatural and natural, the spiritual and earthly and the latent transgression of taboos such as incest and grave desecration that I wished to explore.'

Singer Kate Bush believes she has the ghost of Emily Brontë to thank for the massive success of her debut song *Wuthering Heights* released in the late 1970s. Inspired by the late Yorkshire authoress, Kate said she "felt a closeness to the dead writer which went further than just sharing the same birthday – July 30." As a young girl, she watched an adaptation of Emily's great novel. "I just caught the end where Cathy's ghost was coming through the window to Heathcliff. I had always been interested in spooks and sci-fi and that grabbed me" and that "I often think the song did so well because Emily Brontë had decided to help me. I believe she was promoting her book in a commercial way."

In May 2000, a male member of the British Library had been entrusted with the mission of taking Emily's original *Wuthering Heights* manuscript to a new exhibition called *Chapter and Verse*. He travelled across London by taxi and was stunned by the puzzled driver who, as he was stepping out of the cab, leaned over to ask him where had his lady companion gone? The academic assured him he had been quite alone, but the taxi driver insisted that he had definitely seen a pale looking young woman dressed in black, sitting silently alongside his passenger throughout the journey! Was this the ghost of Emily guarding her precious manuscript?

Brontë enthusiast Sydney Dobell, who at first mistakenly attributed Emily's great novel to Charlotte in the *Palladium*, considered the plot of *Wuthering Heights* to have been drawn from 'a recollection of things seen and heard … written by a baby God.' Perhaps Charlotte was just plain jealous of her sister's talent for writing and did not wish to see another of Emily's works of fiction exposed to the world, thereby overshadowing her own fame? Incidentally, the late Catherine Cookson who penned semi-historical novels beat Emily in the 1999 poll of Yorkshire readers for best novelist. Might Charlotte have secretly been pleased at this … ?

Last, but not least – sweet, strong Anne

Of course, Haworth folk knew that another Brontë would soon follow Branwell and Emily to the grave, for superstition decreed that should death enter a house twice within twelve months it would leave the door ajar for a third. They were, right, for Anne passed away soon after.

As consumption (TB) took a firm grip of asthmatic Anne Brontë's frail body, she desperately tried quack remedies to make her well again. As a last resort, she took Godbold's Vegetable Balsam, which was available from the premises of Mr J. Binns, Leeds. The 'life saving' elixir was advertised in Yorkshire papers thus:

'TO PARENTS – That nothing can be dearer to us than the life of a child, relative, &c. it must be a pleasing satisfaction to the readers to observe the following case, after all the means prescribed by the most eminent of the faculty had failed; and they will have the consultation to know who they may preserve the life of a darling child or relative, pining under a disease that was always fatal before the valuable discovery of
GODBOLD'S VEGETABLE BALSAM, for the cure of CONSUMPTIONS, ASTHMAS, SCROFULA, COUGHS, and COLDS; sold, wholesale and retail, at the Proprietor's, No. 3 Bloomsbury Square; and at S. GODBOLD'S, No. 159, New Bond-Street, London.

A testimonial to the wonderful elixir of life was offered:

SIR,
Among the many surprising cures performed by your medicine, which I have been authenticated by so respectable persons, permit me to bear testimony to that lately happened in my family.
A niece of mine, about nineteen, at Boston, near Norwich, was in a galloping consumption, and was reduced almost to a skeleton; she was given over by some of the most eminent gentleman of the faculty, and her dissolution hourly expected ... recommended to your Vegetable Balsam; I bought a bottle of it and went down myself, and she immediately began taking it. In a week's time she was enabled to walk about, and in the course of a few weeks, to the astonishment of every one around her, she was entirely recovered, and now continues in perfect health.'

Sadly, this magic potion proved worthless in Anne's case. After leaving home on 24 May 1849, Anne and Charlotte stayed the night in York, en route to Scarborough. The sisters took this opportunity to visit York Minister. Anne in awe of the splendid architecture was heard to say before her voice trailed away: "If infinite power can do this, what is ... " Within days, Anne lay dead from tuberculosis in a rented room at Wood's Lodging House, No. 2, The Cliff, Scarborough. Her last words were to urge Charlotte to take courage.

No Final Homecoming

It is hard to imagine why Anne would wish to be separated from her family in death but whatever she might have felt, her sister's manoeuvrings decreed that she should be buried away from her home – there was to be no homecoming for Anne. Old retainer Tabby never forgave Charlotte for burying Anne in a "foreign grave." Anne, aware of her impending death might have agreed to be interred at Scarborough, knowing that the emotional cost of conveying her corpse back to Haworth would have been a traumatic exercise for those left behind.

On the day of her funeral service, held at Christ Church, next door to the lodging house, her coffin, followed by three female mourners (three fates for three sisters?) slowly wound its dreary way through the unfamiliar streets to the waiting grave. For years, the identity of the third woman accompanying Charlotte Brontë and Ellen Nussey remained unknown, until some hitherto undiscovered papers belonging to an elderly lady surfaced, revealing her as none other than Margaret Wooler of Birstall!

Grave Mistakes

Charlotte ordered a headstone to commemorate her sister's passing but was shocked on her return to Anne 's grave to learn that the mason had made *five* mistakes in the lettering including her *age*, which has never been altered! *Lies* was another – what the other three mistakes were can only be guessed at. Charlotte chose a tombstone (made from Cloughton stone) depicting an urn partly draped with heavy material perched on top of two books one large and one small. It is not known whether these carvings are meant to represent the Bible and a prayer book or Anne's two novels *Agnes Grey* and *The Tenant of Wildfell Hall*.

Anne Brontë *(Goodwoods, 1896)*

Her inscription reads:

HERE
LIE THE REMAINS OF
ANNE BRONTË,
DAUGHTER OF THE REVD. P. BRONTË
Incumbent of Haworth, Yorkshire
She died Aged 28
MAY 28th, 1849

Finding her plot in a state of wanton neglect and the protective iron railings surrounding it gone, in the 1920s, Guy Schofield was forced to scrape the moss off the headstone in order to be sure that it actually *was* the grave of Anne Brontë. Writing to the *Yorkshire Evening Post*, he condemned the state of Anne's final resting-place. The grave is situated at the east end of St. Mary's churchyard, Castle Hill, Scarborough. This portion of the graveyard, away from the main cemetery was used for the grazing of sheep.

In the following decade, more Brontë pilgrims complained that they could not find her grave in the disused cemetery, so the tombstone, which was in good condition, was spruced up and the lettering painted black. At last, Anne's grave was brought back to life – although when dusk fell, locals complained that the polished white stone standing proud in the midst of its darker companions in the graveyard appeared to take on the appearance of some ghoulish horror movie backdrop!

However, by 1998, Mark Branagan, a reporter for the *Yorkshire Post* wrote that there were serious fears about the safety of Anne's headstone, for although hers had somehow managed to survive nature's elements, other stones around it had crumbled. After several air gun pellet marks appeared on the monument, there was talk of replacing the original with a replica, which had been made some years previously. Catherine Rayner explained: "we have a reserve stone and whether the day will ever come when the stones will be swapped or not, it is being kept as a possible substitute."

After Charlotte's marriage to Nicholls, legend has it that she wanted to bring Anne's body home where it belonged but he absolutely forbade it.

The Vicar of Scarborough suggested in 1960 that Anne Brontë's remains should be moved closer to the Parish Church, saying that it was not uncommon to re-inter bodies, even those belonging to a saint. However, Scarborough Corporation decided to turn the area around Anne's grave into a garden instead and a grand ceremony was organised to take place after the planting, People flocked in droves to the graveside to listen to prayers read over her remains. The Queen's Chaplain, Canon G.W.O. Addleshaw presided.

Having stood for almost two hundred years, Christ Church, Vernon Road, Scarborough, the sad scene of Anne Brontë's funeral service succumbed to the demolition men in 1979. It seems that when the structure was erected, the builders had made a serious error by placing the grain of the stone vertically instead of horizontally. This caused water to run into the stone, thereby wearing it away with the passage of time. Architects agreed that Christ Church was in such a dangerous condition it had to be pulled down.

On the subject of Anne

It is a curious thing that one day as Charlotte watched over her newborn sister lying in her crib, she called to her father, saying that she had seen an angelic being hovering a little above Anne's head.

Three Angels

They say that life is barren, drear and cold,
Ever the same sad song was sung of old,
Is it then true, this tale of bitter grief,
Of moral anguish finding no relief?
Lo! Midst the winter shines the laurel leaf:
Three angels share the lot of human strife,
Three angels glorify the path of life ...

Frazer's Magazine, Craven Pioneer, 6 Sept 1879

An acquaintance of Anne insisted that she was different from the other sisters. 'Her hair was a pretty light brown, and fell on her neck in graceful curls. She had lovely violet-blue eyes, fine pencilled eyebrows, and a clear, almost transparent complexion.' Tabby Ratcliffe, looking at a portrait of Anne commented, "I think that is a good face."

Joseph Horsfall Turner of Idle near Bradford, author of *Haworth Past and Present*, published in 1879 and devotee of Brontë lore, questioned everyone he could find who had known the family intimately. Devouring their works and reading everything he could about them, he felt especially drawn to Patrick's youngest daughter. Standing alone at Anne Brontë's grave on a windswept cliff within sight and sound of the cold, unforgiving North Sea, Turner knew in his heart that he would have loved Anne had fate been kinder.

The Betrothed

Had I met thee in thy beauty
When my heart and hand were free,
When no other claimed the duty
Which my soul would yield to thee;
Had I wooed thee-had I won thee -
Oh! How blest had been my fate;
But thy sweetness hath undone me -
I have found thee – but too late!
For to one my vows were plighted
With a faltering lip and pale;
Hands our cruel sires united,
Hearts were deem'd of slight avail!
Thus betrothed to wealth and state,
All Love's own sweet prospects faded -
I have found thee – but too late!

Charles Swain, The London Journal 15 Oct. 1853

The three storeys of Blake Hall at Mirfield that were once the home of the wealthy Ingham family and an unhappy Anne Brontë, in her position as governess there in 1839, were demolished in the twentieth century to make way for more modern buildings. Anne made use of her memories of Blake Hall and the Inghams, whose ancestors had been avid supporters of John Wesley's Holy Club, in her novel *Agnes Grey*. The hall's unique yew staircase was shipped to America where it was reported that the ghost of Anne Brontë was seen loitering on it!

Anne's first contact with children in the capacity of governess was with a family named Cuncliffe where she was forced to tie her unruly charges to chairs at lesson time! One of the Robinson children she had taught at Thorp Green named Edmund accidentally drowned before reaching his thirtieth birthday when a ferryboat overturned.

In 1936, The Revd J.H. Brooksbank, vicar of Hathersage, Derbyshire felt drawn to Anne's forlorn grave and the house in which she had died. The owner mentioned that there were still articles belonging to the sisters in the attic. Amazingly, Brooksbank found a number of the girls' personal belongings therein and was able to commandeer them. Among the items retrieved was a lovely silk shawl, two pairs of tiny beaded slippers (authenticated by a piece of paper written in Charlotte's hand found in one of the worn slippers), Charlotte's embroidered purse with the word *Brontë* on it and lastly, a small pearl inlaid writing desk. But, why did Charlotte leave these things behind when she could have collected them on her return visit?

A Final Tribute

From the pages of the *Halifax Courier* printed on the 24 May 1934, came this touching tribute to Anne Brontë, 'She loved the moors, bare, bleak, pitiless. She died by the sea and she sleeps in a little churchyard above the harbour at Scarborough in Yorkshire, a place where we have stood many a time and seen her grave. Poor Anne. Not only poor Anne, but brave splendid Anne, magnificent Anne. One of the three sisters who shook the world, she knew the tragedies of the parsonage at Haworth. She saw Branwell Brontë die standing, a shriek on his lips. She watched Emily fail. She wrote her books and had a sweet, strong nature ...

When she was under the ground, Charlotte opened her desk and found something that Matthew Arnold called a clarion call. It was her good-bye to the world. She wrote it when her hand was almost too limp to hold a pen. It is a hymn now, and it will live.'

> If Thou should'st bring me back to life,
> More humble I should be,
> More wise, more strengthened for the strife,
> More apt to lean on Thee;
> Should death be standing at the gate,
> Thus should I keep my vow:
> But, Lord, whatever be my fate,
> O let me serve Thee now!

The Parsonage

With the exception of Anne, all the Brontës died at the parsonage. 'The old grey house is quiet now', wrote Mrs Gaskell, 'No one comes to the house: nothing disturbs the deep repose; hardly a voice is heard; you catch ... the buzzing of a fly in the parlour all over the house.' Not so today, for literary pilgrims from all over the world are drawn to the parsonage. Their voices now fill the rooms until nightfall, when darkness descends and the house sleeps.

Originally, it was a nine-roomed Georgian house built in 1779 of Yorkshire sandstone and almost surrounded by rows of stark monuments and flowerless graves dedicated to Haworth's dead. It is a place where the wind whistles and the black crows croak. No such darkness creeps within the walls of the parsonage – there are no ghosts here for 'earth had not a sunnier spot than that love lit home.' A sundial marking the passage of time was cut into the parsonage windowsill. When or by who is not known. The front walled garden of the house has been described as appearing to have been 'stolen from the graveyard'. In the backyard was the necessary house (toilet) complete with three seats! Imagine then, if you will, Charlotte, Emily and Anne composing their various writings while relaxing on the loo! Charlotte's bedroom where she wove her dreams was used as a bathroom in the twentieth century.

'Jackdaw', an early pilgrim to Haworth, wrote to *Local Notes and Queries* saying, 'More than thirty years have elapsed since I made my own first pilgrimage to Haworth, and it is no exaggeration to say that at that time hardly anybody showed any special interest in the wonderful story of the parson's daughters. The village itself was then as gloomy and unprepossessing as it had been in the days when the authors of *Jane Eyre* and *Wuthering Heights* trod its single street. There were some faded photographs of Charlotte Brontë displayed in one shop window, and here and there one met with some one who remembered the gifted sisters, and was willing to answer questions about them. But I well remember that on that winter's day in 1866, when I first stood within the damp walls of the old church at Haworth, and read the inscription on the memorial tablet recording the names of Mr Brontë and his family. I was depressed to find how completely they all seemed to have passed out of the lives of their neighbours. It

58

was considered strange that any one should take the trouble to visit Haworth in order to see their resting-place, and the house where they had dwelt and worked in by-gone years ... Melancholy and deserted it looked on that dismal January day, when the snow lay on the moors and the laden skies of winter loomed above my head. I know that it was with a profound depression that I left the place. Little did I think that thirty years after the people of the West Riding, who had shown part indifference to the family of Charlotte Brontë during her lifetime, would be turning to Haworth as a shrine, and that the slender memorials of that pure and noble life would be gathered together and treated as sacred objects.' And to 'a posthumous fame as that which has fallen to the lot of Charlotte Brontë, and of her gifted sister Emily, who died, without having enjoyed the faintest sign of recognition from the world.'

Sir James Roberts, the son of a humble Haworth farmer (born in the week Branwell Brontë died) acquired the property in 1928. This came about because Sir James's wife read an article about the impending sale of the parsonage in the *Yorkshire Observer* and suggested he buy and then donate the property to the Brontë Society. Mulling the proposition over, remembering the blind vicar and his unforgettable daughter Charlotte's kind words to him as a child, Sir James agreed that it was "a jolly good idea." Paying the asking price of £3000, he duly handed over the deeds to the Brontë Society. Harold and Nellie Mitchell were appointed caretakers at about this time and breathed new life into the parsonage with the births of their two sons, Trevor and Eric during the 1930s.

It is Harold we must thank for the world-famous black silhouette sign depicting *a Brontë at work* (probably Charlotte) swinging in the wind outside the museum. Young George Johnson carefully traced and cut round the silhouette at Wood Bros workshop in Changegate and then passed it to Herbert Scarborough, the village smith, who used a sheet of steel to cut out Harold's design, receiving but a few pounds for his labour – and an extra 10s. (50p) compensation for the wear and tear on his nerves! Herbert's ancestors had served as Haworth's black-smiths for nigh on two-hundred-and-fifty years. Mr McCracken of Mytholmes Lane, Haworth paid for the labour and materials, which amounted to around £30. Surprisingly, Harold Mitchell received neither a penny nor any recognition for his excellent creation.

The only time the silhouette has been taken down was during the Second World War, when signposts were prohibited because the enemy would know where he was! It was returned to its rightful place on VE Day.

The oak-panelled infants' cradle in which the Brontë children slept has been re-instated in the parsonage kitchen. It had been given to Miss Greenwood of Haworth, but unfortunately, its hinged hood or canopy was lost at some stage.

Local craftsmen at Scarcroft Antiques were able to fashion a replica of Patrick's half-tester bed in 1987, thanks to Branwell's excellent cartoon ink sketch of it. This is displayed in Patrick's bedchamber, adding to the atmosphere of the Brontë Parsonage Museum.

The parsonage suffered its first theft in November 1947 when a small oil painting of unknown provenance was stolen from a wall in Branwell's room.

Shivering with cold, the 'shades' of Miss Jane Eyre and Mr Róchester attempted to gain access to Haworth Parsonage in March 1964 but were turned away, even though an appointment had been made in advance for the actors, accompanied by journalists and a BBC television unit, to visit the museum. Actress Josephine Stewart told the *Yorkshire Post* 'I know just how Jane Eyre must have felt – unwanted, disappointed and rebuffed.' Rochester stepped towards her, uttering words of comfort for he too was at a loss to know why they had been dismissed.

Apparently, the reasoning behind this rejection was that the two leading actors starring in *Jane Eyre* at the Alhambra Theatre, Bradford had innocently committed a cardinal sin by turning up dressed in period costume. Sir Linton Andrews then chairman of the Council of the Brontë Society explained: 'we have to be very careful about photography in the museum. I think we have allowed it once or twice ... it is a museum of very high standing with very valuable exhibits. We cannot let anyone go along and occupy it, especially if it is a time when we are receiving visitors.' Strange he should say this, for there were no public visitors that particular day.

The *Christian Science Monitor, Boston*, renders us an American view of the Brontë homestead: 'It was the home of the Brontës, hence the museum of memories ... It is almost with trembling that one sets foot in the house that was the rough school of so many geniuses ... The whitewashed walls and simple furnishings speak silently, without need of a guide or interpreter, of the strange and wonderful family who lived there ... The bare walls of the nursery speak more movingly than any relics in the childish drawings that adorn them. They have covered them over with glass, these faint and far-off things, for they are precious ... Into the parlour, where one is standing, after darkness has fallen and the oil lamp is lit, and the wind is blowing outside, used to come the three sisters, talking, writing, planning, till the night grew late and the old servant, Tabby drowsed in the kitchen.'

Brontë Pedigree

The name Brontë does not appear to have an official armorial pedigree and thus there is no family coat-of-arms. Bronty/Brunty and Prunty are among the rarest of Irish surnames. Before Lord Nelson gained his second title of Duke of Brontë in 1799, in recognition of services rendered to the Neapolitan royal family, the Brontë surname had been recorded in old parish registers in Patrick's homeland using a variety of phonetic spellings such as Brunty and Bruntee. It appears likely that Patrick Brunty changed his surname to Brontë in 1799 – the same year that the title was conferred on Nelson by Ferdinand I, King of Naples.

Revd J.B. Lusk discovered the name Patrick Prunty in a book dated 1795, belonging to the famous Brontë family. There is a theory that perhaps Prunty and Prentice were derived from an identical source.

Patrick became Branty (a southern slant?) in the register at St. John's, Cambridge in 1802 but graduated as *Bronte* – minus dots. In 1809 the dieresis was added above the '*e*'. The Revd Morgan at Thornton didn't include any dots on the children's baptism certificates signed by him, whereas Elizabeth and Branwell who were christened by the Revd Fennell appear to have one dot each. Patrick's funeral card reverted to *Bronte*, without the dots.

Sarah Brontë, Patrick's sister, married one Simon Collins. As they were so poor, Patrick was forced to save his sister from the workhouse. Sarah bore a daughter, named Rose Anne, who had an 'unmistakable Brontë face'. She married a David Heslip and in turn gave birth to her own daughter, Emily, named after her well-known cousin. Apparently, the whole family bore a strong resemblance to their famous Brontë relatives. Emily grew up, married Hugh Bingham and went to live in Odsal, a place that had a reputation for suicides. Rose Anne took up the position of housekeeper to her son-in-law after the death of her daughter and died on 15 March 1915 at the age of ninety-three; she was buried three days later at the White Chapel, Cleckheaton, Bradford. It was she who remembered the story of Welsh, son of Welsh, Patrick's nephew who drowned tragically in the Irish River Bann on 22 September 1833.

Aunt Elizabeth Branwell was something of a Calvinistic religious melancholic who firmly believed that some "people were ordained to be saved and bound for Heaven, whereas others, no matter how contrite, were damned and bound for Hell." There is an amusing story about Aunt B's dislike of rats.

Because of poor or non-existent drainage, Haworth suffered badly with rodent infestations. One day a servant complained to Patrick Brontë about them running riot in the house. Taking his pistol, he shot two in the back kitchen. Animal lover Emily found one alive but bleeding. Lifting up the rat she cried, "How could you be so cruel? Just look at its paws; they are like baby's hands." Aunt Branwell, on seeing Emily tenderly cradling the dying creature in her arms immediately fled to her room locking the door firmly behind her. She refused to come out until she was sure the rat was dead. Later that evening at the dinner table, Branwell joked about making a coffin for Emily's rodent so that she could give it a decent send-off. Aunt Branwell quipped that Branwell might "go to Leeds for a suitable black outfit so that he may go into mourning himself."

For more than three decades, the face thought by some to have belonged to "Betty Branwell" stared down at visitors from the walls of the Brontë museum. It later transpired that the copy portrait, which had been admired by thousands, was actually that of a woman named Johanna Sang painted in the late 1700s!

In the autumn of 1970, three girls eventually arrived at the village of Haworth, having trekked from their homes in America. Gloria and Lydia Brontë from Washington DC, accompanied by their cousin Judith Brontë Russo, from New Jersey, believed they were direct descendants of the famous Brontë sisters. Patrick's brother, Billy Brunty, United Irishman and innkeeper at Knock Hill, had a son named John Brontë, who emigrated to Arkansas, America. John was believed to have been the great-great grandfather of Gloria and Lydia. Norman Raistrick, custodian at the Parsonage Museum, confirmed that there was indeed 'a distinct family likeness' after comparing the three visitors to the Brontë sisters' portrait. The trio's next stop was Scarborough to visit Anne Brontë's grave, before flying home.

Each to their own

Whilst visiting the Black Bull in 1879, a rather unsympathetic *Keighley Herald* correspondent wrote about the phenomenal genius of the Brontë family and their tragic life story, claiming the family was, 'a thing abnormal in nature ... . The girls owed much of the misery of their pathetic lives to the boorish selfishness and harshness of their father and to the miserable and degrading vices of their naturally brilliant brother. These wonderful girls were born to die young. They inherited their mothers' consumptive constitution. They only had glimpses of the sunnier side of life, and characteristic of their works are fiction of power and reality wanting sunshine and shadow.'

Haworth owes it to this famous family to preserve their memorials for all time. It is a sad thing indeed when modern day devotees aimlessly roaming the old boneyard are forced to ask, "Excuse me, where *are* the Brontës buried?"

3 | *Tales of Brontë Villagers*

A warming example of how folk looked after each other in times of great want and distress came from the *Yorkshire Briefs, Yorkshire Antiquarian Society Vol. 32:*

> Manufacturers John Pighills and Nathan Wright of Royds House, Haworth suffered a great loss in 1808 when a serious fire broke out in their warehouse. The fire quickly gained control of the whole building, burning it to a cinder thereby destroying all their machinery and entire stock. After viewing the charred remains of the business, principal residents John Brown, John Roper and John Smith informed the Justices at the General Quarter Sessions, Pontefract that they calculated the total loss to be £768 plus one penny. They also stated that since the fire, Pighills and Wright had suffered from "extreme want and poverty." A collection was instigated throughout England, including the Scottish Borders and Counties of Flint, Denbigh and Radnor raising the required amount of £768 0 1d. After deducting various expenses, the men were awarded a total of just over £457 some three years after the event.

A cheerful view of Haworth folk is taken from the text of *The Pious Weaver*, a Wesleyan religious tract published sometime after 1827.

> 'The inhabitants of this neighbourhood are chiefly mill-hands; and very diligent and thrifty many of them are. There was a time when they worked at the looms, or the spinning-wheel, in their own little cottages; but now the looms are to be found in a few houses only ... Hence, many of the people leave their dwellings, at an early hour in the morning, for the mill: and living, as many of them do, under the influence of religion, they go, as we have sometimes heard them, singing the songs of Zion; and return in the evening, when their work is done in the same happy and joyous mood.'

Rent received from the tenants of Top Withens, put in trust in 1723, was to be spent on full sets of new blue clothes, even underclothes and given free of charge to ten poor village children under the age of seven annually, on the "Feast of St. Martin in Winter". For some reason, Robert Heaton paid Joseph Judson to copy out this will on 8 February 1811. At sometime, it was decided that red braid binding should be sewn onto the clothing, but since the brightly coloured braid marked the children out as charity cases, Revd F. Harper put a stop to it. On the Sunday preceding Christmas Day, the chosen children gathered at the top of Main Street, wearing brand new clogs and decked out in their new clothes, cut from the very best blue material. Straight after the morning church service, the lucky recipients, accompanied by their families were treated to a slap up meal at the King's Arms. Tailor and folklorist, John Butterfield, a native of Stanbury, carried on the tradition of making blue clothes for poor children until his death in 1935.

Simple Lives

Somewhat Eccentric

Renowned for his eccentricities, Haworth bachelor George Pickles presented himself before the altar at Haworth church to be united in holy wedlock with his new love Mary Stowe, a widow from Denholme. As soon as George had uttered the words "I will", he asked the parson if he was married. Receiving confirmation that this was the case, George declared that he'd return his bride if she failed to live up to her marriage vows!

Timmy Feather, Stanbury's last handloom weaver
(Keighley Reference Library)

An old woman well acquainted with another eccentric, Timmy Feather told John Dixon, "O he is a good man, is Timothy. He prays to God night and morn. He's trying to live for another world, and always does the best he knows." After a short pause, she added hopefully, "and there is nothing more required is there?"

On the day of his funeral, freezing rain turned into snow as mourners crowded outside his remote home to accompany him on his last journey. His faithful battered hat and the two red handkerchiefs he used to wear lay abandoned on top of his silent handloom. After his death on 30 November 1910, aged eighty-five, 'Owd Tim's' loom, spinning wheel, hat and red pocket-handkerchiefs were removed from his Buckley Green Bottom cottage, where he had lived next door to his older brother 'Owd Jim' and taken to Keighley Museum. It was estimated that between seven and ten thousand people viewed the display of Timmy's loom and other personal belongings the following January. A very good sepia likeness of him can be seen today in the *Edinburgh Wool Shop*, Haworth.

Timmy had been baptised by Patrick Brontë, who signed his birth certificate. He had never married and scrubbed himself religiously from top to toe every Sabbath day. One of his relatives was Susannah Greenwood, "the kindest woman in all Stanbury."

Nancy Ickringill was "a big powerful woman, six feet tall, with a Roman nose." She carted weaver's pieces on her back from her Haworth farm to the market place at Halifax. The job carried with it a serious penalty, for it disfigured the shoulder, leaving the afflicted person lop-sided due to the heavy weight of the cloth. An equally strong Denholme woman, Grace Southwell dubbed "the Packhorse" hired herself out as a transporter of pieces to the highest bidder.

A Malingerer, Methinks!

It was rushbearing time when Jose eagerly set off on foot to Haworth Fair. Taking the steep winding pathway up to the moorland edge, he passed along West Lane with its tempting food stalls selling the famous but now extinct Haworth Feast Pudding. Jose soon found himself drawn towards Main Street by the sound of jolly music issuing from a fairground near Butt Lane. Here he mingled for a time amongst the jostling happy crowds until he was rudely snatched by the 'press gang' and taken off to a Keighley doctor where he was ordered to submit to the obligatory medical examination. The last thing Jose wanted was to find himself spirited on to a man-o'-war or to some foreign land other than America, so he fell quivering and quaking onto the surgery floor, complaining mournfully: "Mi heead warks" (aches) "mi back warks, mi belly warks, mi legs wark, ah wark all ovver. Ah can't stand up, ah can't sit, and ah can only get eease when ah lig" (lie) "dahn. Ah've been like this sin last Mirtinmass, when a load of hay fell on t' top o' mi." The doctor refused to sign the required certificate and sent him home. Safely away from the press gang, Jose displayed no sign of illness and raced off to his farmstead, as fast as his legs would carry him. Ensconced at Betty's that evening he recounted his narrow escape and was dubbed thereafter "Jose Wark".

Local man John Kitson was, by his own account, a bit of a hypochondriac. He and his aged wife actually enjoyed good health and were able to see well. Considering their combined ages, they were able to go about the village and manage their household affairs very competently. For half a century, Mr Kitson was in the habit of keeping a diary, recording events in and around Haworth, together with his worries regarding his bodily functions. John finally breathed his last in June 1869. The funeral service took place at The Baptist Chapel, West Lane, Haworth where his personal thoughts concerning death were portrayed on his memorial card:

> We soon shall have to die;
> We feel this mortal frame decay,
> It soon will breathless lie.
> When death arrives and strength doth fail
> Lord guard me through that gloomy veil

In Memoriam

12 September 1673 brought sorrow to a Mr Ramsden of Haworth and Halifax when Isaac Hopkinson's horse accidentally killed his heavily pregnant wife. Apparently Hopkinson had called out to Mrs Ramsden to get back "but she was heedless, looking at some things in her apron, bought at John Brearcliff's shop, the horse came full but upon her, threw her down, trod on her, she lay with her coats up very shamefully". Ramsden pleaded at the assizes that Hopkinson should be hanged – not because his dear wife was dead but because he had failed to get a replacement to take her place!

Sly Will, a village character knowing he was near death sent for village schoolmaster Jonas Bradley. When Jonas arrived, Will told him that "he wanted a bit of paper writing out", meaning his last will and testament. His life had not been easy, as his wife had been bed-ridden with severe rheumatism for over twenty years. Having no money of his own he had still managed to put by a token amount he got "off't town" to distribute between friends who had been good to him.

Georgina Marley, who came from Leeds, moved to Haworth after her marriage and lived in Timmy Feather's old house. Here she gave birth to three sons, Harold, Thomas and William all of whom were volunteers in the First World War. Tommy, a painter and decorator by trade was ordered by the forces to report to Halifax for the mandatory medical examination. On arrival, he was brusquely ordered to shut the door by one of doctors. The official, repeating himself a second time, was taken aback when Tommy quipped: "Ye mun shut it yersen'. Ah'm not working for yah chaps yet." Tommy was to sacrifice his life for his country. Brother Willie, an intelligent man possessed of a humorous nature, manned the very first tank used in the Great War. Unlike his brother, Willie's days ended not in conflict but at the Old Silent Inn Stanbury where he was proprietor for fifteen years after the war. Every single day of the war their mother Georgina came down from her home on the edge of the moors to find out the latest news of the front line from the *Bradford Daily Telegraph*.

In the village of Haworth on the day war ended, 'Many an anxious mother came to the door and discussed the matter with a neighbour ... a few more people than usual were in the streets, and considerable numbers went down to Keighley. There were very few outward manifestations of rejoicing however, flags and decorations being only very tardily exhibited ... The armistice had been signed and the guns had ceased firing at eleven that morning.'

Three members of the same family died in the tiny hamlet of Stanbury during January 1932. Annie Greenwood, daughter of John Sunderland of Old Bar House was the first to pass away. Within a week George Hutchinson, her brother-in-law died and as he lay fading, John Sunderland, Annie's father died. Annie was the licensee of the Friendly Inn, Stanbury and afterwards of the Wagon and Horses, Dyke Nook, Oxenhope.

Maria Pickles, oldest daughter of overlooker Joe Wadsworth, alias "Owd Waddy" of Griffe Mill, died at her home in Nelson in 1937. She was the widow of Stanbury born "Holmes o' Miles" or "Miles Breed" who had worked at Nelson's Catlow Quarries, where he carted much of the stone that was used to build the town of Nelson. Maria's mother Jane had given birth to twenty-two live infants, although only half of them survived past childhood. Maria being the eldest never knew what it was like to play, having to help with her siblings. One brother, Enoch played the fiddle well and another, James emigrated to America, where he became a prosperous fruit grower. Maria never lost her native Haworth 'speyke', 'redolent of the home of the immortal Heathcliff' and delighted in telling tales belonging to the olden days to any person who would listen.

Jonas Bradley, a retired headmaster, died in June 1943 aged eighty-four. He too possessed a great passion for Brontë lore, God's nature and the children he taught at Stanbury School. Jonas lived at Horton Croft, Stanbury but he was a native of Cowling. For this reason his coffin was carried from his Stanbury cottage to Cowling Methodist Church burial ground. A huge bunch of wild heather was placed on top of the coffin. Bradley was a prominent member of Haworth's Three Graces Lodge and many of his fellow Freemasons attended the interment. The Masonic hymn *Now the evening shadows closing, Worn from toil to peaceful rest, Mystic Arts and Rites reposing ... Mighty Architect Divine* was sung. His remains were buried beside those of his uncle, Ben Snowden, better known as "Spenom" – Ben was depicted as the poacher-weaver in Keighley Snowden's novel *Web of an Old Weaver*. Ben's unusual memorial is a rough limestone boulder from Grass Wood, donated by the Duke of Devonshire.

Little Snippets

The frosty days of January 1664 brought forth revelations from the diary of preacher Oliver Heywood. The musical tone of a mysterious trumpet was heard to echo around Haworth and Stanbury. So loud was the strange noise, it frightened horses and bewildered the bemused residents.

Whilst preaching at Jonas Foster's home, Heywood became aware of what a 'very ignorant and profane' place the village of Haworth really was: an elderly Haworthite, suddenly filled with the Holy Spirit set off for Jonas Foster's, but never reached his destination. Having got half way there, he had succumbed to Beelzebub's temptation of an alehouse, where he was discovered in a terrible drunken state, happily ensconced amongst 'fiddlers and loafers'.

On 11 June 1672, Heywood wrote down the sad story of William and Susanna Appleyard who had two sons and two daughters. The elder son John lived at home, while his brother Samuel, having been disowned by their parents for some reason, had run off, joined the Scottish army and been killed. John wed a Haworth girl, and when his father died, the evil duo turned the mother out of her home. She ended her days in the poor room at Halifax, dying of a broken heart, and the jubilant pair found themselves in possession of a large amount of money to spend as they wished.

There was more news from the preacher, entitled Experiment 27:

> On Easter Monday, 28 March 1692, Heywood rode to the home of John Rhodes; prepared to wrestle with God for the souls of Haworth sinners. It so happened that the vicar of Bradford was 'sat all day in the Ale house, gathering his dues'. Despondent Heywood had nothing but a few sixpences (2½p) thrust into *his* palm. Confiding to his journal, 'I was greatly comforted by my day's work, thought it was far better than his ... Christ ... made me to chuse the laborious, painfull part of the ministry with persecution.' ... This day also brought him John Akeroyd a young swain from Haworth seeking the good man's advice, unburdening his woes and discussing the sorry state of his soul with him in great detail.

Gamekeeper Joe Crabtree, baptised by Patrick Brontë at Thornton, grew up to become the "finest shot in the North of England." He always wore a green, brass-buttoned coat. It was his grandson Arthur Dobson who when working at the parsonage, discovered several childish drawings and writings on the wall of the old nursery.

In the 1920s, young Eric Sawley painstakingly carved a likeness of his screen idol, cowboy Tom Mix, onto a paving stone close to his home at Rock Street, Keighley. Later the paving stone was taken up and was removed to Haworth. It can be seen on the path behind Haworth church past the old cemetery.

Sarah Ann Heaton told the *Keighley News* on the 1 February 1936 how the Clerk of the church, Joseph Redman once fell asleep in his pew beneath the long gallery during Divine Service. He awakened with a start just at the point where Patrick Brontë, warming to his theme as he stood in the middle of the high pulpit, was delivering up the words, "As it was in the beginning, is now and ever shall be, world without end." To the amusement of both parson and worshippers, Joseph, thinking the Sunday ceremony was at an end, called out loudly "Amen", thus bringing the service to an abrupt close!

In the autumn of 1866 James Watkins, a black man from America lectured to a packed hall at Haworth National School. His theme was, *In Remembrance of Slavery*. He spoke of how slaves had been bought and sold amidst great suffering in America. A collection plate was handed round raising a fair amount to aid the cause of freedom.

Providing a Service

William Wood of Newell Hill was Haworth's first and last man, being both a cradle and coffin maker. He was born on 14 June 1844 and died in the house where he had lived for eighty-one years in July 1929, at the age of eighty-five. *Nelson's Leader* dated 2 July 1929 stated that he had married a Clitheroe lass named Ann – who must have been his second wife, unless she gave birth to her eldest child at fourteen!

The Woods, who had served as village joiners and cabinetmakers for several generations, purchased the oak pews from the church when it was demolished. With the wood from these, they made replicas of the three-cornered chair that Branwell Brontë had occupied in the back parlour of the Black Bull Inn, a large number of stools and other items of furniture. William, who was an avid admirer of the Brontës, went out of his way to collect Brontë memorabilia. His sizeable collection consisted of various manuscripts, and antiques, which visitors often tried to wrangle out of him, but he always declined their offers of money for he treasured these relics above wealth. William saw it as an honour when foreign tourists interviewed him about his precious memories of the Brontë family.

John's grandmother used to send him up to the rectory every Saturday with muffins she had baked specially for Patrick and Charlotte. When asked about the Brontë family, John would declare, "We thowt nowt abaht 'em. If we'd a' thowt they'd a' been known, we'd a' noaticed a lot more", adding that he thought stories about Branwell's escapades were overdone.

Joiner and artist Thomas Driver used his talents to help Patrick Brontë 'beautify' the Old Bell Chapel at Thornton. A sum of money paid to Driver for his work in the chapel can be found in the accounts for the old parish. When the job was complete, a board was displayed outside the building, giving the names of the incumbent and churchwardens. Thomas appears to have acquired a fancy middle name somehow, for the plaque was signed at the bottom Thomas *Rembrandt* Driver.

The Village Purveyors

Referring to Charlotte, Mrs Gaskell said – "Mr John Greenwood was the one friend she had in Haworth". Mr Greenwood, a man of many talents began his working life as a woolcomber before turning his hand to signwriting, bookbinding and painting and decorating. He was also the Poor Law Relieving Officer for Haworth during the 1850s and ran a stationer's shop on Main Street, which provided the Brontë girls with much needed writing paper. The Haworth Tithe Award puts his premises on the east side of the street, just before the corner of Overdale Terrace.

Man of many parts Joseph Hardacre (born 1790) from Lees near Haworth opened the first druggist's shop in Haworth c.1828-1834. The shop was believed to have been taken over by Betty Hardacre (probably a relative) and afterwards by Robert and Betty Lambert. Hardacre's premises always attracted the upper classes according to a *Keighley News* report. He also acted as clerk to a firm of Keighley solicitors before having to retire due to ill health.

According to American Claude Meeker, when the first tourists began to descend on the moorland village, the enterprising Samuel Feather sold all the photos of the Brontës he could lay his hands on, from his little shop on Main Street. Meeker also stated, albeit wrongly, that it was Samuel, in his capacity as village postmaster, who handed Charlotte Brontë her anticipated letter from publishers *Smith Elder* & Co., regarding her novel *Jane Eyre*. In fact, Edwin (*alias* Samuel?) Feather did not become the Haworth postmaster until 1862, *after* all the Brontës were dead. William Hartley, postmaster, ironmonger and tinner was actually the rightful claimant to the privilege of handling the precious manuscripts and letters from and to the famous sisters, in *his* shop. His premises stood nearest the church – and are well worth a trip inside, if only to see Barraclough's magnificent Masonic grandfather clock. Next door to Hartley's was the Temperance Hotel, which was Southams bakery until recently and next to this was Edwin Feather's rented watchmaker shop, owned by clockmaker Zerubbabel Barraclough.

Edwin Feather confided to writer Walter White that Mr Nicholls had called into his shop on Main Street soon after the death of his wife 'Currer Bell' in 1855. Handing him a small lock of her hair, Nicholls asked him to fashion it into a ring. However, an hour or two later he returned, demanding Charlotte's hair back, because he deemed it to be very valuable and he feared, "Mr Feather might substitute another lock of hair"! Arthur Nicholls must have taken his precious keepsake elsewhere and had the ring made up for, on 15 December 1916, a signet ring initialled 'A.N.', containing a lock of Charlotte's hair was auctioned for £35, having been purchased for £15 at a previous sale. In 1933 a gold memorial ring containing two locks of hair inscribed on the back 'The hair of Emily and Charlotte Brontë; Haworth' was sold in another London auction room and Emily's burnt toilet comb, which she accidentally dropped into the fire on the day of her death, was withdrawn from the sale as there were no bidders for it.

This shop, now known as Angels still displays an erroneous black and white painted sign stating, 'THIS WAS THE POST OFFICE IN THE TIME OF THE BRONTËS AND HERE THEIR FAMOUS MANUSCRIPTS WERE POSTED.'

* * * *

The job of collecting the famous Brontë packets from London fell to a Kildwick lad named John Tillotson, who was apprenticed to sexton John Brown,

THIS WAS THE POST OFFICE IN THE TIME OF THE BRONTËS AND HERE THEIR FAMOUS MANUSCRIPTS WERE POSTED

This building was claimed, erroneously, to have been a post office used by the famous sisters. It only became a post office in 1862, after the sisters had died. *(Marie Campbell)*

Branwell's friend. John would tramp all the way to Keighley's railway station to collect mail addressed to the pseudonymous 'Bell family'. The 1851 census confirms that the lad, then aged twenty, lodged with plasterer William Boocock of Ginnel, Haworth.

*   *   *   *

Jonathan Wright Moore and Nancy Drake were both baptised by Patrick Brontë. Jonathan, who was born and baptised in 1847, remembered Charlotte Brontë helping his widowed mother to thread needles at her millinery shop on Main Street, where her homemade straw hats drew in customers from miles around. Mrs Wright's sister Mary kept a school on North Street, which Charlotte had attended in her youth.

Nancy, who became Mrs John Feather, was born at Haley Farm, Oxenhope. She could well remember the 'Hungry Forties'. Earning her living as a dress-maker, she made a maximum of twenty pence for each finished dress. Married twice, her first husband was Jonathan Whitaker, a man of letters who had been

Stanbury's schoolmaster. Musing on the Brontë family's widespread fame, she told the *Keighley News*, "But fowk didn't think owt abaht 'em then."

* * * *

The story of Jack Toothill (known as "Jack Tooit") appeared in the *Keighley News* on 9 June 1928. Jack, of Shirley Street, had lived in the village all his long life. He took over the running of his father's barbershop, which was a wooden shack standing on the corner Main Street at the top end of Butt Lane, and the first premises in Haworth to be supplied with electricity. Toothill claimed that Mr Brontë had been his father's most awkward customer. He recalled, "When Mr Brontë was under the razor a well-known Churchman entered the shop and finding a large number of customers waiting he vowed in terms more expressive than polite that he would not have bothered coming had he known the shop was so busy. Patrick Brontë told him off for his less than church like attitude telling him that he should turn to his Bible for instruction. "Nay," said the offender, "I've a book at hooam that taks a lot moor hod o' me than t'Bible." "Oh, and what is that?" inquired Revd Brontë. "Tick book," was the swift response, much to the amusement of the listening crowd. Chuckling at the Yorkshireman's reply, Brontë tossed him two shillings (10p). Jack remembered a carol composed by Patrick Brontë who often "chanted the old music while the wind moaned outside in the Haworth streets." Apparently, Branwell used to get old Mr Toothill to crest up his red hair in the hope of adding an inch or two to his diminutive height!

Jack thought the Brontës were "quiet fowk, an' kept ther fingers aht o' other fowk's affairs. They did ther duty, tha understands, but they worn't forivver interferin' like. We didn't knaw shoo (Charlotte) wer famous, or goin' to be." His father witnessed Aunt Branwell's will.

* * * *

The Temperance Hotel could be found at 123 Main Street. It is a quaint old house, sandwiched between what were Edwin Feather's shop and William Hartley's post office. An oaken panel removed from the interior of Haworth's old church was re-used here as an overmantle above a stone fireplace in the sitting room. The seventeenth-century panel depicts a three-bent scroll in stonework stretched across it. It contained the following Scriptural text, as seen by Harwood Brierley when he called at the house in 1899: 'At the last it biteth like a serpent, and stingeth like an adder.' *(Proverbs 23. v. 32)*. Below the centre of the scroll, six adders are coiled up, spreading out in a cluster from a wine cup and a bunch of grapes. "I heard," said Walter White "that the builder of the house was a rabid teetotaller." The original owner of the property was supposed to have been a reformed drunkard who had the text included as a permanent reminder of his former follies and wicked ways.

'Locals' and their Keepers

'His warmest welcome at an inn' wrote the old poet Will Shenstone and nowhere could that be truer than the Black Bull. Exactly when this fine hostelry was erected is unknown, as the original deeds were lost. Throughout its history, this aged inn, nestling by the side of Haworth church, must have been privy to many an old-time drama concerning its bygone inhabitants. How I wish it could speak and impart them. However, there are still plenty of known tales about this popular watering place to be gleaned.

Charles Hale, an American visitor and friend of Mrs Gaskell, stayed at the inn in 1861. From a corner of the Black Bull he wrote several illuminating letters, describing his time there and the villagers he had met. 'I need not say we had a merry evening – decorous and quiet, of course, but full of pleasant incident. They sang for me some Yorkshire songs and patriotic melodies, and at last our little circle broke up, all well pleased with each other, and I felt as if I almost had a personal acquaintance with Branwell and with the rest of the Brontës. I retired to rest in a very good bed-room, an immense mahogany four-poster bed, with heavy curtains, very high, a little staircase of mahogany carpeted, being provided to get into bed with. The sheets were clean and the covering ample. Altogether one might find a very much worse place to pass the night in, than the Black Bull at Haworth ... '

When Will Carlton paid a visit to the 'Bull' with some friends in 1880, a girl's likeness hanging on the wall caught the attention of one of the party, who asked the elderly landlady who the sitter was. To his surprise, she brought out the same pair of delicate shoes worn by the pretty girl in the picture, who turned out to be her grandmother!

At the turn of the nineteenth-century Dick o' th' Clough could often be found propping up the bar, reminiscing about Branwell Brontë's favourite ale, "I mind th' time when th' 'Bull' watter ran right through th' kirkyard-thick an' strong it war, afore iver it touched th' malt. I tell ye, th' beer hed body in't them days."

Water used for beer making was drawn from a deep well into a wide cistern and then exposed to the air and sun with a little powdered chalk thrown in. The best water to use raised lather with soap, like that in Haworth's graveyard, so vividly described by Dick.

The funeral of Mr William Sugden took place at Haworth on the 20 April 1929. After retiring as licensee of the Black Bull, where his family had been proprietors for generations, William spent his last years living at Darnside, Pilling in Lancashire. He was born on the 19 April 1849 and remembered Patrick Brontë, his daughter Charlotte and her husband Nicholls. It was well before his time though, that Emily Brontë used to run to the old house-of-call to warn her brother of an impending visit by their father. Branwell, quick as mercury would make a dash for home through a little window overlooking the stables. Whilst making good his escape, the inmates of the inn – who harboured a genuine affection for the lad, were busily denying that "Mester Branwell" had been there at all! Sometimes when Branwell's limbs refused to carry him home after a heavy drinking session at the inn, he was deposited in an upstairs chamber for the night.

The late Jonas Bradley, an authority on Branwell thought that if he had been blessed with a more sympathetic father he would not have turned to drink and therefore, would have been a very different character.

Mrs Waller took over the running of the "Bull" in 1939. Previously she and her family had lived at the Old Hall Hotel in Leeds, where her favourite dog was run over and killed after their nursemaid called the animal across the road. Mrs Waller was so upset she sacked the nanny and had her pet's skin cured as a memento, which she subsequently kept in a trunk at the Black Bull! Her daughter, Mrs Crook of Harden wrote 'my mother Mrs Isabella Waller, a licensee throughout her adult life, took over the Bull. She was very untypical of the perceived licensee, a philanthropist teetotaller, respected by customers and employees alike. She died in 1948, her coffin being carried at her funeral by several of our regular customers. My sister Miss Isabella Waller took over the licence and she and I were there until 1952. The Bull had a taproom with iron tables holding brass domino score markers, wooden bench seating and buffets, dartboard and sawdust filled spittoons. The black leaded fireplace always had a coal fire. Prices were cheaper in there. There was a music room with a huge table (where mother was laid out in her coffin until the day of her funeral) – the room was reserved during the forties for the hordes of hikers we catered for. The soldiers billeted in the Chapel and Church schoolrooms used it too for noisy renditions of popular songs of the day. As a child, I went to sleep to the thumping strains of *Run Rabbit Run, Underneath the Lamplight,* etc. A small snug room was little used. The Brontë Room was the one our visitors' (not tourists in those days!) 'gravitated to. They sat in Branwell's chair and rang the tapestry bell pull linked to the bell in the passage. I have that bell linked up to my garden gate here at home, and I'm still polishing the brass and copper round trays on which the drinks were balanced from bar to room. Rumour had it a passage ran underground from the huge cellars down Main Street but although my school friends and me spent hours tapping around we found no trace. One of our guest bedrooms was avoided by returning visitors who claimed they'd been disturbed by footsteps coming upstairs and halting outside the door.' Perhaps this was the ghost of Branwell?

Swedish journalists staying at the inn in the 1970s were so taken with a collection box in the shape of a three-foot high little boy that Billy Kirk, the landlord allowed them to carry the box back to Sweden to raise money for the National Association for the Welfare of the Blind.

Haworth innkeeper Enoch Thomas, landlord of the King's Arms and of the Black Bull suffered terribly from bouts of depression. Patrick Brontë confirmed this, saying that he suffered from "a very severe and great affliction". His good friend Branwell Brontë nicknamed him the "Devil's Thumb" in a letter delivered to 'Worshipful Master of the (Freemasons') Lodge', who was church sexton John Brown. The original letter disappeared in 1874 but fortunately John Brown's brother memorised every line of it and Francis Leyland copied it down.

Enoch's wife Hannah wed Haworth's Dr Wheelhouse at Bradford soon after Enoch's death. Nobody really knows what became of Enoch's property and money other than the fact that Wheelhouse and Hannah moved into a cottage that had belonged to him.

Another landlord of the King's Arms was confectioner Joseph Fox, who provided the fare for Emily Brontë's funeral feast, where no doubt a coffin-shaped seed cake would have been made for the occasion. A Miss Utley

The King's Arms, Haworth, where the innkeeper provided food for Emily Brontë's funeral feast
(Marie Campbell)

acted as a bearer at Emily's funeral. She received a pair of new white silk gloves to wear during the service, as was the custom.

In October of 1863 woolcomber and Oddfellow Jonas Murgatroyd better known as "Jonas o' Rogers" was found dead at Dockroyd, Oakworth. The old man whose daughter who had been landlady of the King's Arms had fallen down a flight of steps in Haworth sixty years previously and had been deaf ever since. He taught himself sign language.

A familiar Haworth figure passed away somewhat suddenly in April 1907. John Hartley, landlord of the King's Arms Inn had been there for forty-seven years, and for some twenty years on and off, had been a member of the Haworth Local Board and Urban District Council. He was fifty-eight years of age when he died and for forty-seven of them had helped to entertain the ten Haworth and Stanbury boys who were annually clothed in blue under the terms of Midgley's Charity, together with their parents and guardians to a most substantial dinner at his house on the Sunday before Christmas.

Hartley had been a member of the Woodlands Lodge (No. 185), of the United Order of the Oddfellows for forty years, and of the Shepherds of the Mount Lodge (No. 1758), of the Loyal Order of the Ancient Shepherds (Ashton Unity), since its formation at the Kings Arms in 1876. He was considered to have been a quiet, unassuming man who believed in calm plodding and honest toil. The King's Arms also doubled as the Manor Court House from 1748 until 1870.

Down the road at the New Inn on Sun Street the landlord once baked his customers a lovely meat pie. When thanked for his kindness, he asked his customers if they had all enjoyed his cooking, before letting slip he'd had a visit from a local rat catcher who had given him a bag full of rodents. It didn't take long for the penny to drop that the tasty meat pie they had just scoffed was in fact rat pie! A few moments later, his horrified regulars charged outside to be sick. The doors of The New Inn were closed for the last time in 1930 and the premises were converted into a private house two years later.

A worn drover's track once zig-zagged its way from Hazel Mill, Stanbury to Haworth Moor, beyond the building closest to the Brontë Waterfall. Passing trade stopped here to imbibe a welcome drop or two of special home brewed strong ale from the Pack Horse Inn, fondly known as 'Betty's, where 'tales much older than their ale went round.' A swinging sign designed to entice wayfarers hung outside the door:

> This inn hangs high upon the moss,
> Refreshment here for man and horse.
> My ale is good, my measure just,
> Come, pay today, ter morn we trust.

One regular visitor to the inn was Smith Bank farmer Joe or Jose Shackleton, described as a 'long loose built fellow', who had spent the whole of his life working on his remote Stanbury farm and liked nothing better than to listen to travellers' tales of America and the like. Thus inspired, he mused of making a butter mould bearing his own initials J.S. thinking that he might one day supply large quantities of his homemade best butter to grateful wealthy American citizens. He never did make his fortune in butter but found he was more than content milking his cows until his death.

Fun and Games with Old Habits

They say old customs live longer in old-fashioned places and this was certainly true of Haworth for each New Year's Eve the streets were alive with jolly music played by a comic music band the *Bingem Bangem Band*, accompanied by a throng of revellers attired in the most outrageous costumes they could find. The Lord of Misrule was chosen from the crowd to lead his unruly mob, complete with marching band into all kinds of wild but harmless escapades. One of the highlights was bursting into Haworth church in the middle of Divine Service.

The last night of April was devoted to a queer old custom by West Yorkshire folk. There was a saying that the first day of April was the "fool's" day and the last the "devil's." The latter being dubbed "Mischief Neet", when imps of mischief set about wreaking havoc on the population in any way they could. Mischief Night is now observed on the 4 November in the West Riding.

Mr James Riley of Coldshaw, Haworth began bell ringing in St. Michael's belfry in 1877. After ringing in four changes of five thousand and forty peals – one each at Oxenhope and Addingham, then two at Haworth, he was interviewed by the *Keighley News*, when he related two amusing incidents:

"In the old days a favourite prank played on the ringers when practising in winter months was the use of burning cayenne pepper, which soon put an end to the ringing, compelling ringers to seek refuge at the top of the tower to escape the fumes. There they had to stay until someone released them as the mischief-makers always made sure to fasten the entrance door with cord."

The second episode James recounted, 'which caused much annoyance to the Conservative Party of that day', was the occasion when six ringers ascended the tower and rang a merry peal to commemorate the return of the late Sir Isaac Holden to Parliament during the rectorship of the late Revd John Wade. '

A son told of his father growing up in Thornton during the mid-nineteenth century where young lads were particularly fond of a game of window tapping. One day at Windy Top "in t' middle house was a little old chap that lived by hissen. He was praying to the Lord to send him some bread. These lads listened for a bit and mi father ran home, got a loaf, wrapped it i' paper and tied it up wi' band, and they got on top of this little cot and dropped it darn t' chimney. It made a din when it dropped on t' floor. He jumped up, oppened it out and 'Praise the Lord, Praise the Lord," the old lad cried out joyfully, 'I've gotton a loaf.'

Old Wives' Tales

Superstitious folk believed that if they touched the warm death sweat of a highwayman, it would somehow transmit a kind of magic spirit to them. The dead scoundrel's hand was brushed against the face of a sick person because it was thought to contain special healing qualities. Ailing people, especially those suffering from throat complaints were allowed on the gallows for this purpose, after paying the executioner a small fee for the privilege. Touching a dead body would prevent a person from dreaming about it and a piece of cloth cut from a gibbeted body was considered an effective charm against the power of witches, as was carrying something that had belonged to the unburied dead.

A severed hand cut close to the wrist and stolen from the body of a murderer or highwayman was highly prized by occultists who pickled the gruesome thing before muttering the *Lord's Prayer* in reverse order. Five locks of hair plucked from the dead man's head were mixed with the fat of a black male cat and made into wicks fixed onto the fingers and thumb of the severed hand. The lighted candle or 'Hand of Glory' as it was otherwise known, was used to charm victims into a deep trance before being robbed of their possessions. There exists a vague story about a Hand of Glory lying hidden below the waters of Backstone Beck on Ilkley Moor.

Hand Of Glory

Now open lock. To the Dead Man's knock!
Fly bolt, and bar and band! -
Nor move, nor swerve, Joint, muscle or nerve,
At the spell of a dead man's hand!
Sleep all who sleep! – Wake all who wake! -
But be as Dead for the Dead man's sake!

The Ingoldsby Legends: Thos Ingoldsby alias Freemason Richard Harris Barham, 1840

Two Very Different 'Sutcliffes'

James Sutcliffe

In a sleepy overgrown corner of Haworth's burial ground is a gravemarker, bearing only the initials of its occupant and the year of interment. The identity of this 'J. S.' remained a mystery until recent investigations with the generous help of Haworth historian Steven Wood. Legend passed down through generations of Haworthites told of this nameless corpse being hanged at York for sheep steal-ing. In reality, beneath this plain marker lie the remains of Haworth's very own Turpin or Nevison – James Sutcliffe. This 'J.S.' used robbery and violence to earn his daily bread. His career on the highways and by-ways came to an abrupt end when he was caught, arrested and committed for trial, being imprisoned at York Castle for "ATTEMPTED HIGHWAY ROBBERY" and "SEIZING WITH

VIOLENCE MONEY BELONGING TO ANOTHER". According to the charge-sheet:

James Sutcliffe alias Freeman alias Smith
For having feloniously assaulted
Mr John Wignall
On the King's Highway, (on Halifax Road) near Keighley in the West Riding
Putting him in bodily fear of his life,
And feloniously stealing from his person a parcel
Containing sixty guineas and several notes and bills.

Sutcliffe was removed from his Majesty's jail, by virtue of a writ of *Habeas Corpus*, taken into custody and charged upon the oath of Mr John Wignall for attempting to steal upwards of two hundred pounds in cash, notes and bills from his person.

At the Lent Assizes held on Saturday 5 March 1796, the highwayman appeared before the King's Justice for sentencing. Among the elected Grand Jury members, were Mr Henry Wickham of Cottingley and Johnson Atkinson Busfield of Myrtle Grove, Bingley. The Crown Bar was closed while James Sutcliffe (alias *Freeman* alias *Smith*) stood before Hon. Mr Justice Heath, accused of highway robbery and burglary – both capital offences. Without exception, Sutcliffe and eight other felons alongside him were found guilty. They all received the maximum sentence the law could hand out – execution. Justice Heath bade the condemned men prepare themselves for the next world, for there would be no mercy in this. However, before leaving York for Lancaster Assizes, Heath saw fit to reprieve six of their number. Not Sutcliffe though, his neck was for Jack Ketch (the hangman). What the highwayman's thoughts were on the subject of his impending public execution, one cannot say, but an account from the pages of *Blackwood's Edinburgh Magazine* dated April 1827, written by a man who survived the hangman's noose gives us an insight into the mind of a person about to die in this manner:

'The mental and bodily sufferings of the condemned man in his cell, his waking dreams, and his dead sleep till the morning of the execution ... I remember beginning to move forward ... I heard the deep voice of the chaplain reading as he walked before us. It was the funeral service – the order for the grave – the office for those that were senseless and dead. I recollect the cloudy, misty morning; the wet that lay upon the scaffold – I can see it all now the whole horrible landscape before me. The scaffold – the rain – the faces of the multitude ... I never saw so many objects at once so plainly and distinctly in all my life as at that one glance; but it only lasted for an instant. From that look, and from that instant, all that followed is a blank.'

This verse also gives an insight:

All you that in the condemn'd hold do lie,
Prepare you, for tomorrow you shall die;
Watch all, and pray, the hour is drawing near,
That you before the Almighty must appear:
Examine well yourselves, in the time repent,
That you may not to eternal flames be sent.

Hones Table Book, 1830

On the allotted day of the hanging, Saturday 2 April 1796 – the day after All Fools Day – the Revd George Brown preached an excellent sermon to James Sutcliffe and his fellow condemned prisoners at York Castle jail from 1 Thess. V 8, 9. *'But let us, who are of the day, be sober, putting on the breast plate of love, and for a helmet the hope of salvation. For God has not appointed us to wrath, but to obtain salvation by our Lord Jesus Christ.'*

Having made sure relatives had obtained a decent coffin, Sutcliffe, according to custom, would have set out his funeral apparel, then shaved and dressed in his best suit, before taking his place beside two other condemned felons on the Knavesmire gallows. The first was Thomas Maclean, deemed 'quite a lad', who had been convicted of attempting to rob one Innocenito Rossi, a Jewish peddler from York. The second was Thomas Birch, a private in the Surrey Militia whose hunger had driven him to steal a hen. All three acknowledged the justice of their sentence and made a confession before dying penitently.

The reader may be interested to know that it was common practice for a criminal's body to be cut down from the gallows and paraded through the streets after their execution. In addition, medical men in those days were permitted by law to cut up these corpses for the purpose of anatomical research. Perhaps Sutcliffe, aware of the dire penalties his chosen line of work carried, elicited a promise from relatives and friends that they would steal his corpse away before it was claimed for the dissection table.

Another Yorkshireman Huffy White was to follow in Sutcliffe's footsteps in 1813, after robbing the Leeds Mail Coach. Huffy kept his nerve and sense of humour to the end though – his last request was for another man to hang in his place!

The first Tyburn gallows erected at York were made by joiner Joe Penny of Blake Street, York and the first person to be executed there was soldier Edward Hewison. Assize records document that between 1379 and 1876 five hundred and sixty-four people were either beheaded or hanged at York, including Sutcliffe. The gallows were removed from the Abbot of St Mary's to Knavesmire, situated close to today's York Racecourse.

Whatever the reason for James Sutcliffe's body being retrieved from York's gallows, it took a day and a night for friends and relations to cart back his broken remains to Haworth. Once there, he was immediately buried in a corner of hallowed ground on Sunday 3 April 1796. No words other than his initials *J.S.* and a date of *1796* perpetuate his memory on a heavy slab of stone designed to deter the detested bodysnatchers of the day.

John Sutcliffe

Searching through a box of old documents in Keighley Reference Library, I came across this illuminating letter dated 16 November 1803, addressed to Mr Timothy Sutcliffe, Haworth, near Bradford, Yorkshire from his son Revd John Sutcliffe (a relative of the nefarious highwayman?), the contents of which I have copied verbatim for the reader's interest:

> Dear Father
> I hope you will excuse me for not writing to you for some time, for bad news comes soon enough, I have waited a few weeks hoping that affairs would put

on a better aspect, but I am sorry to say, they are worse. It is always unwillingly that I write bad news, but at present I must either write it or nothing at all. – My Rector is a Gentleman only in appearance, he minds nothing he says, he refuses paying my Salary quarterly, and I must give him half a year's notice before I leave him, which things I shall never submit to, it being, you know, contrary to our agreement. – I have been obliged to be boarded with him, for which he will keep nearly all my Salary, and hardly content with that, but I am resolved to get a Lodging, whether good or bad, dear or cheap, though my stay here must not be long, as he only cheats me in every way he can. I have wished a thousand times I had never comed, I believe he will never pay me a farthing willingly, he advertised in the newspaper for a long time but could not catch hold of any one, which you are certain, is a sufficient proof of his bad behaviour. The trouble and anxiety which I at present labour under here, is better felt than expressed ... Card playing and other kinds of gaming is the constant evening diversion of him and his family and I am resolved never to follow such practices, and even abhor them. I am looked on as a ridiculous young man and despised by them. He will grudge more at giving his curate five shillings (25p) than loose 5 Pounds by playing at cards with anybody. – From what I have hinted to you, you are certain, that this situation will not suit me, nor indeed can you wish it, if you have any regard for my welfare. – He might well be writing and following after me, because me could get nobody else. I did not think that a Parson would have attempted to use me so ill, but I find they are as bad as other people. He would have cheated me out of the Surplice fees, which are only ten shillings (50p) a quarter or about 2 Guineas (£2.20p) a year at the outside, by saying that the Clerk kept them till the end of the year, and I could not have them. – Be so good as to answer me as soon as you receive this, and tell me what to do, for I am nearly at despair.

I remain, Dear Father, with regard and respect, Your affectionate Son,
J. Sutcliffe.

Please answer direct below

Revd John Sutcliffe at the Revd W. Downing's, Quainton Rectory near Aylesbury, Bucks.

PS: He will not allow me a room and fire to myself, though he might do it very easily, but his ill-natured temper would not submit to it, if it served him nothing. – *I desire you to take off the direction and burn this Letter as soon as you have read it and not shew it to anybody.*

Whatever action John's father took after receiving his son's letter, which he failed to burn, is not recorded; but it is known that John eventually removed to Saddleworth near Manchester, inheriting a small fortune when his father died. After John's own death, his executors found he had badly neglected his affairs and were left to sort them out in the best way they could.

Heather Heaven

'A little higher up the road is the cottage-scene of 'Heather Heaven', wrote Harwood Brierley in *Local Notes and Queries*, February 1899, 'where once lived Emily Northrop with her father, "owd Josewa Northrop," a moor keeper. "Heather Cottage" was an old, cold, decayed little place, with a few raggy beehives, planted above the doors, and the fold, outhouses, and shabby hayrick falling to ruin on each side. A young and energetic farm-servant might within the short space of a week have so rectified things that would scarcely have known itself again. Not that "owd Josewa Northrop" was idle. Far from it. He did what he could, no one could do more. He patched up with his trembling hands, now here and now there, he was, in his way, as industrious as every thorough-bred old Yorkshireman is.' Josewa – or Joshua – always had his faithful dog Shep by his side and more often than not his little Emily. 'Sometimes the girl would lie glorying in her solitude on a heathy bank near her father's door, while not a sound stirred her great purple world – big enough to hold a city like Thebes, Babylon, or Capernaum – except, the fairy chimes of the million heather-bells from their own pretty spirelets of native green. And here, "being old, and under-standing things now," she would read Emily Brontë's lovely poems.

It was not a happy day for Emily when a companion was thrust on her in the person of young Roland Rothsay, 'whose sportsman father wished to get him broken off bad habits contracted in the town, and to this he made arrangements with "owd Josewa." The boy had a miserable time of it at "Heather Cottage." As the time approached for him to return home, this observation escaped his lips: "I wouldn't be paid fifty pounds to come moping up here a second time!" Emily was very indignant. "Oh," said the boy, "you may rile, and pout, and sulk, and ever so much more, if you like, little country puss, but I do hate your nasty ling, which harbours vermin, covers your trousers with shives and burrs, is only fit for besom-makers, and isn't half so poetic, all the blue lot of it, as a leaf of a tobacco plant! I shan't come here again! And if you stay here much longer, you'll go stark mad! What you see in black bogs and coffee-coloured pulps, which attempt to swallow you up directly you put your foot outside the house, I'm sure I don't know. I wouldn't live in a world where the winds are always riving, where there's nothing to see and nobody to talk to, where there are earwigs on every wall, bogs on both sides, and sheep and birds making noises hideous enough to drive anyone silly!' "I love it all, Roland," said the unsophisticated little Emily in reply, "for I was born among it. If I were sent to America or Leeds or Greenland, or any other place. I should think of it every bit of the time, and never be happy till I got back. I shall die here, and I daresay my father will bury me under the heather behind our house."

Roland grew into a man, and went the way of the cosmopolitan roamer. At last the world palled on him, and he remembered Emily Northrop in her moorland home far away in England. Thoughts of her drew him homeward into Yorkshire during the month of August. With a new untried gun he arrived on the Oxenhope moors, expecting that old Joshua would be there, and willing to get him a licence to shoot grouse. But the keeper's house, he soon learnt, had perished in a gale nearly five years ago. Joshua had been killed in his bed, and Emily seriously wounded beneath the flying stones and mortar.

A few months later another Heather Cottage had arisen on the site of the old one. "Who lives here?" asked the lord of the soil, one day, when his agent was accompanying him around the estate. "A young man named Rothsay sir. A likely fellow, too, he having a fancy to build this house out of his own pocket, so I let him. Are we to call sir?" "Most decidedly. I want to see all my tenants today." They were speedily ushered by Roland himself into an artistically ornamented parlour, whose existence here the house's exterior utterly belied. Sir John S.

could not doubt that Rothsay was poor, living on his small earnings, that he was the son of a small farmer, fond of stale country jokes and anecdotes, and pale ale; or that he was – and this, after all, did look more like it – that he was the son of a civilian who had come down into the world. Yet, in either case, where would the young fellow's taste for costly possessions have sprung from?"

"Why, man," said bluff Sir John on becoming familiar with his new keeper. "If you live all alone up here, without so much as a wife, you must feel lonelier than an anchorite on St. Bernard's Pass, even amongst all your treasures."

"But, Sir John, my treasures speak to me of my deceased parents, and the moors speak of precious memories. Not for gold's sake would I rob my soul of them. Within the walls that stood on this very site up to a few years ago I spent three of the happiest weeks of my life. An aged keeper, my predecessor, and his only child, a girl of fourteen, lived here."

"You mean Joshua and Emily Northrop?"

"Yes. For Emily I have sought in vain. Everything points to the fact that she was thrust by cruel Fate from her native hearth, her native heather and..."

"Can she possibly have suffered? If so, I grieve that she never told me."

"What?"

"I say I grieve that she never told me."

"Who?"

The baronet was taken aback by his servant's apparently discourteous address. "Do you know what you are talking about Rothsay?" he asked. But Rothsay now stood up with surprise in his eyes that, to his superior, it resembled fright. He did not speak. "I think," said Sir John S., as to his agent, "that she is unaware that the house has been rebuilt. But I will bring her to see it with her own eyes. She will be pleased."

And now a vision flashed across Roland Rothsay's brain. Emily had become the baronet's adopted daughter! The natural daughter of an old, faithful, and valued servant, was it unlikely that in her orphaned state she would go to the childless child-loving Sir John? God be thanked it was so! Roland felt a relief full fifty times greater than he was used to do, when the drop scene rolled down some spectacular denouncement. And within fifteen minutes he was ready to proceed with Sir John to his Lancashire abode, in order to look at Emily Northrop's face once more.

*   *   *   *

Novelist Halliwell Sutcliffe (1870-1932), whose vivid imagination created numerous works based on his family's native surroundings of Oxenhope, Haworth and Stanbury, died in 1932. He was said to have amassed more knowledge of legend and lore within the boundaries of Old West Yorkshire than any other man. When writing his manuscripts, Halliwell acted out each individual part, speaking in both male and female voices until he was satisfied he'd got the narrative right. Drawn to his beloved Haworth moors day or night whatever the weather, he soaked up the atmosphere so close to Emily Brontës heart – his book *By Moor and Fell*, is a must for Brontë enthusiasts.

Sutcliffe's funeral took place at Burnsall. On top of the coffin, which was draped in a pale blue pall, was a bunch of mauve tulips. After the service, his body was cremated at Bradford crematorium. Relatives scattered Halliwell's ashes to the winds at a secret location out on the lonely wild moors he had so worshipped in life; no doubt an act Emily Brontë would have favoured for herself.

*   *   *   *

Another 'Man of the Moors' was chiropodist Alfred Holdsworth of Hob Cottage, adjoining Stanbury's Old Silent Inn. Alfred was fond of tramping the 'wild and windy heights' whatever the weather or time of day and knew every path and every track. Speaking about the subject closest to his heart, he told the Keighley Photographic Society in 1951 that, 'To understand these moors requires more than a knowledge of their contour and line. They may be seen as wild stretches of heather and ling, of deep valleys and crags, windy escarpments and solitary as a symphony of light, of wild wind and limpid silences. They are like the sea that every change of sky re-creates and makes a new splendour. Word, camera, or brush are utterly inadequate to give shape to the everchanging mood.' It is clear that Alfred felt a close affinity to the moors and Emily Brontë herself could have written these following lines of his:

> 'And I knew a sense of quiet grandeur, in which my being and all beings, even the stones on the moor and the unbending hills, were come to fulfilment; we were one and indivisible.' When Alfred Holdsworth died in 1963 at the age of seventy-eight, a close friend told the *Keighley News*, "He was not of this age, but a man who was outside the normal rat race of this modern day, but still had a sense of awareness of the wonder of life around him."

Upstanding Citizens

Haworth doctor Amos Ingham attended Charlotte Brontë during her last illness. He lived in the old Manor House until commissioning a new home, Ashmount, erected in 1870. The gardens at Ashmount boasted Twelve Apostles (carved stones), thought to date from the Georgian period. With the exception of three that were left to lie in the garden, these curious stones were eventually sold at auction. Another stone in this garden was carved with the demonic face of a jolly Devil complete with horns that peeped out from a wall. Brontë servant Martha Brown worked for the doctor before leaving for Ireland to serve Nicholls, who had pressed her not to marry Jemmy Whitham.

The Revd James Whalley, who was born in Oxenhope, died very suddenly at Coleridge Place, Burmantofts, Leeds, on Thursday 24 August 1882. He was buried in the old Haworth churchyard the following Tuesday. The Right Revd Bishop Ryan conducted the burial service and several clergymen were numbered amongst the mourners. As a young man, Whalley had been apprenticed to a Halifax greengrocer but decided it was not for him; so he forsook the 'knights of the counter' to take holy orders. He entered St. Bee's College in 1857, was created a deacon two years later and ordained as a priest by the Bishop of Ripon in 1861. After a varied career, he moved to Cross Stone, near Hebden Bridge, taking charge of St. Paul's church in 1869. Whalley took up writing, his theme being tales from the area and people he knew best, including Jack Kay –

Haworth's astrologer, who featured in his book *The Wild Moor*. In 1877, he settled at St. Albans Church, Leeds where he stayed until his death. He had been ill for sometime and died from an apoplectic fit.

An essay by him entitled *The Deserted House* was published in 1869. In it, he describes an abandoned dwelling on the moors, not far from the Wagon and Horses Inn at Oxenhope:

> 'The traveller, taking his farewell of the last whitewashed companion a little below the gamekeeper's house, (on Cockhill Moor) does not proceed many yards before he beholds on his left an uninhabited house, which he naturally supposes was built before the business of a glazier was known in the moorland district. I doubt whether a particle of glass of any kind, or an atom of the shavings of timber, can be found in the "window frames." Still, the house appears to be in what businessmen call "a finished condition". When I beheld it, I had not the remotest idea of describing it ... the burglar will probably find more difficulty in making his way through one of these stone windows, than he ever did in attempting to pry into one of these stone windows. This house, like the gamekeeper's, had formerly "*wooden* window frames". But these had been removed, and large flat stones have been substituted in their stead, and now neither wooden nor stone frames are required. Whoever was the builder or occupier of this house, he undoubtedly, after a few years' residence within its walls, began to feel within himself irrepressible longings for the society of his fellow men, and unquenchable desires for the sweets of friendship. It is not at all probable that he advertised the house to sell, or be let, in "the Manchester, Leeds, Halifax, Bradford, Keighley, and Todmorden papers," well knowing that no one would buy, and that no *Yorkshireman* would "take" the house except on one condition – viz., to receive a premium annually for occupying the same! After all, might not this house or place be converted into a splendid country villa for one of the Bradford merchants or manufacturers!'

* * * *

John Greenwood's granddaughter, Mrs Judith Moore of Halifax inherited, among other Brontë relics, tracings of three half-length female figures taken from a painting by Branwell. Her grandfather had carefully written the names of the three sisters below each figure. The tracing of Emily matched perfectly with the portrait in the National Gallery, which had been defaced by Nicholls (apparently, John Greenwood's wife Hannah did not like this Reverend gent at all). It was John Greenwood who informed Mrs Gaskell of Charlotte's death. He died in March 1863, aged 56.

John's son, Mr E. G. Greenwood the younger died in June 1922. For some years, Greenwood Jnr. worked as a piece-looker for Messrs. Merrall's until he and his brother, Richard took up dentistry. He was a member of the old Haworth Band as well as the choir and attended hand bell ringing contests at Belle Vue, Manchester. His brother Brontë Greenwood was born on 12 March 1859. Nicholls was outraged to hear the Greenwoods were bent on having their infant son christened Brontë and flatly refused to conduct the baptism service.

* * * *

In November 1861, Charles Hale wrote:

> 'So she (*sic* he) went unchristened a long time during which she had an illness, which might have been fatal, and her parents were much concerned lest she should die without the ceremony, which their faith makes important. Old Mr Brontë heard of the circumstance, and taking advantage of a temporary absence of his curate, he sent for the child, and although himself more than eighty years old and released from ordinary parochial duties he christened her by the name her parents had selected and entered all in the Church Register (dated 14 November 1859). Mr Nicholls returned, and all seemed well, but the next child (Phoebe Ann Whitham) that was christened by him, caused him to open the Register where he saw of course the obnoxious entry; he flew into a violent passion, bounced out of the church, and rushed to old Mr Brontë whom he scolded well. But the old man is believed to have made good his defence – told his curate that he (Mr N.) would have had a very serious thing to answer for to the Bishop if the child had died unchristened, owing to his refusal for no proper reason to perform the ceremony. But you may imagine that incident affected the popular estimate of the two clergymen. Mr Brontë was seriously and truly beloved. The sexton said he was the most truly kind and considerate man, for the feelings and rights of others, that was ever known ... The sexton by the way, did not tell me this story about his child's christening, but Mrs Gaskell'.

However, our informant made the mistake of thinking the child was a she when in fact it was a he! At seventeen-and-a-half months Brontë Greenwood was described as being a 'puny precocious little lad.'

* * * *

Some possessions found their way overseas. Mr Brontë Greenwood, an American barrister from Philadelphia, came to Haworth in 1930 to visit relatives. He owned Charlotte's writing desk, which was purchased by his family at the parsonage sale in 1861.

* * * *

In the latter part of the nineteenth century, Harwood Brierley – the author of *Local Notes and Queries*, revealed personal experiences of two West Yorkshire villages. He began: 'A flagged causeway leads along the ridge from Haworth churchyard. I travelled this time with the curate Mr Lewis. The last occasion was 26 May 1890. It surprises me to behold in every flag a familiar face. In 1890, my Farsley friend and I were here to enquire of a native the way to Oxenhope. He stood stock still like a post, and more of an indicative nod than an uttered word directed us across "there" and immediately became deaf to our entreaties for further information. We left him staring across the valley into vacuity. In the days of the Brontës there were but few houses in the valley below where there we see an ever-expanding colony bisected by a railway. The curate said that Emily Brontë frequently walked this way on the moors from the parsonage.'

On meeting an Oxenhope rent collector, Brierley described him as: 'A little man, with almost colourless eyes placed somewhere near his nose giving him a ferret-like appearance – who once beguiled a quarter of an hour of my time by relating a strange dream which he had the night before, wherein he saw an unknown enemy rolling a huge stone down upon his head from one of the quarry sides.'

Passing Benjamin Feather's Wagon and Horse and the oddly named Klondike, the intrepid traveller took advantage of the hospitality of the licensee at the Dog and Gun Inn. He was just in time to hear an argumentative farmer claim he did not believe in three things – 'the lawyer, the doctor, and the parson. Before he'd have a lawyer he'd pay twice; before he'd have a doctor he'd die off; before he'd have a parson he'd go to H—- a very bad place.' Harwood thought him a 'hopelessly stupid ox from Oxenhope'. Settling himself in a quite corner of the front room, two pictures occupied his attention. Encased in rosewood frames, the first was entitled, *Two Comrades Before and After the Battle* whilst the other depicted *Cromwell refusing the Crown of England*.

Those who Served

Who was Tabitha Aykroyd, born in 1770 and nicknamed 'Old Tabby Brontë' by the village boys? There is no record of Tabby's christening in the Haworth registers. If she had not been baptised, might Patrick Brontë have performed the necessary ceremony post haste?

For more than thirty years, servant-cum-guardian Tabitha or Tabby Aykroyd gave her heart and soul to the Brontë family. On dark winter evenings, Tabby gathered her motherless charges around her by the glowing embers of the fire, where she related thrilling tales of the phantom black dog Guytrash, fairies and hobgoblins; for Tabby was a great authority on moorland superstitions and old country teachings.

In 1836, Tabby broke her leg, which later became badly ulcerated, so she was sent off to relatives living in Haworth. The pining Brontë siblings went on hunger strike until their substitute mother was reinstated to parsonage life. Predictably, Tabby and Aunt Branwell did not see eye to eye on most things. Nonetheless, she was a loyal servant, refusing to divulge even the faintest tit-bit of gossip about her charges or family concerns to *anyone*.

Where did Tabby hail from? Tabitha appears to have been related to the Wood family of Haworth. A deed brought to my attention by Haworth historian Steven Wood, bearing William Wood's name and dated 1836 (the year Tabby's leg broke), describes her as a 'single woman' – a fact confirmed by the 1851 census. Brontë lore says she moved away from the village after her marriage and returned when she was widowed. However, no evidence of a marriage or husband has ever been located. So, who was George Aykroyd, whose remains lie in the same grave as Tabby? George did not die until 1839 – some thirteen years *after* Tabby's employment at the parsonage, when she was still a spinster. Could the mysterious George Aykroyd have been her brother?

Her grave lies amongst the darkened grey tombstones near to the old gateway (if it ever existed), which superstitious Chinese would dub the 'Gateway to the World of Spirit', amidst tall trees where rooks have made their home.

SACRED to the Memory of
GEORGE AYKROYD of HAWORTH HALL,
Who died Jan. 6th 1839. Aged 76 Years.

Also SUSANNA WOOD, who died
April 23rd 1847. Aged 90 Years.
Also of Tabitha Aykroyd of
Haworth, who died Febry. 17th 1855
In the 85th Year of her Age.
Faithful Servant of the Brontë
Family for over thirty Years.

According to the diary of F.N. Jersey, there was a Primitive Methodist gathering at Mill Hill on 25 April 1821. He wrote: 'Went to open Haworth. I sang a hymn down the street. The people flocked as doves to the windows. I preached to about nine hundred people and two wicked men were awakened. Praise the Lord!'

Was Tabby one of the nine hundred? Primitive Methodists worshipped in a tiny single storey building at Higher Mill, Hill, christened 'The Old White House'. A Sunday school opened here in 1835 and soon afterwards, a brand new chapel was erected on land sold to them for the sum of thirty-five pounds by Haworth butchers John and William Thomas.

Strangely, on the day of Tabby's death Charlotte Brontë, the last of Tabby's charges, accepting her own death was almost upon her, made out a will in the presence of her father and Martha Brown. 'In the name of God Amen, I, CHARLOTTE NICHOLLS, of Haworth in the parish of Bradford and county of York, being of sound and disposing mind, memory and understanding, but mindful of my own mortality, do this seventeenth day of February, (1855) … make this my last Will … ' Charlotte died a few weeks after her faithful Tabby, on whom she modelled the character of Hannah in *Jane Eyre* and who Emily represented as Nelly Dean in *Wuthering Heights.*

Will we ever know *who Tabby really was?* Ellen Nussey described this woman as being "very quaint in appearance." Her face is forever locked within the shadows of the past, for no likeness of her has been found to exist and there is a distinct absence of surviving evidence about her life story before she became a member of the Brontë fold.

*   *   *   *

Stonemason John Brown was more than just the village sexton, he introduced Branwell to the society of Haworth Freemasons, and considered him a loyal and trusted friend. Arthur Bell Nicholls lodged with Brown until his marriage to Charlotte. His daughter Martha served the Brontës until they had all passed away. John died a few months after Charlotte on 10 August 1855, suffering from 'dust on his lungs'.

Historian William Scruton and an antiquarian friend called at Martha's home early in the afternoon of the 15 July 1879. They found themselves in a small but neat little cottage at Stubbing Lane where, except for the time she spent with Mr Nicholls in Ireland, she had resided since Patrick Brontë's death. Martha, described by her visitors as an "interesting looking girl with dark eyes and hair and would be pretty but for the loss of her front teeth" made her guests feel quite at home. "From my first entering the house", she confided to Mr Scruton, "I was always recognised and treated as a member of the family, although I was spoken of by outsiders as the servant-girl." Speaking in a quiet low voice, her visitors listened to her intently, they found her story of Charlotte's love for her younger sisters and "the strong attachment they had for each other" especially touching. Martha told her guests of long rambles on the wild moors around Haworth and the family's regular habits indoors. She reminisced about how the house only seemed to come alive, with them describing plots for their stories, after Patrick had gone to bed at 9pm: "Many's the time that I have seen Miss Emily put down the tally-iron … to scribble something on a piece of paper. Whatever she was doing, ironing or baking, she had her pencil and paper by her. I know she was writing *Wuthering Heights.*" Emily, she said was always thought the prettiest and most intelligent of the girls and the bravest spirited. No one ever thought she would be the first of the three girls to die.

When she heard that Miss Charlotte was the real author of *Jane Eyre*, she burst into the parsonage crying out, "I've heard such news!" "What about?" inquired Miss Brontë. "Please ma'am, you've been and written two books – the grandest books that ever was seen. My father has heard it at Halifax, and Mr T –, and Mr G –, and Mr M –, at Bradford; they are going to have a meeting at the Mechanics' Institute, to settle about ordering them."

At the height of Charlotte's fame, as she was going about her daily chores around the house, Martha could not resist asking her mistress about *Jane Eyre* "Well, Martha," said Charlotte. "I only hope the book may be worth all the fuss that is being made about it, but I am afraid it is not." Shocked by her attitude Martha replied, "Oh, but you must please not forget the good your book must have done in supplying employment to so many people. Look at the printers, bookbinders, stationers, and others who have benefited by its large sale." "Thank you, Martha, for putting it in that light," said Miss Brontë, "I am sure that I had never thought of that."

During the course of the visit, this humble little village woman proudly showed her wide-eyed guests a portfolio containing a number of pencil drawings and sketches belonging to her employers along with letters from Thackeray, Harriet Martineau and other great writers. From amongst these papers they recognised an epistle from 'a great humorist', in which he alluded to his intended visit to Bradford, where he was to deliver a lecture on the *Four Georges*.

Martha's obituary appeared in the death column of *Keighley News*:

DEATH OF MARTHA BROWN, OF HAWORTH
'Martha Brown, for many years the faithful servant of the Brontës died on a Monday after a brief illness. Miss Brown was one of the last survivors of those who were connected to the personal history of the Brontës, having entered into their service as a girl during the youthful days of the members of this family. She continued as housekeeper to the Revd Patrick Brontë until he died in 1861. To the day of her death, she entertained a loving memory of her connection with the family and her memories of her former master and his three gifted daughters abounded with reference to their unlimited kindness to her and others. After retiring, she lived off her savings in her native Haworth and a small annuity left to her by Patrick Brontë.'

She was buried in Haworth churchyard.

At the close of Martha's life on 19 January 1880 aged fifty-one years, she bequeathed her precious Brontë mementoes to various relatives. A veil belonging to Charlotte and a black lace shawl that had been Miss Branwell's were left to her niece, Mary E. Stanton. In 1939, Martha's cousins bought a large assortment of Brontë relics from Alfred Gledhill of Keighley, including an autographed copy of *Jane Eyre*. This collection was to go on display at their quaint shop in Haworth.

Maid Sarah Garrs served in the Brontë household when the children were very young. After marrying her sweetheart William Newsome, the couple emigrated to America to begin a new life together. Her obituary appeared in the *Iowa Weekly Republican* on 25 October 1899 and described how Sarah died yearning for the green hills of her native Yorkshire steeped with memories of family, friends and home. Her last words to her daughter were "Listen, I hear my mother calling me and I must go." Sarah's body was laid to rest in Crawfordsville Old Cemetery.

Sarah's sister Nancy Garrs married twice, firstly to a Mr Malone and secondly to a Mr Wainright of White Abbey Road, Bradford. She too had been employed as nursemaid to four of the Brontë children and always swore that Patrick Brontë was a good-tempered man, although she knew he carried a loaded pistol at all times, even when in the safety of his own house! Nancy said he sometimes shot pigeons when practising his marksmanship skills. Poor Nancy ended her days in a Bradford workhouse.

Abraham Holroyd editor of the *Bradfordian*, wrote in the July 1861 issue of the *Keighley Visitor* that a bitter ex-domestic servant of the Brontës had spoken about Patrick in a nasty spiteful manner *because* she had been dismissed. Those mischievous words were to live on in Mrs Gaskell's first edition of *Charlotte's Life*.

Personal Memories

Oakworth curate Revd James Chesterton Bradley often visited the Brontë household and thought Patrick a good man. Excepting, he said, that he possessed one of most inflammable tempers he had ever witnessed and had "known him so wild with anger at the merest thing that ran counter to his wish that he would take up the rug before the fire and throw it on to the flames." Bradley thought Charlotte guilty of "deep prejudices and of strong will" and Branwell to be "a good hearted fellow when sober and right, but too often drinking and wrong to be of any use to those girls in that lonely parsonage."

Mary Eleanor Stanton (*nee* Ratcliffe) of West Lane, Haworth was directly related to the Brown family. Her mother Tabitha Brown had been employed by the Brontës, so too had her aunt Martha who was present at Charlotte's passing. Tabitha had joked with Branwell about him being so skinny. She teased him for wearing Patrick's coat and not his own just before his death. Mary, not yet ten and her aunt attended the final service held in the old church that the Brontës knew so well and in which her ancestors had served for many decades. Eleanor said that the new church could never replace the old one, even though the smell of death had clung to its ancient walls. When she died in 1963 the memory of the old church died with her, for she was the last remaining regular member.

Mrs Ellen Gillam remembered playing as a child on the flat tombstones in Haworth churchyard and on many occasions, the Revd Patrick Brontë came running out, issuing severe reprimands. "I am surprised at you", he used to say, "running over dead people like that." Ellen, born at Brandy Row, Haworth, lost four members of her family within two weeks, due to a cholera epidemic. All were laid to rest in her impromptu playground. Ellen often saw the famous sisters out walking. She never learned to read or write, having to earn her keep as a spinner at the local mill from the tender age of nine.

Then there was Tom Preston, better known as 'Tom Porridge', a character who hated the sight of a camera. He had known Charlotte when she was a lass and thought her a timid sort, who often appeared to be thinking "o' summat else."

On 19 January 1933, Mrs Sarah Ann Nicholson told a representative of the *Telegraph & Argus* about her memories of living at Withens with her eleven brothers and sisters and of watching Charlotte Brontë tramping over the moors. "We used to see Charlotte walking alone often. I believe among ourselves we used to call her "Our Lady". She wore a shawl and a rather amusing bonnet." Standing up, she demonstrated with her own shawl the two different modes mostly favoured by Charlotte.

Mrs Sarah Ann Heaton (*nee* Binns), aged ninety in February 1936, cast her mind back to the day she spoke to Miss Charlotte. Sarah Ann had been out walking with her friend in Oxenhope eighty years before. As they chatted happily together, her friend pointed to a small lady walking on the dirt track ahead of them. "That's Miss Charlotte Brontë," she whispered. Sarah Ann, quick to notice a bit of Charlotte's skirt hem was undone, ran up to her saying, "Your braid has come off the bottom, Miss Brontë." Charlotte checking the hem replied, "I have nothing with which to fasten it, I'm afraid." Sarah Ann sank to her knees as she said: "I have some pins, let me do it."

James Stansfield, who passed away in 1930, had known Charlotte Brontë in the days of his youth when she taught him at the village school. Born at Pecket Well, Hebden Bridge he joined the postal service at Bradford in 1863, where he was one of only four staff. He was such an authority on Brontë lore that famous personalities specifically sought him out.

One of the few people to attend Charlotte and Arthur Nicholls' June wedding was John Robinson, who could still recall the affair with clarity, seventy-four years after the event. He told a Sheffield reporter he owed a lot to the Brontë family. Mr Nicholls personally educated this bright Stanbury lad at his lodgings every Saturday morning and it was largely thanks to this extra tuition that John Robinson held every public office at Wombwell, affording him the title 'King Wombwell'. John mused that it was Arthur Nicholls who taught him the meaning of lovesickness, after hearing him moan with anguish when his love life took a bad turn.

Mrs Sarah Greenwood Wood's remains were laid to rest in the old church-yard after a long illness that left her completely blind. She was the granddaugh-ter of Jack Kay – Haworth's soothsayer and was seventy-six in 1903.

'With her death another of those few remaining links, which have kept us in living touch with the Brontës is broken for she has been an intimate friend of Martha Brown for many years, visiting the Parsonage, and in this way frequently brought into close contact with various members of the family. She had become possessed of quite a museum of relics of the family, and the visitor to her small, but scrupulously neat and clean home, would be informed that "the substantial hair-seated suite with which the room was furnished had once been the dining-room furniture of the Brontës, and that the small oak table under the window had once occupied a corner of Mr Brontë's study", according to the *Keighley News*.

Mrs Greenwood Wood often related the story of a parsonage cat, "which had a bad habit of sharpening its claws on the legs of the very chair on which you sat, and if you cared to examine the chair leg the story was well collaborated." One of these chairs bearing the cat's claw marks is housed at the Brontë Museum.

Amongst some of the most interesting items this lady possessed, was an antique brooch containing a lock of Charlotte Brontë's hair and a likeness of her father. Mr Brontë gave this trinket to Martha Brown on Charlotte's death and she in turn bequeathed it to Mrs Greenwood Wood. Originally, Charlotte had received the brooch as a birthday present from her father. Another interesting relic was a complimentary copy of the *Life of Charlotte Brontë*, sent to Patrick Brontë by author Mrs Gaskell and presented to Mrs Greenwood Wood by Charlotte's husband, Mr Nicholls. Mrs Greenwood Wood was interviewed many times by admirers of the Brontës, some being well known in the world of letters. These interviews often furnished information that was afterwards reproduced in magazine articles ... Her eyes would twinkle as she told of how Charlotte Brontë was partial to 'high' game, and how Martha Brown would prepare a long-dead hare for the stew pot, with a handkerchief to her nose, which was not sufficient to completely hide her facial contortions.

When asked if she considered the father of the Brontës to have been a stern and unsympathetic parent ... she positively refused to accept the description ... although Mr Brontë was reserved and grave, a certain portion of each day was devoted to his family. He was kind to his children, interested in their work, and proud of their success.

In 1964, a villager wrote to the Editor of the *Keighley News*: 'I, as a Haworth native, shall never forget the thrill as I stood and looked at that tablet' (Westminster Abbey Memorial in Poets' corner). 'The Brontë girls, who lived in our village, talked with our grandparents and friends, are honoured there among Britain's illustrious dead.' Of the eighty people who attended Charlotte's centenary service here in 1955, three remembered the family.

After The Event

On 20 April 1867 the *Keighley News* announced, 'with many a sigh and many a groan Haworth Railway is opened! Henceforth the summons, "All out for Haworth," will only signal the prosaic advent of swarms of visitors, a few on business, but often more on pleasure, who will scale the height and expatiate over the classic grounds trod by the Brontës and associated with the names of

Wesley, and Emmerson, and Hartley Coleridge, and Thackeray. Wuthering Heights will be explored, and the swamp that burst so strangely, and the bolder-footed will roam over the moors to Colne. The little "city on the hill" will cease to be isolated and cease to mask comparatively unknown wilds behind it. A splendid walking country is opened up to pedestrians, who will no doubt receive true Yorkshire hospitality from the natives ... '

If things had gone to plan, Haworth's Main Street would only be half the street it is today. Council planners wanted to knock down thirteen under and over cottages in 1959, at the point where the old cobbled road narrows. They believed them to be unfit for human habitation because of the "gloominess of the rooms" and "bad sanitation." Keighley's Chief Public Health Inspector stated that if folk wished to see the cottages preserved as a "literary relic", they should let them know, but as far as the council was concerned these buildings, home to generations of Haworthites were "incapable of being made fit at reasonable expense."

One man, whose property projected into the hillside, said he was prepared to dig the building out to save it. Brontë author John Lock told the *Yorkshire Post*, "Ideally one would like to see Haworth remain unchanged but it is easy to say that, when one was not required to live in a Jacobean house. Haworth is unique in that the whole village has been preserved, not just some corner of a larger town."

Thankfully, the properties were saved, after a petition containing four thousand names was sent to the council. North Street, Acton Street (the stargazer's old home) and Haworth's tiny prison were not so fortunate, and were destroyed in the 1970s, to make way for a new road and car park.

In 1968, some bright spark in the council had the idea of painting yellow lines on a length of Main Street to deter motorists from parking, but the thick paint refused to stick to the cobbles. A witty local resident, watching a council worker roll up a whole yellow line from the street at dusk quipped, "Ah, I see you take them in at night."

The editor of the *Yorkshire Observer* received a letter from 'Sanity' about the Bonnell Collection in 1929, protesting against Brontë idolatry with regard to a further batch of Brontë relics arriving from America. The writer thought Haworth nothing but a God-forsaken place and the museum a mausoleum containing sad little fading mementos of Brontë memorabilia.

In 1960, British Prime Minister, Harold Macmillan paid a second visit to the museum, accompanied by the Duke of Devonshire. In the forty-five minutes he spent looking round, not one soul recognised him!

On 17 April 1963 The *Yorkshire Post* recounted, how after hearing from Sidney Greenbank that he had parted with 'brass' to get into the Brontë Museum, an incredulous villager indignantly spluttered, "Nay, it's nowt but an 'owd rag an' booan shop! An' tha paid fower bob fer that lot? Lets gan on t'moors!" No doubt, Emily Jane Brontë would have agreed with him.

Haworth villagers do not understand 'all this Brontë fuss', exclaimed the landlord of the Fleece Inn in 1966. He felt Haworth only existed for other people and not the locals, who were not even permitted pull down outside toilets, in the name of preservation! Actually, it is a fact that as late as 1984, almost five per cent of Worth Valley households lacked either an inside toilet or a bath or sometimes both!

Journalist Dennis Booth asked a local resident what Charlotte's centenary meant to the village "Nowt," came the curt reply. "Folk that come here think we're an ignorant lot. They say we're as grim as the scenery. Let 'em think so, that's what I say. We could tell 'em plenty about the Brontës if we wanted to, but they think they know it all ... These 'ere writers will make out it's grim and miserable – but it's as cheerful a place as you can find." The only people to benefit from tourism, said the *Halifax Evening Courier's* informant Jim, were "the big-wigs. Them that take all and pay nowt. Anyway, the Brontë business is all my eye. Half those relics are fake. It took me and my mate four days" (in 1928) "to shift stuff from the old museum into the new one. So where has the rest come from? Don't tell me its genuine!"

Some of the 'stuff' to which Jim alluded, came from the *Wuthering Heights Collection* in the private museum of the late J.H. Dixon of Harrogate. These artefacts included a wooden lion, which Charlotte had given to Tabby Ratcliffe's children as a present and a burnt comb worn by Emily on the day she died. The museum's curator pointed out to the newspaper that everything marked genuine in the Brontë Museum was in fact genuine and anyway she said, "Why should the villagers make money from the Brontës? They never put anything into it. I shouldn't think they did much towards getting the Brontë Society going."

Personally, I think the old village folk (especially the Brown family) did remarkably well in having the foresight to acquire as many items as they possibly could that had belonged to the Brontës – most of which are now in the museum.

4 | *Amen Corner*

From early times, many villagers gathered at the parish church each Sabbath day to give thanks to the Lord. The sexton, armed with his long stick marched up and down the aisles of the church hoping to catch out the odd napper and whack the culprit awake.

For many years, Haworth church employed men from the Brown family. After the deaths of the Brontë family, the guardian of the churchyard was always happy to show visitors around the old Haworth church for a copper or two. During his guided tour, he often quoted a bit of Milton's poetry for added effect. Taking pains to point out the low roof, he would sidle over to the Brontë pew and thumb to the corner where "she" (Charlotte) sat by the wall, drawing attention to the original memorial stone ending with Charlotte's name and leaving but a "narrow blank for those who wish to follow."

When a new memorial stone was put in its place, he complained about the amount of cleaning it required though nobody took his complaints very seriously, considering the ample tips he received from gratified tourists. The cost of the American stained-glass window in memory of Charlotte Brontë could have sustained a poor family for some time, he grumbled.

He maintained that Emily and Anne sat with their backs to the congregation because they were strange oddities. He thought Anne the prettiest of a poor looking bunch saying she was "a nice little thing." Emily he thought was "more prepossessing like and less melancholy." Branwell he declared was almost a "supernatural genius." Following him into the vestry, visitors were shown the marriage register and the signatures of Patrick, Charlotte and Mr Nicholls, after which they could purchase copies of photographs of the Brontës if they were so inclined.

From Ancient To Modern

The first mention of Haworth appears in 1296 when Godfrey de Haworth's name was recorded in the Kirby Inquest. The first known authenticated record relating to Haworth church is a decree dated 1317, issued by the Archbishop of York, indicating that a church had already occupied the site for centuries

In 1337, Adam de Batelay paid 20s (£1) to a chaplain, to celebrate 'Devine Service' for his soul and the souls of his ancestors in the chapel of St. Michael, Haworth.

By 1380, forty persons in Haworth were listed as being liable for Poll Tax. William Midgley and son Joseph purchased the manors of both Haworth and Harden from Nicholas Bladen in 1671, for the princely sum of £80. Lawyer Martin Birkhead of Gray's Inn, London was Haworth's Lord of the Manor in

Old Haworth church *(D.H. Lincoln)*

1559. He assisted the Protestant government in the prosecution of Roman Catholics in 1569. Queen Elizabeth I instructed the President of her Council of the North that Birkhead was to be "their attorney with such reward as he shall deserve." Needless to say, Haworth's sympathies lay on the Parliamentarian side during the Civil War.

Original registers dating from 1645 were so badly damaged by dampness that they had to be copied in 1786. There are supposed to be even older ones in existence but if so, their keeper is silent on the matter.

John Wade took it upon himself to destroy the old edifice, replacing it with his own vision of God's Temple. And so it was that the 'ivy-clothed gable, with its cracked wall, and the bare, square belfry that grew wi' muckin' [1]' disappeared, together with the little windows with their small panes, that let in as much darkness as light and the three-sided black oak pews, capacious in size, and inscribed with their owners' names and places of abode; the oaken roof, the bulging and withal strong and solid walls, the books in the vestry under the steeple, and the pewter communion vessels bearing the Grimshaw's name, and most traces of the Brontë family as had been allowed to remain. These all formed strong attractions, and drew thousands from their homes, often long distances away, up the steep and tortuous Worth Valley Railway, up the precipitous and narrow main street, through the tall spiked gates to the churchyard. As the last days of the church came the visitors increased, and on Sunday, from morning until night, people wended their way to and from the old building, quietly

---

[1]
Foolish parishioners endeavoured to make the tower taller by means of 'muckin' – mixing manure with soil at its base. When this method failed, they tried German yeast!

gazing on it, thinking of its approaching destruction. Many of those who had not been able to gain admission (during the last service) now came in and walked round the aisles before the lights were turned out, and then the creaking doors shut out the last congregation that they will ever open to admit. Darkness fittingly let fall the curtain to hide from view this scene, which cast a sullen depression over the mind, and left one brooding upon dark and dispiriting thoughts' recorded *Jessno*, in *The Yorkshireman*.

Haworth Church

> The church they built with skill,
> And yet stands up on the hill,
> Friends take a walk around,
> And softly tread the sacred ground:
> To pull it down, oh! What a pity;
> Let the sacred place stand-alone
> And never shift a single stone;
> Pray that the dead lie underground
> Till they all archangels trumpet shall sound.

Revd Wade's belief that it was 'his duty that the parish was not to maintain a show place for strangers, but a house of prayer for the Lord his God' caused W.M. from Cullingworth, an occasional correspondent to the *Keighley Herald* to write in 1879, 'For one hundred-and-twenty-five years Haworth church had resounded with prayer and praise until its end.' The *Keighley Herald* in response to a London newspaper article wrote, '*The Standard* in blind wrathful horror denounces Wade as if he harboured a destructive jealousy of the fame of his predecessor's family and laboured with the sick purpose of sweeping their memorials out of sight. This we dare say is all screaming nonsense. On the other hand the present rector of Haworth is probably as devoid of sympathetic admiration of Brontë genius as the great body of clergy and their religious world in general.'

Arthur Nicholls was all for the destruction because the church, he said, was a house of prayer and not a shrine to his wife or her sisters. Wade and his supporters had their way and the last service in the Brontë church was held in September 1879 when the doors opened at 5pm. More than two thousand people bade farewell to those old familiar walls the Brontës had known so well. Latecomers were forced to stand outside in the graveyard.

During the course of the sermon, Wade fervently hoped that "the donors would suffer nothing by giving, and that the workmen would come to no accident while pulling down the church." He prayed for the rising of the "second temple." Voices raised in opposition were easily cast aside and by October, almost nothing remained of the Brontë church, excepting a few skeletal vestiges and the tower. A poem condemning the 'stiff and upright' Wade appeared in the pages of *The Yorkshireman* entitled:

Iconoclast at Haworth

> But have heard the name of one
> Who holds a sacred trust,
> Who's stamp out marks of genius, and lay them in the dust.

One who would raze an ancient church,
And all that is therein -
Each mark and form and tablet -
And deem it not a sin.
"We want no gaping visitors
About the place" cries he,
"No hunting after novelists,
Howe'er the case might be.
Ah! Little man of little mind,
To play so poor a part;
Dost thou not know these names are dear
Unto the nation's heart?
That they will live when thou art gone,
With all thy pomp and pride,
An honour to their moorland home,
With name and fame world-wide?
We love thee not, Iconoclast,
However much we feel
For earnest work and piety,
Religious truth and zeal.
We would have them untouched remain,
Alike to great and small,
A monument to native worth,
A heritage for all.

   J.H. Eccles, 1879.

Practically all that remains of the original tower on the south-west corner is the lower part and a tiny window that has survived from about the fifteenth century.

The new Haworth church, showing the old tower *(William Scruton scrapbook)*

Two fields distant from St. Michael's, a broken stone tablet was unearthed in February 1964, bearing the following inscription: *Jesus came into the World*. It is quite likely that contractors Messrs Crabtree Bros and Sugden of Oxenhope took this stone from the church during the course of Wade's new building programme. At the east end of the new structure, beneath the foundation stone, lies a time capsule in the form of a sealed bottle, put there by George Merrall on Christmas Day 1879. It contains a selection of coins and various documents. More than a thousand people witnessed the laying of the foundation stone by Michael Merrall, who had provided money towards Wade's grand scheme. The new church opened its doors for the "sentence of consecration" on 22 February 1881 but ninety years later, an infestation of dry rot had set in.

Haworth is no stranger to famous personalities and when James Roosevelt, son of the US President, visited the village in April 1939, he was presented with a spill box fashioned out of wood from the old Haworth church. Brontë lover Elsie Stuart of Ilkley said she hoped a spill from the box might "one day light a pipe of peace, which the United States President would smoke." Other bits of wood taken from the demolished church were made into treen and kept as souvenirs. Mr J.T. Reddiough, who remembered Patrick Brontë's farewell speech, owned a large bookcase fashioned from the front of the Brontë church organ. His grandfather was Tom Helliwell, a great friend of Nicholls. He used to sit in the pew next to the Brontës.

Haworth Parish Church was not the only religious building to suffer demolition in the village and in 1964 when Messers T. & E. Waddington were in the process of pulling down Bridgehouse Chapel, a search was instigated for a time capsule. Their diligence was rewarded when a lead casket was pulled out of the rubble. Inside was an English half-crown (12½p) dated 1877, a silver bun two shilling (10p) piece – its date worn away, a Victorian shilling (5p) and a threepenny (1¼ p) bit stamped 1877 as well as an assortment of American coins dating between 1878 to 1882. There were several newspapers including the *Keighley News*, dated 28 April 1883, the Tory paper the *Keighley Herald*, *The Watchman*, the *Wesleyan Advertiser*, *The Methodist Recorder* and finally *The Methodist*, all dated April 1883.

Perhaps the most interesting find was a paper written in the hand of Frederick Butterfield of New York, remembering his brother the late Richard S. Butterfield whose home had been at Woodlands, Haworth. There was also a comprehensive list of all the workers involved in building the chapel and of church dignitaries. The time capsule was duly handed over to the Bridgehouse Chapel Trustees for safekeeping.

As It Was and Is

On the south wall of the ancient church tower above Richard Pollard's quaint gravemarker is a sundial and a stone tablet bearing the words: 'Mr Richard Pollard, of Stanbury gave it to this church 1726'. The sundial is a constant reminder of the passing hour and above its dial and dedication is a curious Latin inscription, together with an English translation set in stone, 'Orate p'bono statu Eutest Tod. Pray for ye soul of Autest 600'. The antiquarian Dr Whitaker believed 'bono statu' referred to the living rather than the dead. Former Rector T. W. Story in his *Notes on old Haworth Registers*, translated the Latin inscription thus:

> Here formerly was a Monastery
> Dedicated to the honour of
> St. Michael and All Angels.
> Autest being the founder,
> In the year of Christ six hundred.

Story thought these characters belonged to a later date and that the inscription did *not* prove the existence of an early place of worship. It is, however, possible that the present church is the fifth to occupy the site. An 1840 sundial to the west of the tower, warns the reader to,

> Remember thy latter end.
> Yea, all round we seem to hear the prophet's warning.
> Set thine house in order, for ye must die and not live.

Have you ever noticed that the clock faces set into the church tower are not identical? The west tower dial was replaced in 1935 after the cast iron original c. 1870 suffered damage during a severe gale. A fragment of this first clock face, in brown and blue and counting the hour of six and six seconds, is kept inside the church as a memorial to the Brontë period.

A carved stone font originally installed in Haworth church by William Grimshaw in 1749 was removed under the direction of John Wade during his rebuilding programme. Restored to the church in 1929, it was placed in the churchyard. Today the font can be seen on the south side of the churchyard, close to the Black Bull Inn. One hopes that this font, associated with a man who did so much for Haworth and religion, may be reinstated within the walls of the church one day.

The black, three-tiered pulpit used by Grimshaw, Wesley and Brontë was relegated to a grimy farm loft at Stanbury for a time, before its top deck was restored and installed in Stanbury's Mission Church. As for Grimshaw's sounding board, which was above the three-decker pulpit, it too was removed from the church after Patrick Brontë's death but later destroyed. Grimshaw's huge pewter communion flagons are no longer on view in Haworth – one being in store whilst the other is out on loan to York Minster. Will the pair ever meet again? The text on each flagon runs thus:

The first:

> In Jesus we live, in Jesus we rest,
> And thankful receive His dying bequest,
> The Cup of Salvation His mercy bestows,
> All from His passion our Happiness flows. A.D. 1750.

The second:

> Blest Jesus, what delicious Fare!
> How sweet thine entertainments are!
> Never did Angels taste above,
> Redeeming grace or dying love. A.D. 1750.

Visitors should take special notice of the stained-glass window, paid for by an American admirer to commemorate the life of Charlotte Brontë – the eyes of one of the male figures are inverted! Eyes were often used in metaphorical language to demonstrate love, pity and wrath, and to signify God's wisdom and knowledge whereby he observes and tries all his creatures.

'I see around me tombstones grey' – *Emily Brontë*

They buried nineteen-year-old classical scholar John Collier in Haworth churchyard on 23 June 1674. A broken fragment from his memorial describes the boy as 'Laureate', according to Turner lore. In Horsfall Turner's day, this piece of stone was reared against the pulpit. Today his gravemarker is outside the church. The remaining words are:

I OHN COL
LAUREAT
SON: TO:
MINIST

His father, Revd John Collier of Haworth, a Royalist supporter was driven out of St. Michael's by Birkenhead's Parliamentarians but was reinstated in 1662. He died on 10 October 1675. Collier was supposed to have taken Mary Heaton, a Ponden widow as his wife although there is no entry in the registers confirming the marriage took place. However, a typed copy of an original legal document dated 1675 can be found in a box at Keighley Reference Library marked BK 105, stating that Revd John Collier and Mary his wife were to give back land to Robert and John Heaton.

From 1726 to 1741 Haworth minister Isaac Smith made it known that, 'Henry Helliwell takes the grass in the Churchyard for Fifteen Pounds of Candles (three in the pound) every year, which are used for Light at Six o' clock Prayers on Saturday Evenings and burying the Dead when occasion shall require.'

To the west of the graveyard stands the Heaton memorial to their children. At the foot of the headstone lies a sleeping babe, which is supposed to have been modelled in the image of one of the seven infants lying beneath. The stone carving is probably James William, James Whitham or little Elizabeth – the last dying in 1885. This touching memorial has inspired generations of Haworth children to gather up wild flowers and place them in the crook of the child's arm, a custom that still thrives today. An almost identical carved child can be seen at Windhill Wesleyan Cemetery, Shipley, dedicated to Sarah Maria Senior who died in her infancy.

When John Dawson Hopkinson died in 1860, his friends erected an elegant tombstone to his memory. This stone depicts the musical instrument he played, alongside an open tune book with *Martin Luther's Hymn* tune inscribed upon it. The stone was designed and cut by the self-taught sculptor W. Hargreaves of Lower Province Mills, Oakworth. During his life Hopkinson had been a gifted musician who played with Wombwell's Show (of Wallace the Lion fame) and led the band at Manders' Menagerie. His music helped to soothe fierce tigers and lions.

In December 1847 Nicholls declared all out war against Haworth's washer-women, they in turn threatened to 'do' for him. The reason for this bad feeling was that he had turned them, together with their clothes' props and wet laundry, out of the cemetery, where it was customary for the women to use the blackened tombstones – Haworth's version of washing lines. One of these washerwomen was pauper Sally Binns of Ropers Buildings. Patrick must have been amused at the hubbub for he put pen to paper and came up with this little ditty entitled *Church Reform*

> The dead all deserted, their ghosts heavy moan
> Oft shakes to the centre each slumbering stone
> The females all routed have fled with their clothes
> They'll lynch him at once, without trial by jury.

Now here's a thought … for many years it was not really known whether the bodies of the Brontë family actually still lay undisturbed in the church vault, until a missing church document was returned in 1935 by an anonymous person. This piece of paper proved that the tomb was not included on Wade's faculty list of 1879 as one of the graves to be removed so the workmen could dig the new foundations. Reference to this can be found in the 1935 October issue of Haworth church magazine where Revd J. C. Hirst stated that the bodies of the Brontë family were where they should be.

Apparently a letter from John Wade's son to one of the Merralls of Law House, Haworth claimed that his father insisted the remains of the Brontë family and other bodies laid to rest *inside* the church were not interfered with. It also revealed that a deep layer of concrete had been poured all over the vaults to seal them.

Haworth's yard-of-the-dead holds thousands of corpses, rich and poor alike packed tightly into the ground. Row upon row of blackened headstones stand starkly against the skyline.

By 1848, Patrick Brontë complained about unsanitary conditions created by rotting corpses in an already overcrowded graveyard and asked the authorities to forbid any further burials, especially since the village water supply passed through the burial ground. Patrick did have a valid point, for it was reported in the 1884 edition of *The Building News* that Dr W. Hesse had conducted 150 trials that year in order to determine ground air quality in graveyards. He found that the air inside new graveyards was far richer in carbonic acid gas than that outside. This was due to the decomposition of the corpses. The amount of carbonic and gas increased from the day of burial, reaching a maximum level within three months. Churchyards in constant use yielded twenty to forty volumes in every 1,000 of carbon dioxide.

Mr A. Wynter Blyth, a Medical Officer of Health wrote the following report on the subject of graveyard air in June 1884:

> 'We might surround burial with whatever impressive religious ceremonies we like; but, considered in itself, burial in the earth was no religious rite, nor did its adoption imply any special belief or cult. The ordinary method of inhumation in this country was to leave the body exposed more or less to the air for a few days in a room or mortuary, to enclose it in a wooden box – this,

among the rich, in a leaden shell – and then bury it in the ground. If we traced the changes that occurred we found that during the period intervening between death and burial the little invisible clouds of bacteria always floating about the air gained access to the tissues and organs, and according to temperature and other circumstances divided and multiplied, and set up those changes which belonged to the phenomena of putrefaction. After death from infectious fevers, added to the ordinary emanations of putrefaction, there were others of an extremely dangerous character. The corpse after death from smallpox, typhus, and plague, was known as terribly infectious; and to a less extent after death from measles, scarlet fever, typhoid fever, and pneumonia. The infection might be carried by currents of air, or by actual contact with the body, or by the common household fly, or by domestic animals. Treating next of the proved effects of graveyards or cemeteries on public health when dwellings were built in proximity to them, he suggested what he considered a rational method of burial. If we continued to bury our dead we ought to begin a new plan entirely – to bury only one body in a grave at a minimum depth of six feet, to abolish the use of vaults, to allow no irremovable headstones or monuments over graves, and at the end of a certain number of years to cause the land to revert to agricultural purposes ... At the end of five years from the last burial the ground in any plot would be cultivated but not built upon ... All persons found dead in the streets and not identified should be injected with a preservative and antiseptic liquid, and remain unburied in some special place for many months, and thus give opportunities of solving the problem of what were called "Mysterious Disappearances." If vault interments were to continue, some modified form of embalmment should be rendered compulsory, so as to lessen the risk of injurious emanations.'

Villagers remembered Charlotte and her father leaving the west door of the church, walking arm in arm up the pathway towards the gate christened the *Gate of the Dead* situated between the parsonage garden and the graveyard. Apparently, pieces of old flagstones could still be traced if one cared to search for them.

Haunted by rooks, the mighty trees we see today in Haworth's churchyard were planted as saplings in November 1864, because the appearance of the graveyard the Brontës knew so well was considered dull and monotonous by Patrick's successor.

J. Horsfall Turner in his *Annals of Wakefield House of Correction* 1904 says that a stone with mortice holes, into which a gibbet-frame was fixed, had been preserved in Haworth Churchyard. He quotes from a manuscript by a Dr Johnson "Two stones, namely, one East and the other West, and the other at the head North and South with three mortices." This stone, if it ever existed, has disappeared. Was it buried in the foundations of the present Haworth church?

It's amazing where some gravestones turn up. During the 1960s, the Civic Trust was informed that gravestones removed from the old boneyard, were being utilised by a thrifty Yorkshire resident as a kitchen flags in a cottage at Changegate, Haworth!

Ashes to Ashes

Joseph Craven in his book *Brontë Moorland Village* tells us that Stanbury folk carried flowers and sang dolefully when accompanying a body taken from the wilds of Stanbury for burial in Haworth. The usual theme was, *Those who had a desire to go to heaven.* Charlotte Brontë gives her version of an impassioned prayer meeting held by folk who were 'all for heaven' in *Shirley*, 'hymns of a most extraordinary description were sung. After an interval of clamorous prayer, accompanied by fearful groans, a shout of 'I've found liberty!' 'Doad o' Bill's has fun' liberty!' rang from the chapel. More hymns, cries, and agonised groans seemed to cap the climax of noise and zeal. The roof of the chapel did not fly off, which speaks volumes for its solid slating.'

Red House, Oxford Road, Gomersal was built in 1660 by William Taylor. Charlotte Brontë was a guest here many times while she was a schoolgirl at Roe Head School in Mirfield, having become firm friends with Mary Taylor, whose family had resided at Red House for generations. Built into the floor of this house was a safe large enough to accommodate a person standing upright! Charlotte would have known that when a member of the Taylor family died they were carried to a private burial ground at Scotland Wood, Gomersal. Mystery and intrigue surrounds the first two burials, here for the funeral processions did not begin until after the stroke of midnight. Why, instead of using the cart track, the bodies were manhandled over walls and dragged across fields before reaching the burial ground, we shall never know.

Whether you were for heaven or not, a person needed a decent send off whatever their station in life, and it was to this end that Revd John Wade wrote to the *Keighley News* in July

THE OLD SEXTON (1).

Nigh to a grave that was newly made
Leaned a sexton old on his earth-worn spade,
His work was done and he paused to wait
The funeral train through the open gate ;
A relic of bygone days was he,
⎯d his locks were white as the foamy sea,
And these words came from his lips so thin,
I gather them in, I gather them in.
Gather, gather, gather, I gather them in.

The maker of dead men's beds *(James Bamforth Ltd)*

1873 about a recent resolution passed by the Board of Guardians, calling their attention to the attitude regarding the cost of pauper burials. The Guardians wanted Haworth paupers to be buried in the cheapest possible manner, even if it meant burying them in ground that had not been consecrated. The 'job', the Guardians argued, could be done much more cheaply at Keighley where poor folk would be laid to rest in a sort of vault or open grave for five shillings (25p) whereas the Haworth sexton demanded payment of seven shillings (35p) – two shillings (10p) extra. If, they reasoned, a relative of the deceased was willing and able to pay the extra two shillings, all well and good. Otherwise, the funerals would be conducted as cheaply as possible. The *Keighley News* valiantly rallied to the side of the pauper, 'we have known circumstances of poor people preserving a couple of linen sheets for many years, that the laying-out might be decent and in order. And we really think the feeling is, as a rule, strongest in those who have least of all to leave behind. Why, for the sake of a paltry two shillings, rob a poor man or woman of a claim expressed or unexpressed, to lie in the dust consecrated by church or dedicated by chapel.'

The Pauper's Box

Thou odious box, as I look on thee,
I wonder wilt thou be unlocked for me?
No, no! forbear! – yet then, yet then,
'Neath thy grim lid do lie the men -
Men whom fortune's blasted arrows hit,
And send them to the pauper's pit.
O dig a grave somewhere for me,
Deep underneath some wither'd tree;
Or bury me on the wildest heath,
Where Boreas blows his wildest breath,
Or 'mid some wild romantic rocks:
But, oh! forbear the pauper's box.
Throw me into the ocean deep,
Where many poor forgotten sleep;
Or fling my corpse in the battle mound,
With coffinless thousands 'neath the ground;
I envy not the mightiest dome,
But save me from a pauper's tomb.
I care not if 'tware the wild wolfs's glen,
Or the prison yard, with wicked men:
Or into some filthy dung-hole hurled -
Anywhere, anywhere! out of the world!
In fire nor smoke, on land, or sea,
Than thy grim lid be closed on me.
But yet, 'twere grand beneath yond wall,
To lay with friends – relations all;
If sculptured tombstones were not there,
But simple grass with daises fair;
And were it not, grim box, for thee
'Twere Paradise, O cemetery.

Anon. *The Keighley Investigator, 1875*

Joseph Hardacre was a friend of the Brontë family and had a number of poetry books published during his lifetime. A sexton of the village came under his scrutiny in 1822 – perhaps that is why he chose to be buried at Keighley in Catholic ground when he died in 1840!

To The Sexton

O, sexton! ye are such a soul,
Ye little care for whom ye toll,
If ye can drain the arvill bowl;
With many more.
Ye'll for a moment sigh and growl,
Then all is o'er.
Before the corpse, in solemn pace,
Full oft I've seen ye pull a face,
As tho' ye were to truth and grace
Nearly allied;
That few would think ye mean or base,
So deep ye sigh'd.
But think ye, old case-harden'd blade,
Knight of the ruthless hack and spade,
Some "lustier brother of the trade,"
Perhaps ere long,
May pop you where you've thousands laid,
Nor think it wrong.

Joseph Hardacre, The Bradfordian, 1861

Haworth's Lady of the Manor, Sarah Ferrand, generously donated land for a new church at Oakworth in 1844. The first incumbent Revd J.C. Bradley was a good friend of the Brontës. In the adjoining graveyard, the family of a maiden erected a memorial warning what can happen if you fall in love with the wrong man.

Pray reader, pause and drop a generous tear,
O'er her sad wrongs whose relics moulder here.
Retiring, modest, thoughtful and reserved,
Of guile unconscious and from guilt preserved.
Blameless and artless with unspotted fame,
The tongue of slander e'en had spared her name.
At length when more than thirty years were passed,
A dark and murky cloud her sky o'er cast.
The spoiler came, fair words on his tongue,
She gave her heart nor thought he meant her wrong.
Guileless herself, she thought him free from guile,
Believed his promise, trusted in his smile
He gained his end, then cast her from his side,
A child was born, she broke her heart and died.

Sadly, this epitaph is no longer visible for the church deemed that it would be easier to bury most of the tombstones and grass them over than leave them standing. Thus, the social history of the graveyard has been lost to us.

Men of The Cloth

A goodly number of Haworth's religious men appear to have possessed brilliant but rather eccentric and unusual personalities. Most of them, as we shall see, left their mark on the village in one way or another.

Coining and Conning

Excommunicated by candle and bell in the seventeenth century, Edmund Robinson, a Colne man who was Haworth curate for a year was supposed to have been a thoroughly bad lot. He was a man with the Devil at his elbow according to a sermon on the subject of Robinson's life delivered by the Revd George Halley, Chaplain of York Castle and published on the 29 March 1691. 'His father, a considerable husbandman, sent him to school, where he made great progress in something besides book learning ... he associated with a lad named Gregson, whose father was a coiner, and the two lads became utterers of false pewter shillings. Gregson took holy orders, and was afterwards hanged at Lancaster for coining.'

Robinson went to University before being ordained by the Bishop of Lichfield. Afterwards he went to Holmfirth, near Huddersfield where he stayed for eleven years. Throughout his time as curate there, Robinson forged church licenses and performed illegal wedding ceremonies – all for a price. As soon as his nefarious activities became known, his name was struck from the list of incumbents. Those who knew their curate well thought him "full of good works and helpful to the poor." With nothing to lose now except his life, Robinson embarked upon a life of crime. Together with his wife (daughter of Anthony Armitage), his son Ben and others he netted a small fortune from clipping gold coins in the cellar of his remote cottage at Bank End.

Prosecuted a number of times for uttering false money, Robinson was usually either imprisoned or fined. His luck finally ran out when on 31 March 1691, he was tried, convicted and condemned to death at York Assizes. His wife and son managed to escape the gallows by a hair's breadth. Ironically, Ben was offered, and accepted a position at the Royal Mint! Prior to Robinson's hanging, a gang of clippers in Lothersdale (Beggars Valley) were very active. From Stock, three miles out of Skipton in the spring of 1681 thirteen men – all coin clippers were delivered to York Assizes for sentencing.

* * * *

Over the moors from Haworth, Heptonstall's church register contains details of a terrible incident concerning a Halifax detective by the name of William Deighton. He was an employee of the Royal Mint and bent on capturing a local gang known as the Turvin Coiners. Returning to his home from Bradford town late on the evening of 9 November 1769, he was fatally shot and robbed of several gold coins.

The premeditated murder of the customs man culminated in these Yorkshire gangs being hunted down by the law. The Marquis of Rockingham, Charles Watson of Wentworth (great-grandson of the Earl of Strafford – executed in 1641) was a great defender of his native Yorkshire and after William Deighton's brutal murder, he travelled from London to Halifax in order to arrest those responsible for the crime. Rockingham and Halifax solicitor Robert Parker got together with gentlemen from Leeds, Bradford and Wakefield in order to put a stop to the counterfeiting of coins clipped from Spanish and Portuguese gold.

* * * *

The grave of the most infamous clipper of them all 'King' David Hartley, whose body swung high on the gibbet after being hanged – to serve as a warning to others, lies in Heptonstall's old churchyard. His counterfeit gold coins were exchanged as far afield as Hamburg in 1767.

Keighley too had its share of coiners, one being a prominent resident – Mr Joseph Stell, a silk mill owner of Walk Mill. Caught red-handed, he was tried at York where the Crown confiscated his entire personal property. Clippers used one of the old Oxenhope Quarry areas to churn out their illegal coinage, mostly passing the illicit tender in taverns where innkeepers dared not say a word, for fear of retribution.

Hellfire and Brimstone

"Yer could ommost smell t' brimstone" said one Haworth parishioner, warming to the theme of the 'Prophet of the Moors'. William Grimshaw, whose ancestors laid claim to being Dragon Slayers in Blackburn Wood, delivered his fiery sermons at St. Michael's from 1742 until his death in 1763. He was Haworth's greatest incumbent, creating a huge following during the Evangelical Revival.

The desolate Grimshaw virtually haunted his first wife Sarah's grave and even confessed to having contemplated suicide after her death. It was commonly thought that he was, 'certainly insane, and had he given utterance at that time to his monstrous and horrible imaginations, which he afterwards revealed to his friends, he would have deservedly been sent to Bedlam'.

Removing to Haworth, he had a remarkable vision that revealed to him Christ's blood and wounds. Fired by God and John Wesley, Grimshaw found a new purpose in life. Whilst leaving his congregation lustily singing the Lord's longest psalm in the church, he supposedly took to scourging the clientele of the Black Bull with a horse whip, causing sinners to tumble out of the inn's windows in order to escape his zealous wrath. Those he captured he drove into church.

Grimshaw and Wesley became great friends and the pair went into the streets of Keighley in a joint effort to save the souls of the 'hard of heart'. They had not long to wait before a wild angry mob came 'pouring down the hill like a torrent' threatening to sweep away the ministers of God, who had by then wisely retreated to a safe house. Hecklers surrounded the premises, demanding that the ministers pack up their books and cease to peddle their brand of religion. Wesley retorted, "I would sooner cut off my hand than make any such promise.'

Riotous gatherings were common in the Haworth of Grimshaw's day, allowing the villagers to add excitement to their otherwise drab existence. The Haworth Tide held on the first Sunday after the 11 October each year, was particularly noted for rowdy behaviour. Brightly coloured peddlers' wagons and drovers with their livestock descended on the windswept moorland expanse.

The following day, revellers celebrated what they called Crowmoor Monday, shifting to Penistone Flats for horse racing events sponsored by the tavern-keepers. This popular activity attracted large crowds and of course gambling was rife.

As October loomed nearer, Grimshaw canvassed the innkeepers to withdraw their support of 'The Tide', telling them that they would reap their reward in heaven, but the innkeepers ignored their preacher. As a last resort, on the day of the races the Minister sank to his knees in full view of the gathering crowds. Lifting his eyes heavenwards, he implored his Maker to intervene. Amazingly "before he had finished his supplication dark clouds gathered, thunder rent the heavens, vivid flashes of lightening lit up the hills, and the rain came down in torrents (for three days). Soaked to the skin, the mob fled in terror from the moor, awed at the sudden frenzy of Nature's power." Horse racing abandoned, word spread quickly of the preacher's powers. No man ever dared to celebrate the October Tide horse racing again.

In 1759 *The Gentleman's Magazine*'s meteorological section recorded, "A very rainy spell in the North from 12th to 17th October.' Preceding Octobers had all been fine. While no exact year of God and Grimshaw's intercession exists, it is thought that this was the year of Grimshaw's triumph.

On Tide Sunday for many years after, Penistone Hill welcomed instead of riotous gamblers, the devout offering of praises to God and "Saint" Grimshaw for putting an end to the unsavoury debacle. The "Prophet" himself was tempted to gamble after reading an advert placed by J. Hasard, Stock Broker of Ludgate Hill, London. Contacting a friend, he begged for money to invest in the English State Lottery Scheme, saying he saw no harm in it and that, "If Divine Providence gives us nothing we are contented. If he gives us anything we intend it for some laudable pious uses." A month later, he wrote to Mrs Gallatin Grimshaw, including for good measure a "dissertation on satanic temptation" and asked whether or not they should register the tickets! Adding, 'We leave the issue to the Lord, in whose hands is the lot.' The winning ticket was drawn in 1759 (the same year Grimshaw brought down God's wrath on Haworth gamblers?), Grimshaw's faith in the Lord was not misplaced for he and two other ministers were rewarded with a cash payout. How much, if anything he handed over to the Trustees – John and Charles Wesley, John Nelson, Thomas Colbeck, Paul Greenwood and Jonathan Maskew, we do not know.

'Haworth is one of those places, which ... owes most of its celebrity to the preaching of the gospel. Its name would scarcely have been known had it not been connected with the name of the celebrated Grimshaw.' Jonathan Crowther wrote this in 1812, long before the arrival of the Brontës. Did stories of this legendary preacher and those powerful men he attracted influence Emily and her sisters in their writing?

Grimshaw's special brand of market place speech was exemplified by his extortion: "If ye will go to hell, ye shall go to hell with the sound of the gospel in your lugs." Fornicators did not escape Grimshaw's wrath either, for poor Esther Greenwood was called into church to serve penance in November 1758, for sleeping with Joseph Wright, a soldier. Esther was forced to shiver in the cold before the congregation for three Sundays running – bareheaded, baré-footed, and barelegged, wearing only a thin white sheet and holding a wand in her hand.

In this manner, she was made to confess her sins and plead forgiveness. Whether Wright received any punishment is not recorded.

Despite Grimshaw's severe modes of punishment, villagers complained that they could not enter the church because it was so full of "off-comed-uns" (outsiders). On 2 September 1763 in the midst of reading a second lesson from the pulpit, Grimshaw collapsed. He was conveyed to the Clerk's home, where his last words – whispered to his housekeeper Mary Shackleton, were: "I have nothing to do but step out of my bed into Heaven. I have my foot on the threshold already."

His work was truly done; he had turned a congregation of twelve into one of a thousand and twelve. He was laid to rest beside his first wife at the Church of St. Mary, Luddenden, near Hebden Bridge.

William Grimshaw, when he died of putrid (typhus) fever on 7 April 1763, left the sum of five pounds to cover the cost of twenty-five pairs of white gloves, a horse litter to carry his body over the moors to

A stained glass window in Haworth church
(Marie Campbell)

Luddenden plus the cost of food and ale for the funeral feast and a pound for his coffin. His own form of burial written on 26 November 1739 stated that he wanted: "To attend my funeral 20 persons invited (of my next relations and intimatest acquaintance) and entertained in the following manner: Let five quarts of claret be put into a punch bowl, and drunk in wine glasses round until gone. Let everyone have a penny roll of bread to eat therewith, let everyone be come, and let all sit down together to the same as an emblem of Christian love. This is at home. Let everyone have a quart of ale, a two-penny spiced cake, and afterwards, immediately before the rising up, a glass of claret and a paper of a biscuit ... This is at the drinking house. In this form I hope my executors will bury me, as I hope to rise again to a blessed resurrection through the merits of my dear Redeemer ..." Grimshaw had secured a good send-off.

During Grimshaw's time, Revd George Whitefield visited Haworth. When preaching one of his eighteen thousand sermons, he solemnly informed Haworthites that man was born to die and after death man would be judged by his actions on earth. In full swing, his powerful voice carried forth tales of Hell-fire and damnation, which would be heaped onto the heads of the wicked and unjust. Amid these outpourings, a sudden "shriek of terror" went up in the church. Grimshaw, taking the pulpit, gravely informed his congregation that of one of their number had suddenly passed away (probably from fright!). Whitefield used the death to make his point; again imploring those present to give up their evil ways and follow the Lord, for the Angel of Death was amongst them. Suddenly another shriek went up. It transpired a second death had occurred. The people quaked and trembled at the Lord's doing and Whitefield held them fast in his grip. On this occasion, the congregation was so great that thirty-five bottles of communion wine were consumed!

Whitefield believed that he had been granted the gift of prophecy, publicly predicting his pregnant wife would give birth to a baby boy and that the child

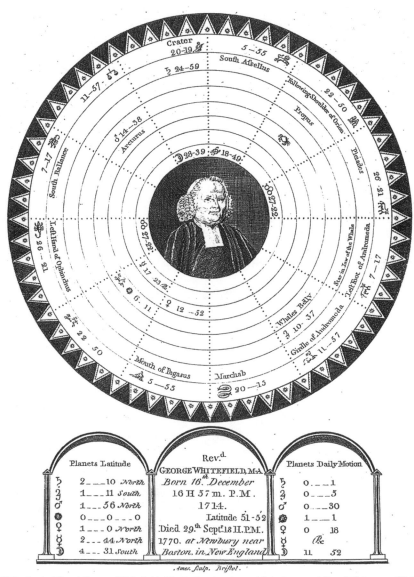

Birth chart of Revd George Whitefield *(Illustration courtesy of Astrology and Occult Sciences, Silsby)*

would grow up to be a wonderful preacher of God's Word. A boy *was* born, but unfortunately died aged four months, after which his father admitted he had been under Satan's spell. Whitefield attended an annual sports meeting (just as Grimshaw had) one Whitsuntide at Moorfields, London. He prayed on the field at sunrise, vehemently denouncing the Devil and all his followers and ignoring the stones, mud and rotten eggs being thrown at him by the brutal mob. His tactics paid off for at the end of the meeting Whitefield gained hundreds of converts to his cause.

After his death in America in the year 1770 a rumour began in 1806 that his body had remained "entire and uncorrupted." This prompted William Morgan to write to the *Gospel Magazine* on the subject saying, 'a few friends were permitted to open the tomb (in 1801) wherein the remains of that precious servant of Christ were interred. After some difficulty in opening the coffin, we found the flesh totally consumed. The gown, cassock, and band, with which he was buried, were almost the same as if just put into the coffin.'

John Wesley, an old friend of both Whitefield and Grimshaw visited Haworth no less than fifteen occasions or even sixteen, if *the Yorkshire Spiritual Telegraph* of July 1855 is to be believed. His first visit was on 1 May 1747. Later he wrote that the 'poor parishioners at Haworth, who hear and hear, and are no more affected than stones.' His congregation grew with each visit.

Decades after his death, the spirit of John Wesley made itself known at one of Keighley's spiritualist meetings. 'The spirit, after giving its name as "John Wesley," said: "I thank God that I am what I am." Someone asked what that meant. The reply came: "A spirit that must live forever in a high state of glory, and Jesus alone is my God." With two short raps, Wesley's shadow was gone.

Excellent Examples

To his servants, Grimshaw's successor John Richardson was a man, "exemplary in his sacred duties." He was very handsome and dressed well, favouring a powdered wig such as that worn by a judge or a barrister. On top of his fashionable wig, he donned a three-cornered hat.

At Folly Spring near Bridgehouse Beck, a secluded spot away from prying eyes, Richardson bathed naked in the cold, fresh clear spring waters. A pursuit, which he firmly believed aided his health. This water was claimed to be "as good as that at White Wells at Ilkley." It is thought that the spring may have been culverted when Ivy Bank Mill (Folly Mill) was built over it.

Richardson was the first pastor to live *and* die at Haworth parsonage. After his death in May 1791, his corpse was taken to the place of his ancestors at Crosby Garrett, near Kirkby Stephen, Westmorland by horse litter – an arduous journey in those times. For many miles, grief stricken parishioners followed behind the coffin of their beloved minister before turning homeward. No special tablet commemorates this good man's memory in Haworth church.

A modern-day Haworth clergyman remembered for his wit and humour is Canon Charles Manchester. In 1962, local and national newspapers took up the plight of the then *Revd* Charles Manchester and his most cherished possession – his car Delilah, a 1937 black Austin Ruby, suffering from serious spring fatigue due to the famous but bumpy stone setts of Haworth's Main Street. Charles informed the papers that, 'We have to move with the times' and called for the cobbles to be covered with asphalt if they deteriorated any further! Rumour had it that the historic setts on which Brontë feet had trodden, could be sold to tourists at a profit of ten bob (50p) each. Villagers though, remained unsympathetic to their Vicar and his Delilah's plight. Billy Kirk landlord of the Black Bull thought the time had come for Delilah to retire. Edward Batt from West Lane said the car was nothing short of a "boneshaker." Brontë author Miss Gerin, a Haworth resident, stated that the "Brontës would grieve in their graves" if the cobble setts went. As a compromise, the Council agreed to mend the offending roadway but by then Delilah had suffered four serious breakdowns. Humorous Zenda Tanner of Haworth sent in a sympathetic poem to the *Keighley News*,

> Cobble stones, aching bones.
> Busted tyres, parson's groans;
> What did the ancient cabbies do
> Who faced the old sett up too?
> Did the carthorse ever hobble.
> When stepping on a wobbly cobble?
> And Charlotte, did she ever chide?
> Though cobbles come and cobbles go.
> To asphalt it would be a blow.
> Each step would chaos invite.
> But readers please now have a heart,
> To help Revd play his better part;
> A silver piece from all who read,
> Could help Delilah's dire need.

>   *2 February 1963.*

The Revd Charles Manchester with his cherished car, Delilah *(The Keighley News)*

Revd Charles Manchester, a good-humoured soul, made up his own parody of a Methodist hymn written by Anne Brontë:

Delilah's Lament

Believe not those who said
That Main Street hill was smooth;
For it has made Delilah dead,
And that's the honest truth.
Though not the only road
Unto the realms of joy;
Yet when she that way bore load,
She'd all her powers employ.
Mend-mend thee for the right!
Cast useless setts away;
Praise be! Before she passed from sight,
Delilah's cause held sway.
To labour and to move,
To flatten and ensmooth;
She moved the Council up above,
Through TV news, forsooth!
If but thy springs approve,
And if, within thy breast;
Thou feel new comfort-give her love.
Delilah's earned her rest.

Delilah's demise was swift and the newly car-less Charles Manchester quipped, "If anyone wants to buy me a new car I wouldn't say no."

Suicidal Reverend

Whatever possessed the Revd Thomas B. Charnock to hang himself in his dressing room in 1847 no one will ever know, or how he came to lose his faith in God. Patrick Brontë, a good friend of both Thomas and his father, the Revd James Charnock (Minister of Haworth 1791 to 1819), read the full burial service over Thomas's corpse, even though Nicholls officiated at several burials. Perhaps Nicholls refused to bury the body for, as a suicide, Thomas Charnock forfeited his right to a Christian burial. Patrick would not deny him a decent burial although no memorial to him can be found in the old graveyard.

All in the Eye of the Beholder

A twentieth-century visitor to Haworth was surprised to hear a Yorkshireman describe the village as being made up from nothing more than a little bit of rubbish God had left over at the end of the day of Creation!

William Grimshaw thought the inhabitants of Haworth in his time were savage in their way of thinking and doing, lacking in morals and intelligence.

Evangelist William Darney, a preacher from Leeds in 1751 wrote on the subject, 'Haworth's a place that GOD doth own, with many a sweet smile; With Power the Gospel's preach'd therein, which many one doth feel.'

'From inn,' wrote Walter White, 'to the churchyard is but a few paces. The church is ugly enough to have had a Puritan for architect; and there, just beyond the crowded graves stands the parsonage, just as unsmiling as the church.'

In Closing

Whilst on the subject of church and religion, perhaps we should not forget a curious chapel known as "t' Bonk", which drew visitors from far and wide, filling all of its thirteen seats in no time at all! One seat was known by the odd title of 'clock seat'. Passing Top Withens and continuing over the moorland track, brought you to Blake Dene Chapel. Mounting the steps, the ground floor was reached first; on descending the steps, the top room was entered. In local terminology "go up th' steps into th' bottom, an' dahn th' steps into th' top." A small burial ground was added in 1902. The chapel closed its doors in 1961 and was afterwards converted into a Youth Hostel.

And finally, did Adelphos have one of the Brontës in mind when he wrote the following melancholic poem about death?

How often in the stilly hour,
My thoughts to thee will fly,
O gentle, loving, hallow'd friend,
Whose graves lin'ring lie.
I cannot chile the happy past,
As prudence bids me do;
Nor lay in an all-quenching grave,
That friendship good and true.
And though thy silence means farewell,
My love will never set;
I'll wish thee nobler heritage,
And memories holier yet.
If beauties stir thy inmost soul,
Thy mind high cultured live
In love with holy thoughts and deeds,
Not more can this world give.
And wisdom should it linger long,
Within poor cottage walls,
May nestle quite as grandly there,
As in proud marble halls.
So prize thy lot, O thou sweet friend;
To thy best moods be true,
So shalt thou keep thy throbbing heart,
Untainted, young and new.
O heed not thou the carping world,
Forsake its narrow creeds,
And undismayed write thine own books,
And trust thine own great deeds.
Be it thy constant wisdom here,
Life's higher paths to tread,
So that at last thou dwellest not
With the ignoble dead.
Be like that child of genius,
Who yet long ere her prime,
On these wild, bleakly moorland hills,
Built up a life sublime.

ADELPHOS, *The Keighley Visitor, 1868*

5 | *Edge of a Shadow*

The talented but sadly neglected Bradford writer James Burnley, alias *The Saunterer*, wrote in 1876, 'I stand on the threshold of the Night ... I look out and watch the darkness stealing over the streaky west, and an awful, unfathomable mystery seems to shape itself impalpably about me. The twilight deepens, the familiar forms of my friends pass me in the street and I know them not, the very houses assume a forbidding grimness, and I feel as if I have been stranded on some desert shore. The lamplighter passes me, and sets the lamps ablaze with his wand-like torch ... night has come but not repose.' And so it is with shades of ghosts who sometimes flit into and out of our lives when least expected.

Plea To A Ghost

Tell us, ye dead; will none of you in pity
To those you left behind, disclose the secret?
Oh! That some courteous ghost would blab it out,
What 'tis you are, and what we must shortly be
I've heard, that souls departed have sometimes
Forewarn'd men of their death; —'Twas kindly done
To knock and give the alarum ... Why might you not
Tell us what 'tis is to die? Do the strict laws
Of your society forbid your speaking
Upon a point so nice? – I'll ask no more:
Sullen, like lamps in sepulchres, you shine
Enlightens but yourselves, Well, 'tis no matter;
A very little time will clear up all,
And make us learn'd as you are,
and as close.

The Grave, Robert Blair 1818

It was customary in Yorkshire to 'Watch the church' on St. Mark's Eve – 24 April. This was the night of the living dead; when restless spirits would rise from their nocturnal sleep to visit places they had frequented in their waking life. A person brave enough to keep watch from a church porch might catch sight of the shadowy pageant of the living, doomed to die within the year. Exactly on the stroke of midnight, the church doors were flung open by invisible agents, allowing undead souls to enter within for one ghostly hour, before returning to their earthly bodies.

The undead were not a pretty sight for they took on the appearance of the death they were about to sufferer. For example, a murderer might have a noose tied about his neck or a suicide would exhibit his self-inflicted wounds. Superstitious Yorkshire folk believed that a person's dead soul flew over to Whinney

Moor. Up until about 1621, a woman was hired to sing this strange dirge at funerals:

> This ean night, this ean night,
> Every night and awle;
> Fire and fleet (water) and candle light,
> And Christ receive thy sawle (soul).
> When thou from hence doest pass away, every night and awle,
> To Whinney-Moor (silly poor) thou comest at last,
> And Christ receive thy sawle
> From Whinney-Moor that thou mayest pass,
> Every night and awle,
> To Brig of Dead thou comest at last,
> And Christ receive thy sawle.

Neighbourhoods Revisited

What drew the Brontë sisters to Wycoller Dene and lonely Barnside near Bouldsworth? Was it because both locations harboured stories of sacrifices and of gruesome murders, terrifying ghosts and tales of the phantom black dog Guytrash and the ghostly horse also known sometimes by the same name? Is this what caused Emily to write in *Wuthering Heights*, 'I have a strong faith in ghosts. I have a conviction that they can, and do exist among us!'

Wycoller

The tiny hamlet of Wycoller, snugly nestled between Haworth and Colne, dates back to the late middle ages and was a tight-knit community of weavers in its hey-day. The advent of the Industrial Revolution wrought poverty and families almost starved for want of work.

When the Brontë sisters dropped down into the nearby thickly wooded glades of Wycoller, perhaps it was to investigate tales of supernatural happenings. Mrs Gaskell wrote this of Charlotte Brontë, *'all the grim superstitions of the North had been implanted in her during her childhood by the servants who believed in them.'*

For several decades, this idyllic place with its pretty, stone cottages was mostly abandoned to its ghostly occupants and the curious. Lancashire County Council granted the village conservation status in the 1970s, thus encouraging a welcome and long overdue revival of the area. The Brontë girls were not the only Haworth writers to be drawn to Wycoller. Halliwell Sutcliffe used this magical setting in his novel *Mistress Barbara Cunliffe*, as well as the Cunliffe name ... the family who had lived at Wycoller Hall for generations.

Wycoller Hall

I paid my first visit to these fascinating ruins, which are best remembered as Mr Rochester's 'Fearndene Manor', in 1997. It is easy to see why the old pile fascinated Charlotte Brontë, with its stories of cruel ghosts, whose souls had fled their earthly bodies long ago and who are said to still haunt the scene of their crimes and tribulations.

Legend has it, that one of the Cunliffes residing at Wycoller Hall during the age of Charles II murdered his wife in an uncontrollable fit of temper. As penance, his ghost is compelled to return to the hall each year and re-enact the awful murder. It is always on a wild, moonless, stormy night when, as the wind howls at its loudest, he appears on horseback, accompanied by a pack of spectral hounds, then gallops wildly across the narrow bridge towards the front entrance of the hall. Dismounting, he opens the creaking door and with heavy measured footsteps, slowly ascends the broad oak stairs that once lead to his wife's bedchamber. A blood-curdling scream is followed by a loud thud and the momentary sound of a woman's dying groan is carried off in a whining vortex of Hunter's Wind. Re-tracing his footsteps, the evil Cunliffe re-mounts his phantom steed and is gone.

Some time before her death, his victim predicted the extinction of the ancient Cunliffe family, so named by a Saxon king. Mrs Cunliffe's prophecy was fulfilled when the only remaining member of the family, Henry Owen Cunliffe – *alias* 'The Baron' died in his sick bed in 1818 from excitement whilst watching a cockfight reflected in a mirror. This scene was captured in an oil painting entitled *The Ruling Passion Strong in Death*.

Interestingly, Cunliffe's ghostly horse was also known hereabouts as Guytrash – is this what gave Charlotte Brontë the idea for the 'Guytrash' scene in *Jane Eyre*, when Rochester comes galloping on horseback at dusk flanked by his huge dog, Pilot?

They say the spectral dog Guytrash often stalked the lonely lane leading from Height Laithe to Wycoller Hall and up to Parson's Lee searching for unsuspecting victims or strangers who had lost their way in the darkness. The name 'Trash' – as he was sometimes called, was enough to send villagers scurrying home to bar their cottage doors against him ... even as late as the twentieth century!

In 1918 Frank Slater, an inhabitant of Colne, felt compelled to write a long poem about the subject as he lay upon his deathbed. Here are a few lines from the mind and imagination of Frank Slater

The Spectre Horseman

The legend says that each year
He must return and re-appear,
Fleshless rider, fleshless steed,
To re-enact his awful deed.
Re-entering once again the hall,
A shriek is heard and then a fall;
Re-mounting up the Dene he goes,
Where to, no mortal knows:
His long atonement now at end
He seeks no face of foe or friend.
On Hallow's Eve, when brown October dies,
And drear November bids her storms rise,
When stormy blasts without do roar,
With shutters fast and locked the door,
In memory of the virtuous dead
Let this memory then be read.'

For all their blood curdling ways, the Cunliffes refused to have a public beerhouse in the village – a restriction that still applies in modern times. Farmers were forced to substitute homemade herb beer for strong ale or face a three-mile hike and the threat of meeting the 'Devil Dog' along the way.

Revd James Carr in his *Annals and Stories of Colne*, related the tale of a courting couple clasped in each other's arms in one of the upper chambers of Wycoller Hall in 1867. His narrative provides the reader with a picture of the hall written some twenty odd years after the time of the Brontës: 'suddenly they heard the sound of light footsteps on the oak stairs and the rustling of a woman's dress. Startled, they held their breath; nearer and nearer came the footsteps; the door opened noiselessly, and in glided a lady, clothed from head to foot in black silk. She uttered not a word, but casting one long, anxious look around the room, and seeing only the frightened lovers, withdrew as quietly as she entered. Years rolled by and the young girl grew to womanhood, living to a good old age, but to her dying day she never forgot the startling apparition of the Lady in Black, who is said by some to be the murdered wife of the 'Spectre Horseman' and is known about Wycoller as Old Black Bess.'

A century later, two men going about their daily work saw a woman dressed in widow's weeds lingering on the Pack Horse Bridge at the front of the hall. They called out to her but to their complete and utter amazement, she faded away right in front of them.

Mr Bracewell, one of the few who had lived his entire life in the medieval hamlet, said in 1948 that the last he'd heard of Mrs Cunliffe's ghost was before the Second World War when his son staged a vigil one night, determined to wait for the phantom to appear inside the ruins. Just before the clock struck the hour of two, Wesley Bracewell distinctly heard the sound of footsteps behind him. Thinking it was his father come to keep him company, he called out but silence was his only answer. The young man didn't stay long after that. It appears that the ghost of Black Bess will never rest until her earthly home has been obliterated forever.

Not all Wycoller romances were doomed to die, for in 1746 a Miss Cunliffe was denied her wish to marry Joseph Owen (ancestor of Henry Owen, last of the Cunliffe family). From then on, she was guarded day and night from her chosen lover, until fate took a hand in the matter. One day as she rode behind her father, she contrived to drop a letter addressed to her beau into the stream running beneath the bridge near the hall. As luck would have it, Joseph happened to be fishing downstream at the time and plucked her note from the water. Thereafter the pair met secretly and were finally married.

Wycoller House

The Cunliffes were not the only phantoms to haunt the village for back in the 1950s a family living at Wycoller House were constantly troubled by the presence of ghostly footsteps coupled with strange noises. Lighted candles were inexplicably blown out in draught-free rooms and doors creaked open of their own accord. In a certain room in the house, it was not unusual for an unsuspecting visitor to be pushed unceremoniously by invisible hands. The family's niece described seeing a woman dressed in bright blue walk down the stairs, as she was going up. Their daughter was almost frightened to death when she saw a man attired in a long black coat with no legs, or hands wearing what appeared to be two caps – one round and one square on top. The most frightening thing about this apparition was that he had "only windows" for eyes. Yet another dark spectre regularly showed itself to the youngster. On asking her parents who it was, they explained the fearsome vision away by telling her it was only her guardian angel!

Barnside

In May 1901 older inhabitants of the area told a visiting group from the Lancashire and Cheshire Antiquarian Society that they could remember seeing the Misses Brontë coming down from haunted Barnside near Laneshaw Bridge. Barnside was where the gruesome murder of pregnant Hannah Corbridge took place in 1789. Her relatives, failing to find the missing teenager, sought the help of a Todmorden wise man, whose crystal gazing led them to her lifeless body, which was lying in a shallow grave. She had been poisoned, then hacked to death – her head almost severed from her body. Nearby was Barnside Farm, the home of her killer Christopher Hartley, who was also responsible for Hannah's pregnancy. He lived here with his mother – known locally as 'Wolf Woman', owing to the preponderance of black hair on her face. Within days of the killing Hartley was caught, tried and hanged on the gallows at York. After Hannah's dreadful death, her pitiful ghost lingered between Barnside and Earl Hall – a farm higher up the track, overlooking Pendle Hill. Hauntings became so frequent at Earl Hall that the tenants were forced to acquire the services of a Roman Catholic priest, to exorcise Hannah's restless spirit from their home. Lonely Barnside Farm remained empty for many years after the murder because folk said the phantom of poor Hannah still searched for her cruel lover.

Stones taken from Barnside Hall, where Christopher Hartley reputedly wiped his dead sweetheart's blood from his hands, were used to repair Laneshaw Bridge. Local inhabitants noted that at a certain time of year these stones appeared to drip blood – the blood of Hannah Corbridge!

Haworth

The Old Hall

The Old Hall stands at the bottom of Haworth Main Street. It was saved from destruction in 1966 by coachbuilder Thomas C. Whittam when, after years of neglect, the property had been condemned. Beneath the old plaster, Mr Whittam revealed stone Tudor doorways and fireplaces. Once the renovation work was complete, he opened the hall as a café and guesthouse. Finding trade poor, he put the Elizabethan property on the market in 1969 for a mere £7750 but was unable to find a buyer!

Tradition has it that preacher John Nelson attempted to convert Haworth folk to Methodism here at the Old Hall, after Grimshaw initially forbade his entry into the church.

The hall jealously guards its secrets concerning the lives of those who once lived and died there. When owner John Emmott died, a loud ghostly groan was heard in the deceased's home, to the consternation of those present at the funeral gathering in February 1648. It is quite possible that these Emmotts were descended from the Duc d'Emot, who came over from Normandy nine hundred years ago.

Author Halliwell Sutcliffe believed the hall's cellars were used as a monks' burial ground in the days when the Old Faith ruled England. He claimed that an old Haworth saying – "by th' Heart", which was used regularly until recent times, emanated from those days. The remains of a male skeleton, thought to have been a monk, were supposedly found walled up near the left-hand side of the main doorway … Strange to say visitors have often complained of an icy cold atmosphere here, even during the height of the hottest summer. A mute dark figure took to standing in the centre of the hall, while monkish figures have been spotted flitting here and there on some ghostly errand.

Folklore, true or not, alleges that monkish hands engineered a secret underground tunnel, running from the church to the Old Hall. And a little girl wearing a crinoline dress of bright yellow was seen standing on the stairway by guests who thought she was real. This little apparition befriended a small child, who terrified its parents when she asked the name of her new playmate!

In the nineteenth century, the footsteps of an old squire who once lived here were often heard in the grounds late at night. And the clatter of horses' hooves pulling a phantom coach has been heard rattling somewhere within the east wing of the old place, no doubt bringing a coach load of unearthly guests in need of a night's lodging after some long forgotten arduous journey across the wild and windswept moors.

Barbara Brooke, a former manager, claimed she saw a monkish spectre on two occasions and felt a strange presence in her upstairs office. One day she was rushed to hospital after she collapsed, suffering from a sensation of being suffocated. Afterwards, she was unable to stay in her office for long periods, without feeling ill. … Mr Gerald Dodd a local psychic and spiritual healer, who claimed that his own life had been saved by his guardian angel, was called in to investigate the odd goings on. A previous landlord's dog was known to bark and growl at "nothing" near the wall between Ms Brooke's office and the nearby sitting room

A legend exists of a tunnel running beneath the hall to Bridgehouse Beck. Sometime during the 1970s, two workmen in the course of their work knocked down part of a cottage wall standing quite close to the beck and were surprised to discover what appeared to be a subterranean passage. Curious to see where the passage led, they knocked out a gap large enough to squeeze through. By the glow of a small torch and a cigarette lighter, they stumbled into the darkness and stale air. After ten minutes, the workman's dog, having tagged behind its owner, suddenly whined and then stiffened, before bolting back to the entrance with the two men following hard behind. Recovering their senses, the pair decided to brick up the wall as fast as they could. They were so convinced that an evil presence haunted the hidden tunnel that they made a pact never to reveal its exact location. One of the workmen has since taken the knowledge to his grave and the full story of what happened that day has only ever been hinted at. The passage leading to the beck from the Old Hall has yet to be discovered but a previous owner believed the entrance lay beneath the main bar.

Before the last owner sold the property, he kindly showed me his bedroom and told of how he lay awake in the darkness one night, watching small mysterious glowing balls of light.

A smooth stone bearing the words '*Go>Mary and Pifs*' was discovered at the back of one of the fireplaces in 1969. This unusual motto now serves as a sign directing ladies to the new ground floor loo! How or why this curiously inscribed stone came to be is not known, however, it is a fact that because of its alkali content, urine once served as a useful scouring agent in the woollen industry. The urine of red haired women commanded a higher price than that of any other, as it was considered the most potent. Piss or Lant stones can still be found incorporated in the old weavers' cottages at the rear of the Friendly Inn, Stanbury, at Wycoller and at Thornton near Bradford.

Beer sellers were wont to water down their ale with urine ... mind you, if Branwell, had contemplated selling the contents of his bladder, he would probably have failed to find a buyer because he stayed up so late and frequented too many inns! Urine was also used as a charm to keep witches and evil spirits from entering the chimney or doorway!

Emily 'Lives' On

Many years ago, a letter headed *Night on Haworth Moors* arrived on the editor's desk at *John o' London's*. In it, the writer (who obviously did not know the legend of Guytrash) described how on New Year's Eve he had walked to the end of a little country lane in Haworth. Up ahead in the distance, through the gloom he could distinguish the outline of an old-fashioned farmstead, where a solitary yellow light flickered through a window, putting him in mind of *Wuthering Heights*. Attracted by the glow and the feel of Emily 's moor, together with the hope of a warm welcome from the farm's inhabitants, he tentatively made his way over the shimmering snow towards the solitary building. That was until a sudden wave of uneasiness swept over him. In the half-light, he swore he could see the black frame of Heathcliff accompanied by Cathy's pale white form. He found himself rooted to the ground – for how long, he could not say – standing between the earth and stars with only Emily's ghosts for company.

It's true that an unknown ghostly lady dressed in white was reputed to wander aimlessly on the track from Stanbury to Top Withens. Could old tales of this lonely moorland ghost have ignited Emily's fertile imagination and thus given birth to the character of Catherine Earnshaw?

Many have felt Emily's strong presence stamped on the wild lands high above her home. One such was the broadcaster S.P.B. Mais who found himself on Old New Year's Night of 1932 standing knee deep in snow on the brow of a hill overlooking the silent world of Haworth moor. "I found Emily," he said, "wandering on the open moor, alight with her presence".

During the course of this lonely night time adventure he'd stumbled upon a piece of abandoned machinery, which he mistakenly took to be a gibbet, causing his muffled footsteps to turn swiftly back towards the welcoming lights of Haworth. On reaching the village, Mais became fascinated by three small shadowy figures, dressed in Oriental type garb and flitting from door to door. His curiosity aroused, he lingered awhile, listening to these strange beings ask the occupants of the cottages if mummers were required (in olden days it was customary for mummers to clean out the fire grate and sweep the house without uttering a word once inside the home). The spell was broken however, when Mr Mais, who had up to that point thought he was amidst a silent world of phantoms, heard them suddenly begin singing that popular jazz song *It ain't going to rain no more*!

A tall ghostly figure, said to be Emily dressed in everyday clothes, with head bowed as if in deep contemplation, has been seen regularly by visitors walking past the waterfall on the path to Top Withens.

A resident of Haworth in the 1960s swore he saw Emily's form huddled in a large shawl, sheltering in a darkened doorway on cobbled Main Street as he and a friend stepped out of the Black Bull Inn late one wet and windy night. Was she waiting for Branwell?

Keith Akeroyd, owner of the seventeenth-century Toby Jug Restaurant, situated on West Lane and Shirley Street, Haworth contacted the *Yorkshire Post*, convinced that a vision haunting his cafe was Emily Brontë. Eight times, always on the anniversary of her passing over to the world of spirit Mr Akeroyd claimed she had appeared before him standing in a 'blue greyish haze' – dressed in a bonnet and a long dress, holding a basket on her arm.

Of his last sighting he said 'Hearing a faint rustling sound, I turned and saw this figure smiling and giggling. She walked across the room to where the stairs used to be and started to climb up to the bedroom. I ran up the new stairs and there she was chuckling in the bedroom. Then she went downstairs and into the street.'

Mr Akeroyd wanted to sell the restaurant but was afraid that the haunted premises might put prospective purchasers off, since he had already lost one sale because of the ghost. And so it was that on the eve of Emily's anticipated arrival, fourteen watchers made up of two psychics, an array of journalists, a teenage boy and a girl all gathered in silent expectation. Wisely, Emily failed to materialise.

After reading in the papers about the strange goings on at the restaurant Revd Eric Davis, Vicar of St. Michael's Church, Morley stepped forward on 1 October 1974 to offer his services to rid the premises of the unwanted apparition but after speaking to Revd Harry Ashdown, Rector of Haworth he decided against exorcism. Instead, Ashdown visited the Toby Jug to perform a blessing ceremony, which took the form of a simple Christian prayer.

The property is known today as 'The Weavers' but a wag at the *Evening Post* suggested it might have been better to keep the ghost and change the restaurant's name to 'Emily's Place.'

Albert Preston whose wife is a descendant of John Greenwood, the Brontë stationer, stated that this was the first he'd known of a ghost here. As to it being Emily he said, "The description doesn't fit any of the sisters. They were a gloomy lot, and Emily was the gloomiest of all."

More Hauntings In Haworth

The daughter of a wealthy manufacturer living in Haworth fell in love with a poor working class boy and he with her. The young couple, knowing her father would put a stop to their affair, met secretly whenever they could. However, news of the romance soon reached the mill owner's ears. Forbidding his daughter ever to meet her sweetheart again, he warned the lad that if he tried to see her he would personally see to it that his widowed mother starved. The lovesick swain took to seeking solace in drink. One evening he swore to avenge himself by damning the cruel businessman and his entire family. Soon after this, the young man died of a broken heart. Following his burial, the manufacturer died an agonising death, the family's once flourishing business failed to prosper and his firstborn son went mad, ending his days in a lunatic asylum, thus fulfilling the curse. In time, the hall was converted into a busy guesthouse but the ghost of a young girl weeping bitterly for her long lost lover can they say, sometimes be heard in the stillness of night in one of the bedrooms.

An intriguing story concerning Branwell Brontë, a phantom ghost and his father's curate Revd William Hodgson written by Mr E. Olridge-DE-LA-HEY, found its way onto the pages of the *Brontë Society Transactions*, in March 1898:

'My father-in-law was a man of a clear head and sound judgement, and little likely to be led away by imagination; yet I have heard my wife more than once, when asked for a true ghost story, relate the following as she heard it from her father: "During his curacy at Haworth my father lodged in an old house occupied by three coeval generations of women – mother, daughter, and granddaughter. The house (at the beginning of West Lane, Haworth) had the reputation of being haunted, but I never heard my father say that he had seen the ghost. His landlady, however told him that when her granddaughter was a child of about three years old she one day came rushing downstairs in a great fright saying that she had seen a lady standing in the middle of the room with something tied around her throat. The ghost made its presence known to my father in several ways. He was returning from a visit when he saw a light moving about from one chamber to another in the upper regions of the house. Although it was not very late he thought the people must be going to bed and hurried on accordingly. To his surprise he found the three females sitting quietly at their work round the kitchen fire and on asking whether anyone was moving about with a light upstairs was answered in the negative. Another time he had gone upstairs in the dark to fetch a book on which he knew that he could easily lay his hand. He found the book, and was just turning to go downstairs, when close to his ear he heard what sounded to him like the shaking out of a silk gown. More than once as he was sitting reading or preparing his sermon he would hear the crack of a whip in the room above him. He would rush upstairs and the whip would resound in the attic. He would follow it there, and then again, it was in the room below.

This ghost had also an unpleasant habit of disturbing him at night. He slept in one of the old four posters, which had an understructure of sacking, instead of the more modern laths or strips of wood. When he had got comfortably settled the bed would begin to heave as though someone underneath were uplifting it. He would get up, light his candle, and look beneath but nothing could be seen. This fact he communicated to Branwell Brontë who was very sceptical on the

subject, and my father invited him to come and test the truth of what he said by sharing his bed. He came, and took every precaution for excluding anyone from entering the room after they were in it. He closely examined the room in every way, and satisfied himself that there was no one there but themselves. He locked and bolted the door, and securely fastened the windows. But they had not been long in bed before the upheaving began. One night's experience was quite enough for Branwell, and he would not renew it. I was a child when my father at my request told me this ghost story, and he precluded it by saying that for whatever reasons they were allowed to reappear upon earth, they were not allowed to do any harm. I say this, he said, from my own experience, for one night, at Haworth, I had fallen asleep while reading in bed, my candle burning on the chair beside me, when an unconscious moment of mine would probably have pushed the bed curtain into the flame of the candle. Judge my surprise and thankfulness when in the morning I found the candle burnt down into the socket and removed to a safe place at the end of the bed."

The curate convinced that the ghost had saved him from a fiery fate decided that it had intended him no harm. Our informant concluded by saying, "It has always seemed strange to me that those who were anxious to unearth all they could of the memory of the Brontës should never have taken the trouble to apply to Mr Hodgson."

Mr and Mrs Glyn White were antique dealers, trading from no. 3 Brontë Street, Haworth in 1974. Their unpaid assistant fondly known as Fred was like no other. For Friendly Fred was a departed spirit and had attached himself to the Whites on their arrival from Thornton in 1971. A family friend described Frederick as a soldier dressed in period costume with a fondness for running upstairs.

One day while serving tourists in his shop, Mr White's eyes widened in horror when he saw a cup and saucer rise up into the air from a sideboard of their own accord and then fall as if in slow motion, clattering to the floor. As Mr White bent down to pick up the china, which had amazingly remained intact, a shocked customer asked what had happened? To which he could only stammer that it had been nothing to do with him. On another occasion, the couple found a mantle clock firmly screwed to a wall. Jewellery was often found broken if left in the shop or the flat above overnight. When someone suggested a priest might rid them of the ghost Mr White said, "To suggest exorcism is like offering a blood pudding to a vegetarian."

Brontë enthusiasts Scott and Mary Hume made the long trek from Chicago to the 'Bad Lands' of Haworth in 1976. Scott, an English literature student was deeply interested in Brontë lore and had come to pay homage at the Brontë shrine. He got more than he bargained for when one dark stormy evening he persuaded his wife to go out against her better judgement onto the wild bleak moor. On reaching the summit of a hill, the pair stood silently in the blackness of the night, listening to the sound of the wind whistling all about them. They were two souls lost in the strangeness of the night – they were Emily's Cathy and Heathcliff.

Caught up in their own world they suddenly felt the ground tremble beneath them. Turning round, they spied four horses (horses of the Apocalypse perhaps?), galloping madly toward them. In the buffeting wind Scott shouted to his wife, "It's the Brontës." Hurriedly retracing their footsteps in the direction of the distant village lights, they were horrified to hear the sound of horses' hooves following on behind, no matter how hard they tried to escape them. Mary missed her footing and would have fallen but sheer terror kept her on her feet. Finally, they reached a wall by the road running alongside the moor, which they scrambled over before stopping momentarily to look back at the ghostly horses. They caught a last glimpse of the phantoms before they disappeared over the hill heading towards Lancashire.

Hophni Bland of Ivy Bank House, Haworth died in October 1907, in his seventieth year. Though a well-respected public figure, Hophni, a West Riding mill owner and magistrate, appears to have had a reputation with women, particularly barmaids. Hophni (meaning "ugliest" in Hebrew) took his name from the Biblical Eli's first born who, unable to resist women, brought down a curse upon his father's house. Rumour has it that Hophni Bland's restless spirit continues to haunt his derelict Ivy Bank Mill, also known as Folly Mill.

Stanbury

Just up the road from Haworth lies the tiny stone village of Stanbury. It too has its fair share of ghostly goings on. A gentleman wishing to purchase a property on the outskirts of the hamlet knocked at the door of a cottage to ask directions. Pointing to a rough unmade track, the lady of the house told him to follow it. Soon after, his figure could be seen scurrying back down the dusty roadway. Intrigued, the lady stopped him to enquire if he had found the property suitable for his needs. However, the man said he couldn't even bring himself to go in, having never felt such evil in one place in all his life. She silently nodded in agreement having heard that a gruesome murder had once taken place there.

An employee of Dean, Smith & Grace, Keighley arrived at his Stanbury home one day to find it ablaze. Disregarding his own safety, he ran into the burning farmhouse and up the stairs to where he kept his money. The fire soon consumed the poor fellow as he stumbled about blindly in the smoke-filled building. Later the property was renovated but they say at times you can hear him re-enact his final moments on earth as he frantically searches for his lost gold, before being engulfed by flames.

In a little stone cottage on the edge of Stanbury, its single occupant found that each time she returned home two china shoes, which lived on either side of the mantelpiece, had been placed side by side in a neat and orderly fashion. She casually mentioned this peculiar phenomenon to a neighbour who explained that an elderly lady who passed away in the cottage had a mania for putting shoes together exactly in the manner described!

Oakworth

As soon as Flora's husband set eyes on the dilapidated White Hill Farm, Oakworth, built by Stephen and Anne Bannister in 1777, he could think of nothing else. When the purchase was complete and while work was being carried out on the old farmhouse, the couple set up a temporary home with their children in a caravan on the site. As time went by Flora began to feel uneasy about her new home often sensing a black shadow near her. She got so used to the presence that she christened it "Anne." After working awhile in an upstairs room, a plasterer bolted out of an unglazed window and ran across two planks to the banking on the other side, before roaring off at speed in his car. Another workman went after him and on catching up with him, asked why he had run away from the site. All he would say was, "I'm not going back there. It's haunted!" Eventually the work was finished and the family moved in but it wasn't long before 'things' began to happen. At precisely 10pm each evening Flora learned to listen for the inevitable rattle of the front door latch followed by the sound of light footsteps on a staircase no longer in situ. Echoing footsteps proceeded across the bedroom floor and past her bed. Flora's husband, a heavy sleeper, refused to believe her story until one night he too heard the sound of trailing footsteps accompanied by a sudden drop in temperature. The petrified couple enlisted the help of an understanding clergyman who agreed to stay the night at their home. He also felt a sudden cold chill and was somewhat startled to hear a sudden burst of *Row, row, row your boat gently down the stream, merrily, merrily life is but a dream* ... issuing from a child's music box in the very place where he was sitting alone. This prompted the clergyman to read a prayer in each of the rooms before performing a special blessing on the house. From that day the haunting ceased but immediately afterwards Flora suffered a terrible bout of depression feeling guilty at having driven "Anne" away from her home.

In the autumn of 1988, Bradford College lecturer Simon Pollard was driving home as usual at about 9.30pm. Having reached the junction of Slack and Slaymaker Lane, he was suddenly confronted by the figure of a ghostly rider on horseback. Mr Pollard told the *Keighley News* "It was a Dick Turpin type figure ... like the negative of a photograph, sepia coloured. I don't know if it was a man or a woman ... the horse was just trotting I swerved to avoid it and it just vanished. If it was real I would have gone right through it." A few years before Mr Pollard's frightening experience, Mrs Shanks of Oakworth suffered an identical encounter at the same place! Another time, she had observed an odd looking figure dressed in a long black coat and wearing a hat at the end of Slaymaker Lane. The apparition vanished when her dog barked at it.

Retired postmaster Robert Sugden felt he knew the identity of the phantom rider, saying the description fitted a man he remembered as a youngster named Seth Burwin. This particular man often wore a Sherlock Holmes type cape and lived in Oakworth. He rode round the village on a big horse named Sam.

Steve Bingham, owner of Seth Burwin's old home – Sykes House, Lidget – turned up an interesting story connected to the history of the house relating to a crock stuffed full of gold, which was supposed to have been secreted away in the cellar of the house. Previous occupants had spent a lot of time searching for the treasure to no avail.

A spiritual healer claimed to have had a vision of an angelic bearer of archaic knowledge "come to advise him on business matters", when he lived at Sykes House. Intrigued by this ghost story I looked through records at Keighley Reference Library in the vain hope of shedding further light on the matter. Within a short period, I came across an article about a well-known Edwardian soprano vocalist by the name of Margaret Ann Burwin of Banks House, Oakworth, who killed herself. She had been found dead sitting in an upright position in a vapour bath with a rubber gas tube pushed down inside her mouth. At the inquest in August 1920 James Rushworth, a family member told the Coroner "I think she had some great trouble which nobody has known but herself."

Just as I was about to return the papers to the slender brown packet marked BK 103 a loose sepia photograph fluttered out onto the desk of *Mrs Burwin seated on her horse in Slaymaker Lane!* Further investigations revealed that she had been an accomplished horsewoman troubled by sleeplessness and was often seen trotting on her horse up and down this lane dressed in a hat, riding coat and long flapping skirt! Is Oakworth's phantom rider Margaret's tormented earthbound spirit? If so, and you happen to meet her on the road, don't worry, for those that knew her in life said she possessed a very caring nature and sunny disposition.

Others claim to have witnessed strange phenomena in Oakworth village as well. For example Olive Foster of Windsor Road, Oakworth reported seeing a man attired in Cromwellian garb riding a horse past her house in broad daylight!

Birstall

Charlotte Brontë used her knowledge of Oakwell Hall to create the fictional Fieldhouse in her novel *Shirley*. She was to make her own mark at Oakwell when she scratched her initials onto a diamond shaped piece of glass – this was afterwards removed for safekeeping.

The hall began its long history with John Tilly in 1311, blossoming into a splendid Elizabethan manor house. A secret passage situated on the western wall near the drawing-room chimney led to a tiny closet hidden above the drawing room. A little window offered welcome light to those forced to use the clandestine staircase, possibly built by a previous Catholic owner named Thomas Hussey. When soldiers searched the house during the Civil War, Royalist Captain Batt hid himself here. In life, Batt "a rogue in spirit" was cast as an evil man of dark deeds, and it is his spirit which is said to haunt the place.

It was late dusk on 9 December 1684 when a shrouded figure resembling that of Captain Batt walked up the Avenue known as the Bloody Lane or Black Walk beyond the bridge to the hall. The apparition slowly entered the property by the door, walked up the staircase to the end of the gallery and the bedroom that contained the hide, before gradually fading away. It later transpired that at the very moment a servant at his home saw Batt's 'fetch', he had been slain in a duel by a Mr Greame of Barnet, near London! His corpse was brought back and buried at Birstall on 30 December 1684. Thereafter, there was a bloody footmark said to belong to Batt's ghost on the wooden floor of the haunted chamber, which no amount of scrubbing could remove until a zealous servant managed to get the mark off with the use of either *Hudson's Soap* or *Brooke's Monkey Brand*. Apparently, a footprint *and* a bloody handmark were hidden beneath the carpet. The last of the Oakwell Batts died in 1707.

In the 1920s, there was a scheme afoot to dismantle Oakwell and rebuild it in America! The plan failed because of the building's strong links to Charlotte

Brontë. In 1928, the house fell into the hands of the old Birstall Council, via the Fitzroy Estate and was restored to its former glory. It is now a museum well worth visiting.

Ponden

Several forebears of the Heatons of Ponden were actually born in Wycoller. Wilfred Heaton built Ponden Hall in 1560. Almost one hundred years later, the estate fell to Michael Heaton who in December 1640 married Anne Scarborough at Burnley church. Anne was the niece of magistrate Roger Newell of Read Hall, Pendle, a man who personally played a crucial part in rooting out the infamous Pendle witches. Michael then aged about thirty-three, mysteriously disappeared at the time of the civil war – perhaps in the burning of Haworth village by Major Sir Richard Tancred of Whixley who fought on the Royalist side. Exactly where or how this Heaton met his death remains a mystery to this day but it appears that he died before September 1643.

Sometime after, the villainous Henry Casson, from Ardsley, Wakefield was made Constable of Haworth and Michael's cousin Andrew Heaton of Old Snap – overseer to Anne's estates, also mysteriously vanished after being arrested by Casson (Casson had previously been employed by the family as farm bailiff). The original marriage settlement made by Michael Heaton was altered, allowing Anne Heaton to marry Casson. Was Anne somehow intimidated or even bewitched into choosing this man as her husband in 1650? Casson had boys from a previous marriage who came to live by him at Stanbury and Anne gave birth to *their* only son, John.

For many years, Casson ruled over the household and estate with an iron fist, until Michael Heaton's natural son and heir Robert, attained full age and his mother was able to retrieve the Heaton property from her husband's evil grasp.

Delving into the Heaton family archives led historian Mary Butterfield to conclude that Emily Brontë's Heathcliff was modelled on the evil Casson, who they say came back to haunt the family as Greybeard. This frightening apparition was often seen skirting the grounds of Ponden, holding a lantern aloft in his skinny hand. The Heaton's, wanting rid of this devilish phantom, sent for a local man well versed in the Black Art to lay the ghost. Holding a lighted rush candle, the occultist confronted the spirit and after reading a passage backwards from a book of Black Magic, he called upon the spectre to depart forever. Dropping the ethereal lantern, Greybeard scurried back across the fields whence he had come and has never been seen again at Ponden, from that day to this. Branwell Brontë was fascinated by the ghost story *Greybeard*.

William Shackleton, in his unpublished 1921 typescript, *Four Hundred Years of a Moorland Family*, believed Emily wove her intimate knowledge of the Heaton family into the story line of *Wuthering Heights*. Mrs Butterfield, author of *Brother in the Shadow*, thought Emily cast the last Robert Heaton as the spirited Hareton Earnshaw. No doubt, Emily had heard tell of the family's ghosts and legends, which had been passed down the generations. The last of the Ponden Heatons hardly ever referred to the Casson episode and apparently were not best pleased when they discovered Emily had let the family skeleton out of the closet in *Wuthering Heights.*

One of the tales told about this place concerned a cousin of the Heatons who was convinced that she not only saw but spoke to the living duplicate (psychic double) of Thomas Midgley Heaton, dressed in his favourite grey suit standing outside in the garden shortly before he died in February 1898 aged 62 years. Family tradition held that whenever a family member was about to pass over, his doppelgänger or 'fetch' would appear before a relative. The Heatons were a superstitious lot, for whenever a death occurred, a member of the family would go and tell the bees of the passing and leave them a saucer full of food from the arvill (funeral feast).

Thomas's brother, Robert, (who, it was supposed by family members had a strong romantic attachment to Emily Brontë and she to him) followed Thomas to the grave a few weeks later. When Robert, son of *Robert* and *Alice Heaton* died in 3 March 1898, it ended the succession of a direct male line of ten generations from the original *Robert* and *Alice Heaton*, AD1560. Robert's chest tomb can be found in Stanbury Cemetery.

Local genealogist, the late Hannah Knowles Heaton, a direct descendant, managed to retrieve hundreds of family documents destined to be burnt after Robert's death. Amongst these manuscripts (now in the care of Bradford Council) were family wills, diaries, old ballads, sealed documents, books and several seventeenth-century copies of *Old Moore's Almanack.*

Patrick Brontë fell out with the Heaton family when he refused to bury Michael Heaton of Royd House, Oxenhope in the same grave as his wife after his death on 6 March 1860. This decision was backed by his son-in-law, which was later to be his undoing. Michael's relatives were forced to seek permission from the Secretary of the State so that they could lay his bones to rest in the family grave. When the order granting permission came, Patrick Brontë still refused to conduct the Burial Service. Eventually the Revd Grant was called in from Oxenhope church to perform the funeral service. The following year Patrick Brontë died. He was buried inside the church, alongside his children without any such to-do and with Home Office approval. Nicholls had hoped to become perpetual curate in his place but was refused because he had gone against the Heatons and "so the widower of Charlotte Brontë had to suffer eclipse at Haworth and go elsewhere."

In 1935 Miss Emily Heaton, of Wibsey, Bradford, author of *White Windows* owned a selection of Heaton relics. These included *Old Bet*, a weird wooden four-hundred-year-old featureless doll said to be akin to a Voodoo carving, having rudely carved ears but devoid of arms or legs. The doll had been fashioned out of stout black oak, probably by the loving father or older brother of its first recipient. Emily remembered seeing the fire being poked with Old Bet at Old House, Ponden when she was a child. Where is Old Bet now?

By 1945, this glorious old pile lay ruinous, dominated by a Spanish chestnut tree and a mass of tangled weeds. In its glory days, it had been a comfortable dwelling place, sporting a huge arched fireplace. In the same year, a *Keighley News* correspondent asked if the dilapidated hall was haunted? Silence appears to have been his only answer.

In 1999, the dilapidated hall rose up from the ashes like the Phoenix, to begin life anew as a hotel. Mrs Muriel Crook remembers the time when "customers sat on old horse hair sofas at Ponden House which prickled the legs, where Mary the waitress chanted out the menu we all knew by heart."

Inn-trusions

At the Old Sun Hotel in West Lane, Haworth, built sometime around 1770, the ghost of a man wearing a felt hat and long dark cape was wont to haunt the bar. No one appears to know anything about this silent phantom's identity or why he was there. The inn's landlord commissioned a modern carved stone head in the 1970s and had it placed above the main entrance in an effort to ward off lurking

The carved stone head above the entrance to The Old Sun Hotel *(Marie Campbell)*

evil spirits – especially that of their dark mysterious figure. Happily, it seems to have done the trick.

The landlord may have got his inspiration from a similar, but far older head situated on the opposite side of the village carved above the Old Hall's main doorway on Sun Street. While another stone head can be seen, protruding from the gable end of a cottage dated 1757 in West Lane. Either it was put there to commemorate the death of a builder at the site or it would have been built into the fabric of the cottage to ward off witches.

Stanbury's Old Silent Inn once boasted its own brew-house and was famous for its 'Sad Cakes' baked on the premises. The hostelry was known as the New Inn until the 1820s, when it became The Eagle. Halliwell Sutcliffe, in his novel *Ricroft of Withens*, romantically re-named The Eagle as the Old Silent.

It was here that two Lancashire men murdered an innocent traveller after robbing him of his valuables, throwing his corpse into a stream close by. At the Brewster Sessions in 1926, the Old Silent's licence to sell alcohol was refused after the Licensing Committee heard that the place was utterly unsuitable for visitors, owing to years of neglect and rising dampness. The last pint was pulled on Christmas Eve the same year. The building then served as a café until 1965, when new owners were granted a restaurant licence, against the Licensed Victuallers wishes. Mr Cockcroft, speaking on their behalf, went as far as to say to the Licensing Committee "You are being asked to assist at the birth of a white elephant, you are being asked to deliver it, and it is my submission that it will be stillborn." Fortunately, Cockcroft was proved wrong, for the Old Silent complete with phantoms is still a popular venue among locals and tourists alike.

Decades later, after suffering two serious fires within the space of five days, the old hostelry was once again forced to close its doors. In 1992, two frightened

The Eagle, Hob Lane, Stanbury – renamed 'The Old Silent' by Halliwell Sutcliffe

workmen employed in renovating the property told former licensee Philip Duncan that they had seen the ghost of a man. A cleaning lady complained of a ghostly presence in the living quarters above the bar. Guests have protested about experiencing a sudden feeling of coldness and having their hair stroked, while lying in bed. This particular ghostly presence is believed to be that of a former landlady who adored cats. She would go out on the moors at night dressed in a long dark cape calling to the cats. Sometimes the faint sound of jingling bells carried on the wind can still be heard in the distance. A previous landlady was relieved when a waitress questioned her about the noise of bells, because it confirmed she wasn't losing her mind.

Two house guests, Julie Barrett and her partner Gary Chatel from Bolton, Lancashire were rudely awoken from their slumbers when the bedroom they were sleeping in began to shake. They watched in horror as a glass flew across the room before crashing to the floor. The couple fled to pub manager David Stanton's room for the night but within the hour all three witnessed a painting vibrate, then fall from the wall and slide across the floor. A table was pushed over and a glass danced in mid-air. On top of all that, the curtains opened and closed of their own accord, accompanied by the sound of rustling noises. Mr Stanton was not put off living at the Silent by the ghostly demonstrations because he felt the presence meant no harm.

If that's not spooky enough, Mr Joe Narey, another licensee told a reporter for the *Keighley News* in August 1999 about the inn's spectres: "One which seems to appear downstairs, mainly to women, is of a tall man wearing a big hat and old-fashioned long coat. One male customer claims to have sat up all night talking to the ghost of a young girl, and another said his keys had been moved from the floor to a mantelpiece while he slept."

In the old days, suppers used to consist of pies and pints in a gloomy flagged stone room. Today the Old Silent can proudly boast of winning the national Pub of the Year Award in 1999.

They say an unexplained presence is often felt at the Dog and Gun Inn, Oxenhope especially in the ladies' toilet. In 1995, the landlord Michael Roper looking out from an upstairs window at the pub thought he was seeing things when he saw a bright pink lurcher-type dog wandering about. He and John Sawood caught the frightened animal and discovered its unusual colour was due to household paint! Mr Roper offered to provide the distressed dog (which he'd christened Duncan) with a loving home.

Spoofed by Spooks

As soil was shovelled down onto the remains of 'careful-solemn sides', Revd James Charnock, Incumbent of Haworth Parish Church gravely announced:

> "The friends of our dear brother, Kossuth Batty, now laid to his long last rest, are bidden to attend the arvill" (funeral feast in honour of the dead) "at the Black Bull Inn, at three o' clock."

Two days before this miser's sudden departure, Kossuth had warned his brother-in-law Tobias Todd that on no account must there be an arvill after his burial, otherwise he'd come back to haunt him with a vengeance. Furthermore, he promised to "rise from the grave, and make in Tobias's house his immortal abode, to the terror of all who slept there."

According to Joseph Wright's *English Dialect Dictionary* the word arvill means 'a funeral repast, usually consisting of bread or cakes with ale. Also applied to funeral ceremonies in general.' In Yorkshire an arvill was an excellent excuse to celebrate the dead person's life in great style with lots of good food and plenty of ale. Should this not be the case indignant mourners might be heard to say, 'Ah didn't call that much of a *do*; they buried him wi' cold ham! Aw've putten away three children an' they were all buried wi' roast beef an' plum puddin.'

Funeral feasts were particularly popular affairs in the Worth Valley and Tobias firmly believed in making merry whenever he got the chance. Choosing to ignore Kossuth's dire warning, he set about organising the arvill at the Black Bull as soon as he heard of his relative's sudden passing.

According to Harwood Brierley's story, there were seventy-six mourners in all. Most couldn't wait until the funeral service ended, for no sooner had the cleric uttered 'ashes to ashes, dust to dust' over the coffin than the hungry crowd made off to the inn where two long tables groaned with the weight of the banquet. The menu consisted of seventy-eight spiced rolls, three cold possets, two dishes of stewed prunes, seventy-six sprigs of the herb rosemary – signifying remembrance and one tremendous currant cake complete with a doleful black paper flag flying at half-mast, added for effect. While the adults tucked into the feast, children waited patiently in the little parlour to take their turn at the table. In the corner of this room stood an elderly high-cased piano on which some semi-musical soul banged out the *Dead March in Saul**, which sounded as "flat as a German band trumpet."

When it was almost over, the crafty Tobias demanded payment towards the meal, much to the annoyance of the crowd. To avoid arguments, the landlord intervened, telling Tobias he would have to pay the bill himself ... aye, and pay it within a week.

Neddy Watmouth, having taken exception to Tobias trying to wangle money out of him and his friends, devised a plan to punish their miserly host. Waiting until Tobias was in a drunken stupor, Neddy went over to him and reminded him of Kossuth's threat to come back and haunt him. He dared him to go to the grave in the darkness and shake hands with Kossuth's waiting ghost. Tobias declared he had "no fear 'o flay boggarts-devils or wraiths and that be so-*hic*-Ah'll shak' hands wi' 'm ... Ah love the good grip o' a ghoast ... But I dinna think he'll come-*hic-hic*-Ah'll go to Backbummer ef he do!" Neddy though, had already been to the grave, leaving behind a friend holding a clothes' prop and draped in a white sheet to look like Kossuth's phantom!

Tobias fell out of the Bull and into the frozen churchyard, lit only by the rays of a full moon. Lurching unsteadily towards the opening of Kossuth's grave over on the south side of the church, he came to an abrupt stop for he could make out something ahead of him flapping about in the wind. "Damn 'em! That's a heffigy o' mysen them divils ha' been puttin' oop ower ahr Kossewth's hoil (hole)" he muttered to himself. Bravely venturing a few paces forward, he moved cautiously towards the 'ghostly thing', then gave it a good licking with his clenched fists, knocking the 'phantom' bang into the opening of the yawning hole and onto Kossuth's coffin. Neddy and company who had been watching and sniggering from a safe distance, seeing their prank had backfired made for home as fast as they could.

The ghost of Kossuth Batty rising from his grave in Haworth's old graveyard *(The Yorkshireman)*

Did you know that it was against the law for anyone to hum, sing or whistle the tune entitled the *Dead March in Saul* except at church or in the grounds of a cemetery? In olden times, this law was strictly enforced and miscreants imprisoned or fined. During the First World War a soldier caught playing the *Dead March* other than at a military funeral found himself in front of his commanding officer and given barrackroom duties, or even worse.

132

Handel was the composer of this piece of music. There are some however, who claim that a musician named Steibelt wrote it when he was dying. The story runs that as the composer sat dozing fitfully in an armchair, he fancied he caught sight of his dead father standing at the far end of the room silently beckoning him to come forward. His actions were accompanied by the muffled strains of strange mournful music followed by a phantom funeral possession, which paused and turned in the centre of the room. It was then that Steibelt realised they were carrying *his* coffin. Without a sound apart from the mysterious music, the procession continued on its way until fading from his view. Now fully alert, the musician jumped up and while the doleful music was still swirling round in his head, immediately committed it to paper. Picking out the tune on his pianoforte, he thought it sad but beautiful. After he had finished writing, he sank insensible to his seat, where his servants found him. He later died on the couch to which he had been carried. It was at his funeral the famous *Dead March* was played for the very first time.

Mystical Manifestations on the Moors

It was one late September when the heather turns purple, that three young male students set out from lodgings near the village of Oxenhope, intending to spend the day sketching on Haworth Moor. Finishing off their picnic lunch, the friends decided to split up and find a subject of their own to paint until dusk, when they planned to meet at the inn where they had left their bicycles.

One of the youths, Michael Brookes lighted on a lonely stream in a desolate valley with only the distant sound of curlews and the rustle of a warm autumn breeze for company. Revelling in the silence of the day, he followed the stream uphill until he reached a waterfall lit by the rays of the sun. He got to work on his painting, putting everything from his mind and was soon so engrossed in his work that he failed to notice the dark storm clouds gathering at an alarming pace, until the first drops of rain ran down the canvas. Quickly collecting his belongings, he turned to go back but a heavy mist descended and this, along with the ever-increasing gloom, caused the lad to lose his way. He stumbled, fell down a ravine and broke his ankle. Cold and wet, he managed to crawl from the muddy bottom onto a nearby rock and thence up onto a rough track. By which stage, he was so confused and exhausted he lay down to rest. Just as he was about to fall asleep, a deep voice roused him. Opening his eyes, he was confronted by the shadowy figure of a man attired in old-fashioned garb. On coming to his senses, he asked the stranger if he too was lost. The man, who had introduced himself as Paddy, told him the moors were his home and proffered a walking stick. As they travelled together in the blackness of the night, Paddy wished he had something strong to drink but admitted that he had given up alcohol after a long hard struggle. Paddy urged Michael to hurry for he was afraid his three sisters would be waiting up for him at home. He described his eldest sister as straight-laced, the youngest very religious and of a sad disposition; whereas his middle sister, who he thought should have been born a man, wouldn't think twice about setting her brute of a dog on you if you tottered home drunk!

133

By now the path had become more even and lights twinkling in the near distance lifted the darkness of the night. Paddy continued to talk about himself, saying he had failed as a tutor and was in the process of finding a new position and how all his misfortunes in life had been the fault of others. The journey continued in this manner until the darkened silhouette of the parsonage loomed up ahead. Straining his eyes, Michael was able to make out the slim figure of a girl framed in the doorway, dressed in a long gown and holding an old-fashioned lantern aloft. At this juncture, his new friend quickly advised him which way to go and then faded away in a light swirling mist!

His mind numbed by what had taken place, Michael stumbled on until he reached the Black Bull, where he collapsed unconscious to the floor. An ambulance whisked him off to hospital and, while plastering his injured ankle, the doctor inquired where he had obtained his ash walking stick, saying he hadn't seen one like it since his grandfather had died. Feeling awkward, Michael muttered something about finding it on the moors. The night before leaving hospital, he woke with a start at about 2am to find his saviour Paddy standing by his bed, "I've come for my stick, I need it in my work", he said. Lifting his hand by way of farewell, Paddy was gone. Michael called to the night sister on duty to ask if she'd seen his late night visitor but she told him he'd been dreaming as she'd been in her office with the door ajar and not a living soul had gone past ...

*   *   *   *

One Saturday afternoon, several school friends went wandering as usual on Haworth moor where they stopped to admire a low-slung cottage nestling against a hillock some distance from the road. Looking at the tiny mullioned windows and a quaint stone arched doorway they wondered why they had never noticed the old dwelling before. Pushing open the rickety door, they saw that a narrow stone passage led to a staircase – quite worn away by generations of clogs trudging up and down – and this they gingerly ascended. At the top of the stair-well, dappled rays of summer sun played inside a room, which they happily explored until a sudden feeling of dread descended upon them. All fell silent, no longer giggling at this unexpected adventure.

The spell broke when one of the girls screamed and then ran towards the downstairs entrance. The others tumbled after her until they too reached the safety of the open air. No matter how many times the girls tried to locate the eerie cottage afterwards, they never found it again.

*   *   *   *

Mr and Mrs Emsley were travelling from Stanbury to Hebden Bridge during the 1960s. Having reached the weather station high up on the bleak windswept Yorkshire moors near Oxenhope, they spied an old codger carrying a heavy looking sack filled with worn blankets slung across his back. Since it wasn't a good day, the couple agreed to offer the man a lift. Slowing the car until it came to a smooth stop, the driver was about to open his door to attract the wanderer's attention when his perplexed wife exclaimed, "There's nobody there." Both agreed they had definitely seen the lonesome traveller but the stranger appeared to have melted away into thin air.

Was this then the ghost of 'owd Charlie' who had gone missing after his adopted family, the Midgleys of 47 Park View Road, Heaton, Bradford, lost him one Sunday afternoon? Charlie, as they liked to call him was in the habit of watching popular Westerns on television with his adopted family Bertie and Muriel Midgley. The couple never saw Charlie but could always tell when their guest was about because of the awful smell of the pipe tobacco he always smoked. Despite this, they had become very fond of their ghostly companion, although Charlie's continued presence became too much for a young priest who was staying with them ... he was driven to flee the haunted house.

One fine day the Midgleys, with Charlie settled in the back seat of the car as usual, set off for their customary weekend drive. Having reached the wastes of Oxenhope moors, Bertie stepped out of the car and opened the back door to release the pungent smell of Charlie's pipe smoke. However, it wasn't until the couple returned home that they discovered Charlie was missing.

Thinking he must have got out the car to go for a walk when the door was opened and then lost his bearings, the couple went back to the same spot several times, in the hope of finding him. When this bid failed, they were forced to contact the local paper, begging for his safe return ... but he never did go back. Perhaps Charlie found another family who liked watching John Wayne films ...

Bothersome Beasties

A fearsome ghost dog was once believed to prowl the streets of Haworth. A passage from Halliwell Sutcliffe's book *By Moor and Fell* published in 1899 sets forth a wonderful descriptive account of Guytrash, the death dog: 'Yet the November Grey is better. Standing at the road-foot here with the dun fields climbing to the rounded skyline, it is easy to understand Barguest, the ghostly Dog who holds first place among all the moorland superstitions. Barguest – they call him Guytrash sometimes – is of a piece of with the drear look of the land, with the shrewd breeze that whimpers out of the silence and is gone again before the chill is realised. His coat is shaggy and dun-brown, this phantom dog's, his feet are shod with silence as he passes you, and in his wake, an ice-cold wind advances. Old faiths retire discomfited, but Barguest is dying hard, and fear of the Dog is half-slumbering terror yet, in woven in the brain and nerves of men whose fathers learned what panic waited upon the Brown Beast's steps. Such a dread strikes deep, and manifests itself in many a curious guise, the honest cheery dog of the flesh-and-blood has been known to take on a borrowed signifi- cance from his ghostly cousin, and the malignity which folk attributed to his bite had in it, one suspects there is something of a superstitious vividness, separate altogether from such physical danger attended it. Superstitions lead one far afield; they fatten on loneliness and storm, and the marsh candles which lighted unwary travellers to bog brinks have led men's fancies also into eerie places.'

Harbinger of death and destruction, this silent phantom dog – also known as Clatterchains and Black Shuck, often wandered the Yorkshire and Lancashire hills and dales deep into the night. The animal was usually described as a large shaggy Newfoundland type of dog, coloured black and/or white or dun-brown having saucer-like eyes of burning red and the ability to change into a horse or a white calf!

Both Patrick Brontë's dogs Plato and Cato, purchased in 1855 shortly after Charlotte's death, were black Newfoundland types and would undoubtedly have caused quite a stir if they had been out at night. Superstitious folk dreaded the sound of a lone dog howling at night, for this was a sure mark of a death and should a strange dog divide a couple on the day of their wedding it was the sign of a sad parting.

Charlotte Brontë demonstrated her knowledge of Guytrash when she described him as "a lion-like creature with long hair and a huge head." Not all dogs were heralds of doom though as there have been reports of ghostly dogs safely guiding lost strangers over desolate and dangerous moorland hereabouts. Guytrash is not the only phantom animal to haunt the district; in the hamlet of Hainworth near Haworth, a cottage is supposed to be visited by a white horse and a house in Bradford by a 'spectral bear'.

One winter's evening, a little Haworth body nicknamed Grace Serious made her way home aided only by the light of the moon. It was chilly and thick snow lay heavily underfoot. Leaving the safety of Main Street, she passed the Black Bull and cut through the old cemetery. Walking steadily on, Grace took care to look neither left nor right, for she was afraid of ghostly apparitions, it being very late and the streets so empty. She could not help but notice the black outlines of tombstones standing out in stark relief against the white background of the snow. Suddenly, from out of a dark corner, Tombstone Tom – a huge white longhaired phantom cat appeared. Catching the glint of his eyes Grace noted that the cat followed her, stopping and moving only when she did, stalking her just as it would a mouse. Terror took charge and Grace made for home in record time. Afterwards, a relieved Grace told her friends, "Thanks to heavens it disappeared instantly as the old church clock in the tower did break the deathless silence by solemnly announcing the midnight hour of twelve!"

Just above Wycoller's village café was, until recently, a piece of wood taken from Roughlee Hall, once home to the infamous Pendle witch Alice Nutter. This building is sometimes visited in the dead hours by a ghostly cat.

During the 1970s, Big Tom – a village character and regular of the Black Bull, often nipped though the churchyard to imbibe a beer or two at his local. Ensconced in his favourite chair and surrounded by his friends, Tom would relate many tales of daring-do.

The villagers were shaken out of their easy and peaceful existence when one night an ashen-faced traveller burst through the door of the Bull. "The dead have spoken," spluttered the wild-eyed visitor. At first Billy Kirk the landlord, hesitated but it was plain to see that his agitated guest had undergone a fearful fright. A kindly Tom with two of his dearest companions was soon in comforting attendance.

Observing this scene whilst measuring out a strong tot of whisky for the hapless soul, Billy perceived a stricken victim amongst angels of mercy. Despite Tom's reputation for having a wild and fanciful imagination, he and his friends restored calmness and tranquillity within the walls of the old inn. The afflicted party, grateful for the help he had received, insisted on repaying their kindness by buying drinks for the rest of the evening.

The following night the inn was buzzing and trade was brisk. The merry sound of clinking coins played to a background of terrifying new reports of banshee-like screams rising from the tombs of those long dead. Tom and his stalwarts remained unruffled throughout. Long before last orders were called, Billy noticed that Tommy and his band of angels, as he now liked to think of them, had disappeared. His suspicions, aroused he went outside to see where they had gone.

Right enough, strange sounds *were* coming from the direction of the cemetery. Creeping forward he found Tom and his drunken cronies tangled up, helpless with laughter, in a complicated array of wires and devices. The end of the trail led to Tom's house and a tape recorder!

Mischief at Work

Professor Tyndall had been employed to survey the Worth Valley for the coming railroad. "A time" he stated "of terrible toil." Later he was to write in his autobiography, 'One of my last pieces of fieldwork in those days was the taking of line levels from the town of Keighley to the village of Haworth. On a certain day, under grave penalties, these levels had to be finished, and this particular day was one of agony for me. The atmosphere seemed full of mocking demons, laughing at the vanity of my efforts to get the work done. My levelling staves were snapped, and my theodolite was overthrown by the storm. When things are at the worst, a kind of anger often takes the place of fear. It was so in the present instance. I pushed doggedly on, and just at nightfall, when barely able to read the figures on my levelling staff, I placed my last 'bench-mark' on a tombstone in Haworth Churchyard. Close at hand was the vicarage of Mr Brontë, where the genius was nursed that burst forth and astonished the world.' One gets the feeling that Tyndall felt there was some kind of supernatural agency at work in the graveyard.

This story concerns a portrait of Charlotte Brontë, bequeathed by Arthur Nicholls to the National Portrait Gallery that had adorned the centre of his drawing-room wall at Hill House at Banagher in Ireland. One day as he and his second wife Mary Bell were entertaining their nephew, the portrait suddenly fell off the wall for no reason at all, hitting the table below it with such a force that it catapulted towards the sofa where Mary was sitting and struck her. Fortunately, neither Mary nor the picture suffered any damage. Everyone present was too shocked to comment at the time but later Mary remarked that it was an odd thing to happen. The memory of the incident must have stayed with her, for when Arthur died she had his coffin placed directly beneath Charlotte's picture – acknowledging that the two were no longer separated by death.

This ghost story reminds me of the haunting of Grimshaw's friend John Wesley's family home at Epworth Rectory. The story begins and ends between December 1716 and January 1717. The Wesleys claimed that a loud banging and knocking could be clearly heard in the upper chambers of their home but as soon as someone went to investigate, the noise would stop immediately and issue from an entirely different place below! The swishing sound of a lady's silk dress was distinctly heard at night in Wesley's sister Emily's room and the heavy bed, complete with occupant, was shaken and lifted off the floor by an unidentified invisible intruder, without any apparent effort. On being advised by his fellow clergy to flee his residence, John's father Samuel declined, saying: "No, let the Devil flee from me; I will never flee from him." This story can be found amidst other eerie tales in a book previously owned by Dr John Milligan of Keighley now in Keighley Library enticingly titled *History of Magic* by Joseph Ennemoser, 1854.

A young Bradford girl, whose identity has never been revealed, awoke one night to find a male ghost leaning across her bed. For some unknown reason the appearance of this unwanted vision began at the exact time her sister was born. The girl often heard footsteps. Always the same tread: one, shuffle, two, shuffle, late at night on the stairs leading to the attic. On creeping into her parents' room one evening she found that a heavy wooden wardrobe had been inexplicably moved into the centre of the bedroom but by morning it was back in its original place. Flowers and plants always died as soon as they were brought in and an awful heavy atmosphere permanently pervaded the house.

The girl's younger brother asked to swap his attic bedroom because he was afraid of the man who stood outside his door. Yet, strangely the family's two bulldogs never seemed affected by this unearthly presence. Tearing off antiquated wallpaper in order to re-decorate, the family came across an old door set deep into the staircase wall, leading to the house next door. Intrigued by their find, they got out the house deeds and found that their haunted home had been St. Augustine's Vicarage in days gone by.

Eventually, having had enough of sharing their lives with the uninvited visitor, the family packed their bags and left. Two years after the move the family paid a visit to the Brontë Parsonage Museum. As soon as the girl saw the portrait of Patrick Brontë in clerical attire, it dawned on her that the spirit haunting their old home had been wearing clerical garb. Following the family's departure, no one ever seemed to stay at the old vicarage for very long.

Final Thoughts on the Theme of Ghosts

'Substance and shadow-mind and matter-real and unreal-are very ordinary phrases, but to draw a dividing line between any two of them is a much more difficult matter than many are apt to suppose. Of course, to our limited minds, nothing is actually real that is not patent to our senses – we must see it, and feel it, before its reality can be determined. Such evidence I say, is necessary for our finite minds, but when we give heed to the teachings of our higher and spiritual nature, I think we shall soon discover that there are far greater realities than those that must be confirmed by our earthly senses. Is that wonderful storehouse which we call memory not a reality! Is the wind not a reality, though we only hear the sound thereof? Is conscience not a real thing, though a material part of our being? Yet, we are apt to conclude that our thoughts and actions are governed exclusively by our contact with tangible objects, whereas our manner of life is moulded and determined by influences, which are not seen, and which, in our ignorance, we sometimes presume to call ...

Shadows

The past is gone, but still it lives
In shadows round us thrown;
We hear the voice, and note the smile
Of those we have once known:
For though the eye no form can see,
The heart no solace find;
Yet shadows, draped in moral guise,
Parade before the mind.
And on through every stage of life
These phantoms dog our way,
As harbingers of hope and joy,
Or heralds of dismay:
Each heart can for itself predict
What likeness they shall wear;
A comforter of angel form,
Or demon or despair.
The miser sits with one dim ray
To lighten up the gloom;
He hugs his gold, but can't shut out
The shadow of the tomb:
No hiding place can moral find,
Where shadows do not roam;
But thanks to God, no shadows fall
In heaven's "unclouded home."

T.F. Hartley, Halifax Guardian, 27 Nov. 1886.

If you are phantasmaphobic (have a fear of ghosts) or find yourself troubled by unwanted manifestations, some say that you should try leaving your Bible open at the 23rd Psalm. Worth remembering, if you can find a Bible at the critical time!

6 | *Darker Than Death*

Prior to the advent of proper registration and police intervention in suspicious deaths, murder was easily covered up. For example from 1763 to 1791, numerous deaths in Haworth were recorded in the parish registers as either dropsy, fits, colic, the spotted fever (smallpox) or decline (whatever that meant), this last being a favourite term irrespective of the deceased's age. To illustrate just how lax the authorities could be in these matters there was a woman walking around Sheffield in 1878 with a death certificate in her pocket. Apparently, her doctor was so sure she was dying, he wrote out the certificate of death to save him the bother of a return journey!

Hidden among Haworth's tombstones is a curious inscription warning all those who pass by that:

> All the world's a city, full of crooked streets,
> Death is the market-place where all men meet;
> If life were merchandise that men could buy,
> The rich must live, the poor must always die.

What follows is a selection of bygone tales concerning family tragedies and sudden death.

Blighted

Neither herbalists, bona fide medical men nor quacks could cure the sudden outbreak of scarlatina, which caused a number of deaths in Haworth in 1874. The illness concentrated itself on the right-hand side of Main Street up as far as the Black Bull Inn, including Gauger's Croft where six cases occurred in one family alone. Two young children under the age of three died of the disease in their parents' one-roomed hovel, situated almost opposite the church gates. Another child died at Well Street during the Easter of that year.

Dr John Milligan visited the village at the height of the outbreak. The church sexton informed him there had been a heavy rainstorm a few days before and water from the graveyard ran down Main Street for two whole days. Milligan's findings caused him to write several reports to the local newspaper concerning the old churchyard, which had been the burial ground of the district for many centuries and where the entire ground was filled with human remains in every process of decomposition. He said, 'The digging or new re-opening of old graves, which at the first rainfall washes the poisonous elements and distributes them through every grate that opens into the covered channel below'. Towards the end of June, Dr Milligan and Burial Board Commissioner Mr M.P.H. Holland surveyed the graveyard, accompanied by a concerned Revd John Wade. Based on his findings, the doctor sent a copy of his report to the *Keighley News*, which appeared in the newspaper four days later. He demanded an immediate stop to any further burials in the cemetery. In response, the Haworth sexton declared, "all the bodies were entombed and made air-tight." This was strongly refuted by Milligan, even if charcoal had been deposited with the corpses. Apparently, when water from pumps in the vicinity of the church was left for an hour or so, it developed a greasy substance so thick that it could be skimmed off the top. This "greasy substance" was the effluent from putrefied corpses!

In answer to Milligan's report, a vigorous reply to the allegations concerning the unsanitary conditions arising from Haworth's churchyard appeared in the *Keighley News* on 4 July 1874 entitled, *Haworth and Mrs Gaskell*, and signed Sexton, Haworth.

This keeper-of-dead, described elsewhere as an intelligent man, demanded to know 'If Dr Milligan wants to report fairly and honestly why does he single out inmates of the parsonage to the exclusion of other families equally close to the crowded churchyard? If Mr Brontë lost his six children, did not the sexton (alluding to his late brother John Brown) in the very next house bring up six young girls who are all still living, and with one exception (Miss Martha Brown) mothers of large families. Why then does he refer us to Mrs Gaskell's *'Life of Charlotte Brontë'*? Can we not learn more in 30 or 40 years spent here than from a few pages of a lady who only spent a few hours in gathering hurried information wherein to embellish her book? There are those among us who could have told Mrs Gaskell of many a little incident happening in the family circle which combined to undermine the health of those ladies more than all the black tombstones and poisonous gases which she could conjure up ... '

Twenty cases of smallpox were reported at Shipley and at least eight in neighbouring Saltaire in May 1874. All but one could be traced back to source, for on 7 May a man named Mitchell – keeper of the Baptist Chapel on Rosse Street, Shipley, succumbed to this fatal disease. The man's home, immediately beneath the chapel, adjoined the Sunday school. It was through a gap in the wall of the room in which Mitchell expired that the deadly virus escaped to infect children in the classroom next door. In no time at all, several further cases occurred and the unfortunate victims were removed to the fever hospital, where they too died. Placards were posted about the town, warning of the sudden outbreak and arrangements quickly made for the burials of the victims.

At least two of these funerals took place at Haworth. "In one instance," said Dr John Milligan "the stench was so horrible that the people could not bear to walk behind the hearse." – This coffin was refused entrance to the Baptist Chapel on West Lane, where the other Shipley victims had already been interred. Even worse, "Two decomposing bodies trailed fourteen miles through the entire towns of Bingley, Keighley and Haworth" wrote an incredulous Milligan, risking further infection to the populace. At the time of writing he'd heard that yet another Shipley smallpox victim's funeral from Shipley was to have taken place at Haworth but an active member of the village Burial Board got wind of the plan and put a stop to it. The impudence of Shipley and Saltaire, endeavouring to send its pox-riddled dead away for burial!

According to the Heaton family bible Miss Elizabeth, the eighth child born to Robert and Betty Murgatroyd Heaton (a relative of the Mugatroyd's of East

Riddlesden Hall) made her entrance at Old Ponden House on Monday 16 November 1795 at precisely 6.30am. Born just seven days after her grandmother Sarah Murgatroyd an 'exemplary Christian' died to 'walk with Jesus clothed in white.'

In July 1813, young Elizabeth found to her horror she was carrying an illegitimate child and was thus forced into a loveless marriage to Bradford shopkeeper John Middlebrook Bakes of Gomersal. The unhappy couple were wed at Haworth church on 2 August 1813. In those days, it was customary for the bride to carry her dowry with her in a strong box when leaving home to begin married life with her 'future lord'. Elizabeth's dowry amounted to two hundred pounds but within two years, the money was all gone and her health wrecked. No longer able to live in constant fear of her abusive husband, she fled back to her childhood home in November 1815, taking baby daughter Elizabeth Matilda with her. Her mother Betty was gravely ill, having been diagnosed as having breast cancer by Dr Mossman, who recommended she "go out on horseback as much as possible" to help keep the illness at bay. However this did not stop Bakes from making a thorough nuisance of himself at Ponden, demanding money from his in-laws which, when he got, he either drank or gambled away.

The ill-starred Elizabeth died in March 1816 and her mother in July the same year. Baby Elizabeth Matilda died the following January and Robert Heaton, her grandfather was committed to the earth in November 1817.

Elizabeth's eldest brother John Murgatroyd Heaton was born at his maternal grandparent's home at Royd House, Oxenhope on Saturday 5 April 1785 at 2.10pm. He embezzled a staggering five hundred pounds from his father's cotton mill at Pitcher Clough. John's sudden death appears to be a bit of a mystery – was it suicide or a premeditated murder by person or persons unknown? What we do know is that almost one hundred people attended the funeral bidding at Ponden where his corpse lay rigid upon his four-poster bed. After the burial, a funeral feast was held at the Black Bull. Unfortunately, his childless wife's name has been lost in the mists of time along with the facts behind the crime committed against his own father, no doubt covered up by the grieving family. Thus, Elizabeth, her baby daughter and brother John Murgatroyed were all buried together in the same grave. A carefully chosen inscription reads:

Here lieth the Body of
John Murgatroyd Heaton Son of Robert and Elizabeth Heaton of Ponden:
Who departed this Life on
Friday the 6th Day of February
1807 and In the 24th Year of his Age.
Also here lieth the
Body of Elizabeth their Daughter
who departed this Life on Tuesday the 12th Day
Of March 1816 in the 21st Year Of her Age.
The wicked case (cease) from troubling here,
The weary are at rest,
Sorrow and Sin and Pain and Care.
No more approach the Blest.
Also Elizabeth Matilda her daughter who departed this Life at
Ponden on January 25th 1817 in the 2nd Year of her Age.

Their burial place can be found in Haworth churchyard directly in front of the parsonage. Take the fifth row up from the bottom path, look for an end grave inscription of Pratt, and then count fourteen graves in until arriving at the Heaton headstone.

The Brontë children, listening to country gossip heard that both mother and daughter still "walked and weeped in the garden, though both had long mouldered in their graves." It was at an upstairs chamber at the head of the stairs of the Old House, Ponden, that the ghost of Heathcliff's tormented Cathy piteously wailed outside the window *"Let me in! Let me in!"* professes the family's historian William Shackleton. Could this have been the very bedchamber where Elizabeth came into the world in 1795? Might the life and times of tragic Elizabeth Heaton, fleeing from her unhappy marriage and her family living as they did in the same period as *Wuthering Heights* have helped serve Emily Brontë with ideas for her characters, including the pitiful ghost of Catherine Earnshaw?

By Misadventure

Cold As Ice

On the night of 15 November 1648, one Harrison, a tailor by trade was found drowned. Having drunk himself stupid, he stumbled and was swallowed up by the icy waters of the North Beck, Oxenhope. Haworth's parish register warned all drunkards to avoid drinking on a Sunday.

Two companions, a carrier by the name of Green and a dealer in shalloons, had been travelling the long mountainous road between Oxenhope and Heptonstall on 5 November 1754, where there had been a heavy fall of snow. Caught in the sudden storm, they froze to death before they could reach the safety and warmth of a public house perched high above Heptonstall.

Martha Heaton of Oxenhope remembered the following narrative, which was handed down through generations by word of mouth. It concerned the tragic death of a little boy: on a bitterly cold February day in 1801, a farmer left his home at Enfieldside to attend a business meeting up at Pecket Well. Unbeknown to Thomas Helliwell his two-year old son Joseph quietly tagged along behind him. Farmer Helliwell travelled swiftly on foot by way of the old Haworth Road known as 't' stairs' and it was not long before the little lad was left on the moors, alone and lost. His thin frozen body was discovered the next morning on the bleak moor above Harbour Lodge.

Haworth sisters Sally and Hannah Feather were on friendly terms with the Brontë girls. Hannah had in her possession a letter from Emily on the reverse side of which was a picture of a robin, drawn in about 1836. Emily wrote a sad little poem a year later, entitled *Redbreast in the Morning*, about a lost child found dead in winter on the moors (was this a reference to Joseph?).

Redbreast In The Morning
'What woke it then? A little child
Strayed from its father's door,
And in an hour of moonlight wild
Laid lonely on the desert moor.' *Emily Brontë 1837*

By a terrible quirk of fate, an identical occurrence took place on Saturday 27 January 1849 and was reported in *John Mayhall's Annals Vol. 1*. Another Joseph Halliwell, aged four years was reported lost on the same moor. He was the son of farmer William Halliwell of Far Intake Farm, near Top Withens. His frozen footsteps eventually led a party of searchers to his body the following Wednesday morning, three miles from his home. The second Joseph's memorial can be seen in Haworth's old churchyard and reads:

In Memory of Joseph,
Son of William Halliwell of Far Intake,
Who died Jany. 28th 1849
In the 4th year of his Age.

How bizarre that both children had identical names apart from the spelling of Ha(e)lliwell, lived in the same area and met their deaths in exactly the same manner!

Richard H. Hodgson became a partner in and eventually took over the old established firm of Richard Medcalfe, Solicitor of Keighley around 1853, accepting the position of Magistrate's Clerk at about the same time. A staunch member of the Royal Yorkshire Lodge of Freemasons he was to became a firm favourite of Charlotte Brontë. She hinted on more than one occasion that she had based her character Dr John in *Villette* on Richard, who was loved by everybody because of his humorous and obliging nature. In *Leisure Musings with Portrait and Memoir of R.H. Hodgson Esq. by Silas Cryer, 1876* he is described thus: 'moral without asceticism, religious without bigotry, a party politician (Conservative) without party bitterness, a patriot with sympathies truly cosmopolitan, a lover of social enjoyments without degenerating into an epicure … In short, here was a man with a unique character that, appealed to the universal heart, and won it.'

In 1876, Hodgson and a party of friends left Keighley on a fishing expedition. They travelled to Carlisle and hired a cab from the station to take them to their hotel at Armathwaite. Two miles before their journey's end a blinding snowstorm whipped up and the carriage turned over, spilling the occupants out onto the frozen country lane. Hodgson came off worst with a badly fractured leg. His friends carried him to the King's Head at Armathwaite where a local doctor examined his injuries. Blood poisoning set in within seven days of the accident, whereupon five surgeons decided to amputate the affected limb, but Hodgson passed away on Sunday 7 May, before the operation could be performed. An undertaker provided a shell and on the Monday, his remains were taken back to his home at Highfield Lane, Keighley. The funeral took place on Wednesday 10 May at Bingley Cemetery. The coffin was flanked on either side by three police officers. Behind the hearse were two mourning coaches and fourteen private carriages containing local dignitaries. A special train was laid on at Keighley, to accommodate the large number of mourners. Two beautiful wreaths were placed on top of his polished oak coffin; one was in the shape of a cross. After the funeral service, as the coffin was lowered into the grave, the grief of many mourners made a visible impression on the silent crowds.

R.H. Hodgson had one son, Harold H. Hodgson. At twenty-nine he advertised his skills as both a chemist and a phrenologist (a person who practised

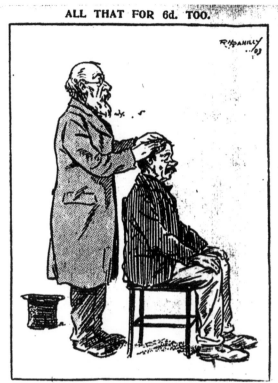

ALL THAT FOR 6d. TOO.

Phrenologist. Now, you're full o' nerves—you are. What you want is iron. You must drink beer—you must drink Burgundy.

Timely advice from a phrenologist! *(Leeds Mercury)*

fortune-telling by reading the bumps on a person's head – a test that Charlotte favoured). In Slater's 1891 Trade Directory, Harold was listed as a boarder at the home of insurance agent William Wright Shaw of 13 Crossroads near Haworth.

A Fatal Mistake

John Place, an eleven-year-old Haworth lad, was sent by his father, Francis Place, to purchase some worming powder from the premises of F. Tidswell, Chemist and Druggist. The boy thought nothing of dosing himself with the dark brown powder, which had been stirred into a glass of water, before going to bed. When asked if the powder was nasty-tasting John replied, "Yes, I should think it is." Within two hours of swallowing the medicine John called out from his bed "Father, come and rub me." Francis Place immediately hurried to his son's room where he found John's limbs stretched and stiffened. Young John complained of terrible pins and needles and begged his father to rub his hands and feet harder as he couldn't feel them. Dr Ling was sent for but by the time he arrived, the boy's body was in spasm. The doctor attempted to administer salt water, but try as he might, the unfortunate child could not part his lips. Although his mind was clear, his pupils were dilated and his jaws remained clamped shut. Mustard plasters were put on his limbs in an attempt to ease his suffering. The doctor ran to fetch a stomach pump but alas, he was too late for by the time he returned, John William Place had already breathed his last.

It transpired at the inquest that the powder, bought in a small paper packet from Tidswell's, should have been coloured blue not dark brown. Seemingly, the chemist had mistakenly wrapped up a lethal dose of poison instead of innocuous worming powder. The verdict of the inquest was that the boy had died as a result of accidental poisoning.

Act of God

A gravestone in Haworth Cemetery records the tragic death of Elizabeth Hartley. She was one of almost three hundred passengers bound for the sunny shores of Melbourne, Australia aboard the Steamship *London* when it capsized and sank in the Bay of Biscay on 11 January 1866. Only nineteen people were to survive this terrible catastrophe. Elizabeth, who purchased her ticket to a better life from Barwick's Emigration Office at Keighley Market Place, was not listed amongst the survivors. It came to light that the ship had been tossed in violent seas before sinking to a watery grave. The ship's engineer John Greenhill explained, 'We left Plymouth on the 6 January. On the 7th we experienced heavy weather with rain. On the 8th the same. On the 9th we lost jibboom and foretopmast, topgallant mast and royal mast. About 9am we lost the port lifeboat, a heavy gale prevailing at the time. On the 10th at 3am the ship put about, intending to run back to Plymouth. About the same time the starboard lifeboat was washed overboard by a heavy sea ... At noon ... we were shipping heavy seas, which carried away the engine-room hatch, the water going down and putting the fires out. The passengers were baling water out of the ship with buckets.'

11 January – the last terrifying day of Elizabeth Hartley's life: 'The gale was still increasing, with heavy cross-seas, nearly all coming over the ship. During the morning, all that could were trying to stop the leak in the engine-room hatch, but to no purpose. At about 4am four of the stern ports were stove in; efforts were made to stop them, but it was found to be impossible. At 10am we could see the ship was gradually sinking, it being then as low in the water as the main chains.'

The company put up a brave fight to the end, frantically bailing with any receptacle they could lay their hands on, until the captain told them it was useless and they must expect to die. As the ship went down Revd Draper and his wife prayed calmly.

Greenhill tells us that at 2pm, just five minutes before the end, most of the crew abandoned the foundering ship in a port cutter. Two other small ships were getting ready to leave but it was too late. Those in the cutter watched the Steamship *London* go down taking two hundred and seventy souls with her. The *Marianople* picked up the exhausted crew and a handful of passengers, twenty hours after the doomed ship had succumbed.

Strange Goings On

The following poem is dedicated to all those gone before, who might have seriously contemplated the act of suicide.

The Suicide's Rest

When the midnight wrapped city,
And the candles gutted down,
Was there not a sigh of pity?
In the wind across the town?
In the chimneys hollow answer
To the towers aeolian wail,
Were the poet and the romancer?
All that noted down a tale?
Was there none to be the wiser?

As the night-wind bore it on?
None to be a sympathiser,
Till the story's theme has gone?
None to guard the fatal portal
None to idle o'er,
None to serve the soul immortal,
None to pass, in time the shore
Ah! The candle flares and flutters
Like an imprisoned human soul -
Watch it as it shrinks and gutters
Dealing out its dole.
As the embers glimmer faintly,
Could the watcher picture there
One small face all sweet and saintly,
Would he mourn out, Despair!
Would he then, beyond the distance
Of his gaze into the fire,
Trace a mortal's last resistance,
Trace a scene so dark and dire?
Would he then among the embers
Cast the lock of golden hair?
Ah! he well, the face remembers
Through the groans "Despair – Despair."
Swiftly through the silent city
Steals a man – alas, how young?
Is there not the sound of pity in that?
Steeple's iron tongue?
As it clangs its echoing quarter,
(First born quarter of the year)
Does the sound upon the water
Wake no lightermen than in fear?
When a sunbeam lit the city,
Or the first rift in the cloud,
Still the wind with voice of pity
O'er the forest wailed aloud,
Then the stealthy, hurried marches
Speed the rivers sleepless tide,
Through the grey of village arches,
Bearing on a suicide.
Is there *more* behind the curtain?
'Twixt Eternity and Time?
Hear we not some voice uncertain
Calling from a spirit clime?
River, thou hast wrought thy mission,
Heartless, sinless is thy breast,
Secret portal of perdition
The soul that sought for rest?

H.E. Spencer, *The Craven Pioneer, October 1874.*

Note: There are two different versions of this poem; the first appeared in the *Keighley Visitor* on 2 September 1872.

Man versus Mill

Mr Thomas Lister, a cotton manufacturer purchased Hollings Mill, Stanbury, from either Michael Cousins or William Hollings who had first erected the premises around 1810. The mill thereafter was known as Lister's Mill. By 1839, this property had been sold to a Mr T.B. Brown who took rent from the previous owner Thomas Lister. After struggling to survive for some twenty years the business took a turn for the worse and in a dire fit of depression Lister took a piece of rope and hanged himself in the mill on 26 April 1842.

It appears that the premises lay empty for nine years until William Thomas, whose family resided at Balcony, Haworth, re-occupied the place. Bad luck constantly dogged his one-hundred-and-thirty-five employees and when one particular series of calamities occurred, they decided that the place was hexed.

The next leaseholder was Will Turner who seems to have rented out a portion of the premises until 1864, when the mill was gutted by fire late one Thursday evening. A brave individual risked life and limb to release gas from the nearby gasometer, which stood just two yards away from the burning building, thus averting a major catastrophe.

The firm of Tim Feather & Sons re-built the mill but almost before the ink was dry on the contract, late one night in December 1865 the premises inexplicably burned to the ground again. The fire had started in an upper room and in *exactly* the same manner as before. A messenger was despatched on horseback to Keighley to raise the alarm but the fire brigade was delayed because of a shortage of horses needed to pull the cumbersome engine. In the meantime, a man entering the blazing premises had to be rescued by the police when overcome by thick smoke. The mill, where upwards of two hundred folk earned their livelihoods, was once again destroyed and the causes of both late night fires remained a complete and utter mystery. In 1866, Lister's Mill was restored again and was occupied by several different businesses but, by 1878, the entire property was up for sale.

The next occupant was George H. Merrall of Manor House, Haworth, whose business failed to thrive here, forcing him into liquidation. Young Seth Hudson, an employee at the mill, committed suicide rather than attend court as a witness in an affiliation case. He threw himself into Churchill's reservoir, where his corpse lay decomposing for several weeks; meanwhile the villagers of Haworth had been drinking the water!

The mill was included in a Halifax auction in 1882. Three years later Joe Lightowler, an engine overseer was accidentally killed during the course of his work there. In January 1889 disaster struck again when a third fire wiped out the mill, now belonging to Keighley builder Robert Sugden but occupied by spinners Fred Townend & Bros. The fire started in the boiler house after the boiler mysteriously exploded with great violence at 11.45 one night, leaving only the bare walls standing. Travelling home on the 11.20pm train from Keighley, auctioneer James Ackroyd's attention was caught by an unusual orange glow in the sky midway between Stanbury and Haworth. In the process of running through the village, he awakened several persons by shouting 'fire'. On reaching the scene, Ackroyd and the others with him noticed there was a

148

light in the bedroom of Townsend's cottage next to the blazing property but saw no sign of the tenant or his family. Townsend claimed he had sprinted to Sladen Bridge in his stockinged feet to fetch help as soon as the alarm was raised and that when Ackroyd arrived he was in the cellar trying to save what stock he could. After finding out that both Townsend and Sugden would be due a massive settlement from the Norwich Union, the auctioneer was convinced the whole thing was an insurance dodge and actually challenged Townsend's version of events in the local press.

Mr T. Greenwood, who purchased the ruins of the fated mill, razed them to the ground, leaving only the tall chimney intact and re-built it yet again. One day an employee of his, a warp dresser misplaced his tobacco tin. Some time later he located his brass box, took out a bit of tobacco and put it in his mouth, as a result of which, he immediately fell down in a fit. A quick thinking workmate gave him a dollop of oil, making him sick and in doing so, saved his life. It turned out that the tobacco had become poisonous because of the length of time it had been left in the metal box. Dogged by bad luck for so long, the workforce felt Thomas Lister's restless spirit had been in action from beyond the grave.

The jinxed mill was offered for sale again in 1891, as a freehold property with shooting rights on Stanbury moor attached to it. By 1906, it was offered at auction but was withdrawn after failing to reach its reserve price.

Two years later a firm of tanners bravely moved into a brand new mill erected on the site of the old one. It wasn't long though before the firm of S. Raistrick & Son began experiencing serious water problems, which effectively shut down their tannery business. Just when these had been resolved to their satisfaction, the landlord ordered them to leave the premises.

Lister's Mill was almost levelled to the ground for the very last time at the beginning of the First World War.

*   *   *   *

Gillson's modern windmill towering high above Haworth cannot claim to be the first windmill in the district, as there was once a wooden windmill standing on Penistone Hill, Haworth.

A man working here on Plot night in 1926 got his clothing tangled in the mill's drive chain. He subsequently died from the terrible injuries inflicted by the machine. After the tragedy, the mill was dismantled and taken away. Wind power from this contraption had been used to run cranes at Dimples Quarry, an industrial stone saw and a blacksmith's shop. A photograph of the windmill taken by Bram Rose of Wesley Grove, Idle in 1927 shows the head being moved by a pole. According to a newspaper report, the water-well itself was covered over by a huge piece of mill stone grit for safety reasons. Mr Rose's photograph appeared in Bradford's *Telegraph & Argus* newspaper dated 26 November 1983.

Up and Away ...

The next sad story centres on the lady balloonist and parachutist Miss Lily Cove whose life came to an abrupt end at 7.45pm on Monday 11 June 1906. It was Haworth's gala time and Lily's balloon ascent was billed as the main attraction. She had travelled from Cambridge accompanied by her employer of three years, aeronaut Captain Frederick Bidmead. The pair reserved separate rooms at the Old White Lion Hotel, Haworth.

The Old White Lion where, in room 7, Lily Cove spent her last night *(Marie Campbell)*

Lily was booked to star in the gala the following day at the fairground site on West Lane football ground. Several thousand excited spectators gathered in anticipation of the great event. All eyes focussed on daredevil Lily, dressed in shirt and knee tights as she climbed onto the platform. The balloon had been filled with gas from the local gas works but unfortunately, no matter how hard Lily tried to get the cumbersome apparatus into the air it simply refused to ascend. Ninety minutes later, she was forced to abandon the attempt, after discovering a tear in her balloon. The disappointed crowds were promised another attempt at the beginning of the week, which turned out to be perfect for aeronautical adventures.

There was a warm summer breeze as a white-faced Miss Cove again stepped confidently onto the air balloon's platform. Ascending at precisely 7.40pm this pretty, flaxen-haired, girl smiled sweetly at her cheering audience who strained their necks to watch her fluttering the white handkerchief she'd borrowed from the captain as the balloon shot up and bobbed its way slowly towards Stanbury.

Captain Bidmead accompanied by local mill owner Mr C.E. Merrall followed on land in a horse and trap. Jonas Bradley a well-known schoolmaster was standing on Haworth Moor when he saw the balloon for a brief moment as it dipped over towards Laneshaw Moor. Cowling Heaton of Oxenhope saw the balloon right above him near Scar Top Refreshment Rooms at about 7.45pm. Having lost sight of it for a few seconds, he then heard a terrific explosion and watched as Lily somersaulted in the air at least twice before hitting the ground

150

headfirst, at which point, "A cry of horror was heard from the throats of the anxious assembly". Cowling was the first person at the scene and he swept the bleeding girl into his arms. Laying her head on his knee he pleaded, "My good woman if you can speak do so" But she uttered not a single word. He sent a boy to fetch water. Next on the scene were Bidmead and Merrall. They were just in time to witness the dying girl taking her last breath. Her corpse was picked up by the men and carried on the trap back to Haworth; the crowds there had been ignorant of the tragedy that had befallen her. A little girl stood by and watched Lily's yellow hair tumble over the back of the cart as it turned towards the road.

Dr Robert Thompson examined the corpse at 9pm. He found a fracture of the tibia in the left leg, a fracture to the right leg, a fracture to the right thigh and severe bleeding caused by a skull fracture. Lily was the fourth woman to die in this manner since the first lady balloonist took to the air in Paris on 20 May 1784.

It was rumoured that Lily was hopelessly in love with a local mill owner's son (Merrall?), who did not return her devotions and because of this unrequited love she had deliberately taken her own life. A more likely theory was that non-swimmer Lily had 'an absolute horror of dropping into water' and rather than falling into the nearby reservoir, she loosened herself from the parachute in order to escape drowning. During the inquest it came out that at the same time Cowling Heaton witnessed Lily's frightful fall, so too had Robert Rishworth of Stanbury who was monitoring the balloon's progress through field glasses. Robert, the last person to see Lily alive, observed her "shrugging her shoulders" out of the safety harness just as she neared Ponden Reservoir before losing her grip or letting go of the safety straps.

I think it is highly unlikely Lily intended to take her own life because shortly before her death she had planned to re-visit Haworth in her holidays and to this end had fixed an appointment with a Keighley Friendly Society gala official for Tuesday, the following day. Cowling Heaton said that if she had remained in her parachute, which landed partially open twenty yards from her body, she would have lived. Whatever the truth of the matter, it died with Lily.

As soon as Lily Cove's death became common knowledge, a large number of sightseers flocked to the village to seek out the exact spot where she had met her end. Haworth natives stood by on street corners, watching the sudden onslaught of rushing journalists with morbid interest. Locals drew their blinds as a mark of sympathy and respect for the relatives of "that dead poor lass."

Many of the village women looked upon Lily's face before the coffin lid was nailed down forever. On 14 June, the Revd T. W. Story held a short but touching service in the presence of her father, Thomas Charles Cove and her friends. The funeral cortege departed from the Old White Lion. Mourners stretched along both sides of the road right up to Haworth's new cemetery, where she was interred and which overlooks the scene of her last jump. Members of the Haworth Gala Committee carried the pitch pine coffin containing Lily's remains on their shoulders in relays. Almost every person in Haworth walked behind her coffin as it wound its way along the road. The only sound en route was that of occasional sobbing. Men working at Dimples Quarry close to the cemetery ceased working to take off their caps and bow their heads as the coffin passed by. The crowd had swelled in number and only a few were able to witness the actual burial take place. There had been nothing to match this public show of mourning in Haworth since the day of Patrick Brontë's funeral in 1861. Revd Story met the procession at the gates and led the way between grief-stricken mourners to the open graveside. With the uttering of "ashes to ashes, dust to dust" the corpse and coffin were lowered gently down into 'the silence where hath been no sound.' A lark was heard singing signalling a message 'of love and sympathy' to those left behind. A card attached to the wreath presented by Mr C.E. Merrall bore the words, 'for a poor girl who lost her life in the cause of charity'. The District Nurses' Association took up a collection, which paid for her granite headstone.

> In Loving Memory
> Of Elizabeth Mary Cove
> (Miss Lily Cove,) (Parachutist,)
> Daughter of Thomas Cove of London,
> who died 11 June 1906
> aged 21 years.

Carved at the base of the stone was the doleful reminder '*In the midst of life we are in death*'.

On the day of Lily's funeral, Parliament was already preparing a *Dangerous Performance Bill*, introduced by Mr H. Samuels under the guidance of Mr Gladstone. The coroner's jury brought in a verdict of accidental death even though it seemed clear that she had for some unknown reason deliberately detached herself from the safety of her parachute harness.

A Tragic End

> All was ready then up she went,
> 'Mid cheers from the crowd below,
> And when she reached a certain height
> She drifted a mile or so.
> "She's made a leap," cried the people
> And they watched for her return,
> But little knew the sad tidings
> That they were so soon to learn.
> Yes! She had leaped, 'twas certain,
> But oh! What a tragic end;
> For some strange reason none could tell,
> When she began to descend.
> Unbuckled the straps that bound her,
> And then took the fatal leap
> Into the icy arms of death
> Which were open at her feet.
> Strong men were stunned and women wept,
> And the town was wrapt in gloom,
> When news was brought to the people.
> Of the dear young lady's doom.

> *Miss Ethel Denby*

Some two years after the tragedy Captain Bidmead was back in the area with his balloon, selling tickets for *A Journey to Cloudland on Captive Balloon with Captain Bidmead, return tickets 2s 6d.*

In June 1992, on the eve of the anniversary of Lily's sudden end, a Scottish ghost hunter arrived in Haworth having specifically requested the room she had taken at the Old White Lion Hotel. Convinced that a restless Lily Cove had called out to him from beyond the grave he felt his 'mission' was to discover the cause of her distress by psychic means and thus finally put an end to the speculation and mystery surrounding her death. He believed the answer was somehow linked to a stone on the site of a demolished Sunday school close to the Brontë parsonage. Drawn to the hotel's cellar he claimed to encounter a strong psychic energy saying that he thought she wanted to say it wasn't her fault and explain what had really happened that fateful day. Armed with a photograph of the girl he stayed the night in room seven (known by staff as the *Ghost Room*) where Lily had spent her last night. The next morning he announced that during his vigil he had *sensed* but not seen Lily sitting on the end of his bed. Referring to his brief stay at the Old White Lion, he told a poker-faced *Keighley News* reporter, "I experienced sudden shivers down my spine and I knew straight away that it was haunted because this has happened to me before. Ghosts have a purpose in appearing. They are troubled by something but they never appear to just frighten people. They want to find out something or change something." He appealed to readers of the *Keighley News* to contact him if they had actually *seen* Lily's ghost.

Leaving Lily behind and the mystery unsolved, he returned to his home from where he dispatched a good luck card on Valentine's Day. The envelope was carefully addressed to Lily c/o the Old White Lion and contained instructions to the landlord that the card must be left open in room seven so that Lily could read the contents and send him a signal from the world of spirit.

The sign he was waiting for arrived in the form of a playing card, the two of spades lay face up on the floor of a friend's bathroom. This card not only represents a desire for knowledge it also signifies fear and a deep-rooted anxiety of the unknown. It is a card that encourages the enquirer to continue his investigations in order to attain spiritual peace and holds the *power* to unlock hidden secrets. However, if inverted the two of spades may signify manipulation, obsession and intrigue where truth has become distorted out of all proportion and developed into pure fantasy.

Now to continue the story:

Our ghost hunter immediately returned to Haworth. After outlining his extraordinary quest, he went to the old football ground at the rear of West Lane Haworth Methodist Chapel, accompanied by the late Mrs Kathleen Cole – manager of Haworth Tourist Information Centre, a photographer and a reporter from the *Keighley News* and another person who wished to remain anonymous. Lily's grave was easily recognised by the balloon carved on the grey granite headstone, a tiny plot planted with London Pride and a vase containing two artificial white lilies. On grasping Lily's headstone the man declared, "Dear God! It's loose! It could fall down at any time!"

His quest over, he felt compelled to visit the place of her death. To the consternation of those present he threw himself to the ground where he lay with his eyes closed for several minutes before asking the reporter to help him to his feet on account of his being "magnetised." The truth seeker explained that he was actually able to feel the girl's fear. Standing in the mud-spattered field amidst those who by now must have fervently wished that they were elsewhere, he silently bid his Lily adieu.

This was not to be the end of the bizarre story though for in 1999 our supernatural inquirer returned to Haworth with fresh news of Lily, who he claimed had recently contacted him from beyond the grave. Apparently, she told him that unbeknown to everyone another girl named Elizabeth had secretly taken her place in the balloon that fateful day so that Lily and her lover Charles Merrall could elope to Droitwich!

Brothers, Beware!

Staunch Methodist churchgoer, seventy-seven-year-old Miss Marion Stansfield had lived in Haworth all her life, helping her father with his antiques business and keeping house for him until his death. Miss Stansfield then opened her own little shop on Main Street, selling sweets to children and Brontë books to tourists. In 1969, the old lady decided to rent the cottage she owned next door to two brothers, in order to earn a little extra cash.

On 12 September, one of her tenants met up with his brothers in Keighley but afterwards returned home alone. Shortly after 1am, on hearing strange noises emanating from his landlady's home, he placed a 999 call to Keighley Police and arranged to meet a policeman in front of the sweet shop. Calling out her name, the constable was answered by a man's voice. Reinforcements were summoned and after kicking down the door, they found the crumpled body of the frail Miss Stansfield on the living room floor close to the fireplace, clad only in a nightdress. Two intruders stood by – both brothers of the man who had placed the emergency call.

In a police statement one of the men described what had taken place. 'We went round the back of the houses and were making for Miss Stansfield's house. She had some money and we intended to break in and get some. I took away a sheet of glass from a window and I heard Miss Stansfield scream. I panicked and saw her going down the stairs and I went in after her. When I got into the living room I saw the outer door was open and Miss Stansfield was standing in the doorway she was still making noises. I went up to her, put my right hand round her mouth to stop her from shouting, pulled her back out of the doorway and shut the door. My intention was just to keep her quiet. She was struggling a bit and trying to pull my head down. It must have been not a minute and she collapsed and I laid her down on the floor.'

Both were charged with murder. The first was given a life sentence whilst the other received a four-year term in prison for burglary. At their trial Mr David Savill for the prosecution said, "Marion Stansfield was a quaint old lady of extremely frugal habits. She kept her money in tins and purses about the house." A Haworth shopkeeper said, "Miss Stansfield lived very quietly and I think people thought she had plenty of money because she did not spend very much." Jack Moore barman at the Black Bull told the *Keighley News*, "I awoke during the night when my dog barked. I heard someone running down the street. Whether it was connected with the death of Miss Stansfield I do not know." Mr Moore had been the last person to see Miss Stansfield alive when she had been standing in the doorway of her shop at about 7.15pm the previous evening.

After Marion Stansfield's cruel and unjust end, the premises stood empty for some time. Squatters eventually made the cottages their home using the property to practise witchcraft and black magic. Unable to control the demonic forces they had summoned by various means including an ouija board, they were forced to quit the property with its awful deathly smell. The cottages were exorcised twice, ordering demons out by the power of prayer, firstly by the Canon of Bradford and then by a priest, after the wife of the new owner was horrified to discover a large pentagram etched into the black bitumen surface of the floor. The priest was convinced that there was more to the strange goings on than met the eye.

Nevertheless, the property underwent extensive renovations and the couple settled into their home. Mrs 'X' recalls, "I remember walking into the house for the first time and telling my husband I didn't like it because it made me feel cold inside. No matter what you did, you couldn't get warm. It wasn't clothing – it was a cosy house – it was a beautiful house." A friend of theirs, a vicar from Menston found he could not go to the upstairs lavatory when he visited the couple's home for it seemed as if an unseen force lurked beyond the first stair, blocking his way. He was obliged to take himself off to the nearby Fleece Inn instead, where he ordered a half of lager so he could avail himself of the inn's conveniences! Thirteen months after taking up residence the couple moved out of their haunted home with its brooding atmosphere and troubled ghost.

Murder Most Foul

Tales of Young Innocents

A sad story comes from the pen of seventeenth-century Nonconformist preacher Oliver Heywood, 'I was returning home from Rawden calling at Bradford, MD would needs have me to goe discourse and pray with a sinking and sad family. The case was this, one Nathan Clegge near Bradford Kirk had a daughter that bore a child in his house on Saturday night … and her father made a grave and buryed it in the barn on Lord's day night. Some suspecting, a search was made for the child, found on Wednesday after. Nathan Clegge and another daughter were apprehended, carryed to York that week, the mother I found weak in bed, the daughter that bore the child I found walking by her, I discoursed as God helped, and prayed, but was much bound up in my spirit, pittyed them, two fellows were watching them day and night, designing to take them to York, the assizes beginning on Munday following … the father hath been a great professor for many years and a great talker … Mr Pemberton, vicar, and Mr Gleadston lecturer at Bradford did both discourse seriously with him after this business fell out, he thankt them for their good words, desiring their bowels might work and their bones drop some fruits of charity on him, thus consulting self he went to prison … the young woman saying the devil had given her up, it may be meaning God hath given her up to the devil, wept sore.'

Sometime back in the 1840s a well-known local doctor claimed that he had heard that the body of a deformed child had been dug up on the moors at Cockhill many years before. This may have been the murdered child.

Another folktale exists of a child (or simpleton youth) living at New Westfield, Oxenhope having been murdered by its parents simply because the little innocent let slip to a police constable that his mother and father had hidden gold in a meal jar. When the constable left the farmstead, the child was immediately set upon and beaten to death. The evil pair carted the corpse off to a nearby quarry where, it was claimed, they dropped it down to the bottom. When this cruel act was uncovered the farm was renamed Drop Farm. Drop also means hanging from the gallows. It must be said however, that there is no evidence to support either of these two stories.

The Sagar Saga

Just off the path beneath a flat stone in Haworth's old churchyard lie nine babies with dates from 1838-1854. At the end of 1857, their mother, thirty-nine-year old Barbara Sagar (*nee* Scarborough) was also dead after six days in bed suffering from arsenic poisoning. The poison was believed to have been administered by her one-handed husband John Sagar, described by one person as a "short, dull, vulgar looking man ... a low, spiritless despicable man."

Whispers of suspected foul play soon reached the ears of the district coroner, Mr T. Brown of Skipton who immediately put a stop to the ongoing funeral preparations, ordering Keighley surgeon William Ruddock and Bingley surgeon William Ainley to carry out an immediate post mortem on the corpse. Superintendent John Cheeseborough of Keighley Constabulary, who had barely been in the job twelve months, personally searched the Sagar quarters for clues at the time of John Sagar's arrest but could find no incriminating evidence against him. Keighley Council had employed the Haworth couple in the capacity of Master and Mistress of Exley Head Workhouse, Oakworth since 1851. These premises, which had served as the town's poorhouse since 1739, were between Occupation Lane and Wheathead, Oakworth near Keighley.

During the sensational three-week court case, it was revealed that whenever her husband was in a foul mood, he beat her in the dead-house (this was the mortuary, which had previously served as a coal hole) after locking her in 'mad owd George's' chains. It also came out that Mrs Sagar often procured young girls for the couple to bed. One of the girls, Ann Bland – a Guardian's daughter – was arrested after admitting she had slept with the Sagars on a number of occasions. Apparently, this was acceptable behaviour in some lodging houses. In 1866, the visiting Local Keighley Board of Health surprised a seventy-year-old married lodging-house master in bed with a teenage girl, while her unconcerned mother lay next to them. Above the door of one Keighley brothel and tramp quarters, a motto earnestly advised the reader to '*Study to be quiet, and mind your own business, and work with your own hands*'. Hanging on the wall of a prostitute's room in another local house of low repute run by a nameless 'cunning female', was a picture of Our Lord on the cross.

Before her demise, Mrs Sagar claimed her husband was endeavouring to administer poison to her. Confiding in Mary Ann Scarborough, she whispered, "If owt happens to me you might think it murder". She asked pauper Martha Bland to pray with her and complained to her "That doctor's stuff is like as if it burned my inside out" – Milligan's elixir, a supposedly simple saline solution had been prescribed for inflammation of the stomach.

Dr John Milligan, a Fothergillian gold medal winner for his essays on health and disease, was employed as Keighley's Union Workhouse doctor. He had been a friend of the Brontës and followed Jack Kay (Haworth's crystal and stargazer) as vice-president at Keighley Mechanics' Institute.

Standing before the magistrates at Keighley Dr Milligan was careful to say that Mrs Sagar had definitely *not* died from external arsenic poisoning. Later at the Assizes, he swore the death was due to natural causes. During his trial Sagar tearfully claimed that Milligan, after examining his wife in his presence, assured him she was not dangerously ill. Yet somehow two grains of arsenic had found their way into her stomach and other vital organs – a fact discovered during the post mortem examination performed by Leeds police surgeon George Morley – an amount he stated which was more than enough to kill a person. For legal reasons the police surgeon's evidence was not taken into account and because of Milligan's conflicting court evidence the case against John Sagar collapsed. The Jury's final verdict was that, "Barbara Sagar came to her death by poison, but by whom administered they could not find." Sagar was therefore acquitted of the wilful murder of his wife at the Spring Assizes of 1858, walking out of court a free man. After the trial, John Milligan regularly attacked George Morley publicly in the *Leeds Intelligencer* on the subject of poison.

Mrs Sagar went to her grave in a Keighley public cemetery minus her heart and innards. The public was outraged at the outcome of the case and never forgave the doctor for his part in this sorry saga, blaming the conflicting evidence of key witness John Milligan for Sagar's escape from the hangman's noose.

At one point it was suggested in the *Bradford Observer* that Sagar, who had previously kept a druggist's shop at Cullingworth during the time when several of his children fell ill and died, could easily have murdered them too. This suggestion was swiftly dismissed.

A number of questions remain unanswered:

Why was Milligan's evidence totally at odds with the police surgeon's report?

What was behind the doctor's insistence that his patient died a natural death?

Was he defending Sagar because he himself played a principal role in the murder by procuring and/or administering poison to his patient – a woman who may have procured young girls for *him* and therefore knew too much?

Did Sagar himself have some secret hold over the so-called respectable doctor? Were the two men bound together by a clandestine pact or were both members of the same secret fraternity?

Interestingly, Milligan owned a personal copy of at least one work on the subject of Freemasonry entitled: *Masonry* by William Preston published in about 1846. Beneath the heading *The Advantages of Friendship* in section two, the writer advises the reader that 'Friendship is traced through the circle of private connections to the grand system of the universal benevolence, which no limits can circumscribe, as its influence extends to every branch of the human race. One individual connects his happiness with the happiness of his neighbour and a fixed and permanent union is established among men ... friendship ... exerts its influence more or less powerfully, as the objects it favours are nearer or more remote.' If both men were connected to the Order of Freemasons or more likely some rustic fringe organisation and either one or both were responsible for the cause of Mrs Sagar's death, perhaps they took the meaning of 'Union and harmony constitute the essence of Freemasonry' much too far.

Whatever the truth of the matter we shall probably never know and we will never know if the despicable Sagar did in fact murder his children unless the case is re-opened and their bodies inspected for telltale traces of poison

CULLINGWORTH

TO BE SOLD

BY AUCTION,

On Saturday the 12th April, 1851,

At the House of Mr. John Sagar, of Cullingworth, in consequence of his having left the premises,

All the Valuable Household

FURNITURE

And other Effects, to be sold without the least reserve,

Comprising 4 Poled Bedsteads, 1 Camp do. with Chints Hangings; Wool and Tow Mattresses, Flock Beds, Feather Pillows, Blankets, Quilts, and Sheets; Painted Dressing Tables; 3 Chairs with Cane Bottoms; 6 Mahogany Chairs, 1 Armed do. in Hair Seats; 1 Armed Oak Chair, Carved; 2 Armed do. with Cushions; 1 New Mahogany Sofa, in Hair Cover and Pillows; 1 Mahogany Side Board; 1 Round Table and Cover; 3 Tea Trays; 1 Glass in Mahogany Frame; 2 Rolls of new Bed Room, Stair Case, and other Floor Carpets; 1 Stuff Piece or Delaine; 1 Kitchen Table; 1 Round do.; Cupboard and Drawers; 1 Clock in Oak Case, and 1 American do.; 2 Coffee and 2 Metal Tea Pots; 1 Swing Glass; 1 Set of China; Glass Sugar Bason and Cream Pot; 2 doz. Tumbler and Wine Glasses; 1 Metal Quart; Iron Candlesticks; Wash-basons and Pitchers; 1 Stand Scale, brass ends; 1 Copper Kettle; Fender and Fire Irons; Clothes and other Baskets; 5 Oil Paintings; 6 Silver Tea Spoons, Metal Table do., 1 Silver Watch, 2 Toast Jacks, Brass Fire Irons; with a great variety of Earthenware; Iron and Tin Pans, Water and other Cans, Brass Stair Rods, 1 Barrel Organ, 1 Musical Box, 1 Stomach Pump, 1 Time Piece, 20 Volumes of Books, 1 Work Box, 1 Glass Lantern, Hair and Clothes Brushes; 1 Set of light Gig Harness; 3 Bridles; 1 Hackney Saddle: also, all the

Stock-in-Trade of a Painter & Glazier

Consisting of 8 Diamonds, Cans, Bottles, new and other Brushes; Oil Paints and Colours; Oils and Varnishes; 2 Sash Windows and Doors; Paint-stones and Mullers; 8 sundry strong Painter's Ladders; 1 pair good Steps, Poles, and 1 Window Squirt, with every other article connected with the Trade.

Sale to commence at Ten o'clock in the Forenoon precisely.

WILLIAM DEAN, Auctioneer,

28, Malvern Place, near the Railway Station, Keighley.

J. L. CRABTREE, PRINTER AND STATIONER, CHANGE-GATE, KEIGHLEY.

William Dean's poster advertising the sale of the Sagars' household effects *(Keighley Library)*

There is yet another mystery attached to this case. What drove the Sagars to auction off their valuable household furniture and effects from their large and prosperous Cullingworth home in 1851 *without any reserve?* Why leave their beautiful home and thriving business to work in a stinking, flea – ridden, rundown workhouse in a dank seventeenth-century farmhouse, living alongside down and outs for a mere pittance of a wage? Judging by auctioneer William Dean's catalogue of household effects, the Sagars were extremely well before their 'voluntary' move to the workhouse. Sale items that poorer families could only ever dream of included quality flock beds, feather pillows, a set of china, an American clock, silver watch and teaspoons, a barrel organ and music box, five oil paintings, twenty volumes of books and *one stomach pump!*

The Most Foul of All

Towards the end of 1888, a small boy was found dead in horrific circumstances. Johnnie Gill should have celebrated his eighth birthday the following February. His mother, Mary Ann last saw her boy alive on the morning of the 27 December 1888, when she stood outside her home in Thorncliffe Road, Bradford and

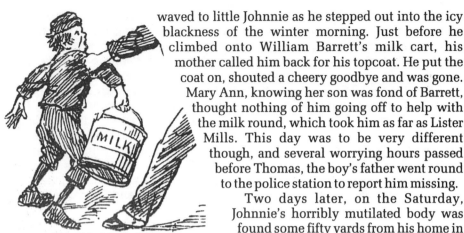

Who stole Johnnie Gill away?
(The Yorkshireman)

waved to little Johnnie as he stepped out into the icy blackness of the winter morning. Just before he climbed onto William Barrett's milk cart, his mother called him back for his topcoat. He put the coat on, shouted a cheery goodbye and was gone. Mary Ann, knowing her son was fond of Barrett, thought nothing of him going off to help with the milk round, which took him as far as Lister Mills. This day was to be very different though, and several worrying hours passed before Thomas, the boy's father went round to the police station to report him missing.

Two days later, on the Saturday, Johnnie's horribly mutilated body was found some fifty yards from his home in Back Mellor Street by apprentice Joe Bucke at about 7.00am. He immediately fetched Burt Teale from the bakehouse next door, who in turn summoned P.C. Haigh. The corpse was lying face down in the corner of a deep recess filled with rotting horse manure, at the back of butcher James Berwick's stables (Mr Berwick lived at No 5 Burlington Road). The boy's own braces and a piece of string were wrapped tightly about his neck, thighs and feet (the string was later lost by absent-minded police). Haigh untied the braces and saw the body had been ripped open right up to the neck. The thighs had been placed on either side of the face, the feet protruding from below this point, where the body had been separated. The heart was under the chin (a scrawled 'Dear Boss' note, dated 30 October 1888 and signed 'Jack the Ripper ' had threatened to kill a child and extract its heart). The boy's boots had been pushed partly inside the abdominal cavity. Several stained wet rags were found underneath the now bloodless torso. The boy's clothes lay neatly arranged close by. A coat covered the remains of the naked body giving the impression of a 'compact soldier's knapsack.' Drs. Major and Miall had the body photographed after a quick examination and an excellent likeness of the boy's face was taken.

Bradford Coroner Mr J.G. Hutchinson opened the inquest at the Town Hall. Women were not permitted to listen to the details of the crime and were ordered to leave the courtroom.

Police Surgeon Samuel Lodge thought the cause of death to be two stab wounds on the left side of the chest, inflicted by a strong, sharp pointed knife, the second having just missed the heart. Yet, there were no knife marks in any of the boy's clothing. Every large blood vessel had been sliced. Both kidneys were intact but the liver had been cut loose, handled and replaced inside the body – Lodge noted that it had been dried out and did not look like a liver at all. The stomach, pancreas and intestines had been disturbed but not pulled out. A 'piece of red tape and some fragments of printed paper were found in among the coils of the intestine.' I think the torn pieces of paper mentioned were from a 'Penny Dreadful'. Worst of all, the boy's private parts, including part of the iliac

159

and pubic bones had been completely removed (similar to 'Ripper' victim Mary Jane Kelly 's case several weeks previously, apart from their gender). The fleshy attachments were missing altogether. It would appear that the boy's last meal had been currant cake, as there were undigested currants in his stomach. The corpse gave the impression of having been washed inside and out and looked as if it had been completely drained of blood. Lodge was unable to determine with any certainty the time of death but thought it had taken place within the last twenty-four hours. He concluded that several sharp instruments had been employed to dissect the body and a hammer or mallet had been used to smash and separate the thighbones. The doctor found difficulty in getting blood for analysis. He saw that one lung had been detached and the other was missing. The ears had been cut as "cleanly as the doctor could have done it" the left ear being carefully sliced. The right ear had been cut round and "very neatly and prettily" scooped out. A second post mortem revealed the right ear, hidden inside the chest along with the missing lung. It was only human, the sickened doctor concluded, to hope that mutilation had not taken place until after death.

Keighley's Local Board medical officer Dr Arthur Roberts took part in one of the post mortems but he was not called into the witness box. Bradford police knew that his opinion as to the immediate cause of death went against that of Lodge. Roberts did not believe the stab wounds had killed the boy. He was confident that the 'stabs', which in his view were not stabs at all in the ordinary sense of the word, were actually inflicted *after* death and that the cuts had been made purely to pluck out the heart. He maintained that it would have been impossible to stab this way in life without harming the left lung, which was intact. It was Roberts' considered opinion that, "whoever committed the murder had some skills in using the knife. The incisions were 'clean and business like" he added, "I never saw anywhere a better section that was shown in the slicing of the scrotum. It is no easy matter making a good section, and skill is required as well as a good sharp knife. The cuts elsewhere were clean sweeping cuts and not hacking cuts. The man however could not have had any knowledge of human anatomy for where he tried to cut the thigh joint or amputate the leg – the cuts showed he did not know where that joint lay exactly … "

If Johnnie was alive during the mutilations, why did he not cry out? Had he been plied with alcohol, drugged, or even trapped in a place where no one could hear his cries for help? The crime was so like Whitechapel's 'Ripper' murders that London's Metropolitan Police despatched H. Division's police surgeon Dr. George Bagster Phillips, who had personally inspected the work of 'Jack the Ripper' on at least four other occasions and so was familiar with the murderer's distinctive trademarks. Ordered to perform special examinations of Johnnie Gill's remains, the doctor carefully measured and calculated wounds and checked each organ. His conclusion was that the murder was *identical* to those in the East End, except that in this case it was a child and therefore much worse than the Whitechapel atrocities. This was not the first time Phillips had been called to a *possible* 'Ripper' killing. In late September 1888, he had gone to Birtley, near Gateshead to examine the mutilated corpse of Jane Beetmoor but declared that this clumsy piece of butchery was definitely *not* the work of the 'Ripper'.

An in depth discussion followed between Phillips, Dr Lodge and Chief Constable Withers followed by a short visit to the stables at 11 Belle Vue, a possible scene of the crime. Having arrived by the 6pm train on 2 January 1889, Phillips left on the 9.15pm night train the same evening. London Metropolitan Police authorities promised to send Withers a copy of Phillips' report within a few days.

Meanwhile Bradford police refused or were unable to say where they thought Johnnie might have spent the last hours of his life or where he had met his untimely end. Those 'in the know' speculated that the deed had taken place in the vicinity of either Thorncliffe Road, Barrett's cottage in Bateman Street, or where Barrett kept his horse in Wolfenden's stables at the back of Belle Vue. It later emerged that the authorities believed the mutilation had been performed at Wolfenden's, after the killing but no trace of blood could be obtained. Alternatively, perhaps it was Bertram Street or Walmer Villas, where Johnnie was last seen alive by servant Annie Kershaw, who was standing by the gate of number 10 when Barrett claimed the lad had told him he was going home for breakfast. The milkman said that the last memory he had of Johnnie was of him gleefully sliding down the slippery causeway with a group of boys, in the direction of Thorncliffe Road.

On the evening before Johnnie's sudden disappearance, a family acquaintance by the name of Elizabeth Craggs saw a suspicious looking person enter the Gills' home when both parents were out. She watched as the man bent down to say something to Johnnie but could not hear the conversation. When the stranger left, Mrs Craggs went over and ordered the boy to bolt the door until his mother got home. Who was this person and what did he want with the boy?

A letter posted in one of the town's pillar-boxes on Wednesday the 2 January 1889 was received at Bradford Post Office a day later. It was addressed to 'THE BOSS, BRADFORD.' One of the chief officials at Bradford Post Office opened it and after reading it, thinking nothing wrong of it, intended throwing it onto the fire. Written on both sides of the paper the contents ran something like this,

'DEAR BOSS, LOOK OUT! ARRIVED ON *WEDNESDAY. MY STEAL (?) IS FINISHED. SHALL KILL FIVE. RIP THE – – s FROM HEAD TO HEAL. YOURS JACK THE RIPPER.'

The writing was very clear, and evidently the work of some person who was a good calligrapher, although there was an element of doubt attached to the word 'steal' or 'steel', which was on top of some other word previously written on the back of the paper. Before the letter could be consigned to the flames, another Post Office official, aware that Thomas Gill had received a similar communication, postmarked Plymouth, handed it over to Bradford's Chief Constable James Withers – who ignored it. Mr Gill's letter, opened by Johnnie's sister Ruth, contained a chilling threat to do away with Johnnie's younger brother Sam. It had been written in red ink (or was it the blood of the Gills' dear dead child?) and signed 'I AM JACK THE RIPPER'.

These were not the only letters received by the Chief Constable and signed the 'Ripper', for a few months earlier, in October 1888, he had received a certain communication attributed to a twenty-two-year old Oldham woman Maria Corroner, then residing at 77 Westgrove Street, Bradford and employed as a mantle hand by Messrs Illingworth, Newboult & Co., of Westgate. She stood charged of writing the following (as it turned out, prophetic) letter on unusual black edged notepaper, claiming the 'Ripper's' next victim would be in Bradford; this she posted to the *Bradford Daily Telegraph* and Bradford's Chief Inspector. The latter, having received his missive posted on the 15 October, did nothing until the newspaper inadvertently forced his hand by publishing the letter *it* had received.

> Dear Sir,
> If the Bradford police would like to make another gallant capture now is the time. I have arrived in the town for the purpose of doing a little bit of business. Bradford is the field that requires my labour. Of course, knowing as I do that your men are so clever, it is not necessary to give my address, nor yet describe myself minutely. I will simply state that I am here alone, quite near to the Town Hall.
> I am, my dear sir, yours in the light against wickedness. *J. Ripper.*
> P.S. – perhaps you'd like my portrait, but you see I am in deep mourning for those ladies that I put to sleep, and do not wish one to be taken.

A covert tip-off instigated a search of Corroner's lodgings by Det. Inspector Dobby while his partner Det. Inspector Abbey went to her employer's shop to arrest her. Amongst Corroner's possessions were several drafts of the letters – a visiting card belonging to the Public Executioner – James Berry of Bradford, a number of articles from newspapers describing the Whitechapel murders and a part written letter about the recent murder of a warder from Strangeways Prison, addressed to the governor there. Corroner claimed "I did it for a joke." Found guilty, she was remanded for a few days, bound over to keep the peace for six months and fined £20.

Twenty-three-year-old milkman William Barrett, employed by dairyman Mr Wolfenden whose business was on Manningham Lane, was swiftly accused of Johnnie Gill's murder by Bradford detectives King and Butterworth, despite them having no evidence of his guilt, other than one or two vague statements from unreliable witnesses … Mrs Rose Ann Cooper of Abbey Road (a woman well known to the police) claimed she saw a man fitting Barrett's description in Manningham Lane at 6.15am on the morning that Johnnie's remains were found, carrying what looked like a bundle of clothes in his arms.

Another trumped-up police witness who did not come forward until 9 January was a simpleton by the name of Dyer who didn't even know if his name was Thomas John or John Thomas, nor could he recall his date of birth! Apparently, Dyer – who had never met Barrett, was told "Withers is wanting you to give evidence in the Barrett case." The entire chain of circumstances was based on Dyer's false statement.

The police even suppressed vital evidence given by James Head of 592 Bolton Road, who had made a formal statement to the effect that he had heard the lad telling the milkman he was going home for breakfast just as Barrett claimed he had. They also refused to surrender three milk books to the court, which could prove Barrett's whereabouts at the time of the disappearance.

In court, Barrett denied the assertion that he was the murderer, insisting he had only been on the lane to deliver milk. "It looks as if it's somebody who had more time than me, and it looks as if it had been planned beforehand," he said. On the morning of Johnnie's disappearance, he told of walking in the shadow of a broad-shouldered man wearing a dark coat and a hat. Barrett described to the court how a few months previously he had overheard a discussion about the London Whitechapel murders in a railway carriage, which "made his blood run cold."

Bradford folk were convinced that Barrett was innocent and his imprisonment a scandalous injustice, calling for his immediate release. *The Globe* wrote: 'The poor boy was killed by a person who possessed more knowledge and skill than a man in Barrett's position. The true killer was a dextrous operator and the circumstances go to place the crime in a similar category with those in the East End of London.' Only one person went against Barrett ... while he was awaiting trail in Armley jail, he received a threatening letter from an anonymous source demanding he confess to the murder or prepare to die.

Bradford police were eventually forced to admit they had got it wrong when the case against Barrett collapsed due to the lack of evidence. The prisoner subsequently obtained his final discharge on 12 March 1889, but not before being dragged from the Magistrate Court to the common jury on a charge of 'wilful murder.' On his release, Barrett left Bradford immediately and returned home to his native Cross Hills, where the Kildwick Band struck up the tune *See the Conquering Hero Comes* as he stepped onto the station platform from the Keighley train. A cheering crowd waved an effigy of "Owd Withers" dressed up in a policeman's uniform coat and hanging by the neck! I doubt if this action would have bothered the Chief Constable much since the Fenian Irish Secret Society had already threatened to murder him! Withers, incidentally, lived at 57 St. Paul's Road, Manningham, only a few streets away from the actual scene of the crime.

Barrett accused Bradford's police of "sparing no pains neither in lying nor prompting other people to lie" in their attempt to convict him, thereby giving the real murderer every chance to escape justice.

Fresh evidence came to light from butcher Richard Manuel – who ironically lived only a few doors from the residence of England's official executioner, James Berry. On the way home from a billiards match in Manningham Lane, he noticed candlelight in the coach-house and stables of Wolfenden's stable, 11 Back Belle Vue at about 11.45pm on Friday 28 December. A tall man stood holding the stable door nearest to Lumb Lane ajar with his left hand. Manuel thought nothing of it, since the stranger did not attempt to conceal his presence in any way. He was close enough to observe that the man was dressed in a dark Italian cloth sleeve-waistcoat (an all-in-one-coat) and a pair of worsted cotton trousers.

This large house, previously occupied by solicitor Mr A.W. Robinson, was also a Friendless Girls' Home, The Free Registry Office – an agency where females could register for domestic work and The Lodge. The building later housed the Bradford Theosophical Society Headquarters – a Lodge indirectly linked by its members to the Golden Dawn Movement which claimed knowledge of Secret Doctrines and Divine Wisdom – but what 'The Lodge' related to in Johnnie's day, I have yet to discover.

At about 6.30 the following morning, domestic servant Lizzie Jefferson, who resided in the Servants' House of number 11, looked out of the scullery window and saw a flickering light in the coach-house. She knew that was the time because just before her attention was claimed for two or three minutes by the sound of a man whistling, accompanied by a dull hammering sound, she had heard the distant Town Hall clock strike the half-hour after checking the clock in the back room.

Lizzie's matron, Mrs Eliza Jane Kendall, whose back bedroom overlooked the coach-house, described how she had heard a sawing noise in the stable. Fearing burglars, she had listened intently to unfamiliar scraping sounds, followed by water being swilled in the yard and then a hard sweeping brush moving backwards and forwards, stopping and starting at intervals. She estimated that this lasted for fifteen minutes or so before the stable door was closed and rapid footsteps faded into the heavy early morning mist, down Belle Vue in the direction of Manningham Lane, which was then a dark and lonely highway. The matron fixed the time at somewhere between 1am and 3am. At the same time, she stated that she had not heard customary measured footsteps of a police constable on his beat at any time that night. At the mortuary, Mrs Kendall recognised Johnnie Gill for she had seen him on Christmas Eve hanging around the stables with his friends.

PC Kirk patrolled the Manningham area, as usual, between 9pm and 6am on the Friday and Saturday in question. Kirk maintained that he had called at Berwick's stables (where Johnnie Gill's mutilated body was found) every hour during that time, to make sure the doors were locked. He added that there were no notes in his book to corroborate this, because there had been nothing unusual to report. However, the policeman's pocket book did confirm that he had visited Wolfenden's to check on the door at 10.25pm, 12.25am and 2.25am, and again at 4.25am. How could Kirk possibly claim the stable was secure? It opened out onto the back of a cobbled causeway where people walked by and anyway, it was impossible to lock the door because it had been broken for three weeks. A fact upheld by photographer Harry Ledgard, who passed the stables at 10.30pm (just five minutes after the policeman). The dim glow of a candle from within enabled him to discern the outline of a stooping man who was inside. In fact, *anyone* could have got in and even spent the night there, since the hay chamber was big enough to accommodate a man. Why then did Kirk lie on oath?

The public was informed that two Bradford detectives had been despatched to Liverpool in connection with the boy's murder, to make specific enquires regarding a bloodstained sack bearing the words *MASON, DERBY ROAD, LIVER-POOL*, which had been found underneath the body in Back Mellor Street. The outcome of these enquires was kept quiet. My own investigations revealed that in 1888 there was a corn merchant by the name of William Mason who was trading in Derby Road, Kirkdale. More interesting though, is the listing of one William Mason, provision merchant of 18 Leigh Street, *Whitechapel*, Liverpool. Was this a sign as to the murderer's identity, a possible connection perhaps to James Maybrick, ('I AM JACK') supposedly respectable cotton broker of Tithebarn Street, Liverpool by day and self-proclaimed 'Jack the Ripper' by night? His journal – if it was a genuine account puts him in Manchester at around the time of the Bradford murder and boasts of planning an even worse atrocity than his previous acts of sickening violence and murder. He also revealed how heartsick he was of his children, one being a boy who was similar in age to Johnnie.

About this time, an elderly woman spiritualist held a séance at her home with five others present. The medium summoned the spirit of 'Ripper' victim, Elizabeth Stride. Her spirit obliged them with her presence, telling them her murderer was a middle-aged man living in or near Commercial Street, Whitechapel ... as it happened, a place well known to Maybrick and his famous brother Michael Maybrick, a high ranking (thirty degree) London Freemason, better known in his day as music composer Stephen Adams.

Arsenic addict Maybrick died in May 1889. The circumstances surrounding his death caused an enormous sensation for his wife Florie, niece of Jefferson Davis, ex-President of the Southern Confederacy stood accused of poisoning him. Florie's mother was concerned that a number of documents had 'gone missing.' Is it possible that James Maybrick's journal had been hidden by one of the remaining Maybrick brothers under the floorboards of Battlecrease House when Florie's papers were stolen?

If this man really was 'Jack the Ripper', it is fitting that his own body was violated in the dead of night at Anfield Cemetery, Liverpool, when medical men took away his head, heart, lungs, kidneys, a femur and some flesh from a thigh. Replacing what was left of his remains in the coffin.

Although Johnnie's life was insured for £5, his parents gained little from his death, as the money only paid for his burial. Kind friends and neighbours collected eight shillings (40p) for flowers and a deal coffin was acquired from undertaker and cabman Mr Whitaker of Thorncliffe Road – Thomas Gill's employer. The coffin had silver mountings, draped in black material and covered with beautiful wreaths of lilies, ferns and white flowers. The plate on the lid simply recorded, "BURIED ON 4th JANUARY 1889 BORN 5th FEBRUARY 1881. FOUND DEAD 29th DECEMBER 1888."

Tom and Mary Ann Gill laid to rest what remained of their first born in Windhill Wesleyan Cemetery. Although only close family members, including his younger brother Samuel and sisters Ruth and Jane attended the actual funeral sermon, hundreds turned up to pay their last respects. Bradford sent ten policemen to control the crowds, which lined Manningham Lane, Frizinghall Road and Valley Road.

When the cold clay had settled on the grave, his bereaved parents erected a fine stone memorial to their son, bearing the inscription:

JOHN GILL, WHO WAS FOUND DEAD DECEMBER 29TH 1888, HAVING MET HIS DEATH AT THE HAND OF SOMEONE WHO WILL SOME DAY SEEK REPENTENCE. IN HIS 8TH YEAR.

Shortly after the tragedy, a letter 'from some kind friend living in London' was sent to Bradford's Lord Mayor at the Town Hall. He then forwarded it to the Gills, along with this note:

'Sir, Will you oblige me by remitting the enclosed sum (£2 postal order) to Mr and Mrs Gill, the parents of the murdered boy, as a token of sympathy in their misfortune from a former inhabitant of Bradford. E.B.'

Eventually removing to 11 Fairfield Road Bradford, Johnnie's distraught mother Mary Ann continued to visit her son's grave until her own death in June 1932. She had to live with the fact that the murderer was never brought to justice for, after Barrett's discharge, Bradford police astonishingly dropped the case.

On January 18 1889, the *Keighley Herald* announced, 'The police have still before them the fact that the murder of poor John Gill remains unavenged, and that the real culprit is still untraced and at large.'

Furthermore, a journalist from the *Bradford Observer* pointed out that had someone bothered to notice the muddy footprints (still recognisable in March), which lead to and from the back yard of an empty house between Burlington Road and James Berwick's stable, the evil perpetrator might have been caught.

The *Star* rightly observed, 'To all appearance the Bradford police have cut as poor a figure in this investigation as their Metropolitan brethren in the worst crimes which we have had in London.' This total lack of interest (or incompetence) by both Bradford and London police authorities lends credence to the statement of Robert Anderson, former Assistant Commissioner of London's Metropolitan Police, claiming that they knew the true identity of the 'Ripper' but it had been kept hidden from the public.

* * * *

A Foolish Freak was the title of the following bizarre story that appeared in the *Keighley News* on 8 January 1889 and seems to be connected to Johnnie Gill's murder.

Mr Cahills, a tailor of 324 Heaton Road, Manningham and his wife attended the servants' ball held at the Alexandra Hotel, Great Horton Road, on Boxing Day. (Incidentally, the manager – Carlo Faro, happened to be an initiate of the newly formed Bradford Horus occult group the Order of the Golden Dawn. At that time, the Golden Dawn and subsequently the Theosophical Society gathered here each week). The couple did not arrive back home until 10:00 the next morning – exactly two hours after Johnnie Gill was last seen alive in the same suburb, only half a mile away from their rented house.

The Cahills were in the habit of keeping the front door key on a hook behind the outhouse door, which was where they found it on their return. Stepping into the sitting room, they saw an open umbrella on the floor (an unlucky omen). It did not belong to either of them. Another open brolly was discovered behind the door leading from the room to the back of the premises, but that one *did* to belong to the couple.

The first thing Mr Cahills saw when he entered the living room was his wife's dress, suspended over a table from a hook in the ceiling. At first, he thought it was a woman hanging. Pieces of women's clothing were draped neatly across the back of a chair with a bonnet placed on top (as in the case of 'Ripper' victim Mary Jane Kelly). The table had been piled high with various household items, together with two used but now empty glasses. Furniture was strewn about and a cupboard emptied of its contents.

On a table close to the front window lay two crossed carving knives (to stir up strife?) and upon them was placed a card, which Mr Cahills read out, 'HALF-PAST NINE. LOOK OUT. JACK THE RIPPER HAS BEEN HERE.' On the reverse side appeared the words 'I HAVE REMOVED DOWN TO THE CANAL SIDE. PLEASE DROP IN. – YOURS TRULY, SUICIDE.' Although pen and ink were on the table the originator of these few but chilling words had used a lead pencil instead. This was reminiscent of another message – 'DEAR BOSS – I AM STILL ABOUT. LOOK OUT – JACK THE RIPPER.' – which, on the day of Kelly's funeral, had been scrawled onto the gable end of Newsome Street, Whitechapel (the home of a 'Ripper' informer) but later partly obliterated by London police. A clock had been set to the time on the card and then stopped. Some boxes of matches were placed on their ends in a circle around the crossed knives. A large tin basin filled with water was also on the table where the knives had been placed and the tabletop was saturated with water ... someone was playing a nasty sadistic game. Nothing was missing except a bottle of rum and the contents of another consumed by the intruder, judging by the empty spirit glasses left on the table. The police were informed immediately, but opted to keep the matter 'strictly silent' for four days.

From that moment, on Mrs Cahills refused to set foot in the property again. Later it was reported – as a throwaway remark – that the whole thing had been a silly prank played on the couple by a relative. However, Mr Cahills claimed that only their employer knew they would be at the Alexandra Hotel that evening and staying there until the following morning.

Incidentally, some of Johnnie's remains supposedly turned up near St. Mark's Road, situated between the Cahills residence and Chief Constable Withers abode.

*   *   *   *

Several tormenting questions about this unsolved crime remain:

Was John Gill sacrificed as part of an occult ceremony that demanded the blood of an innocent first-born male child? James Monro, Commissioner of the London Metropolitan Police thought that there *was* a strong likelihood of occult links concerning the Whitechapel murders, even going to the extent of investigating the possibility.

Could the 'Ripper' have been associated with Dr William Wynn Westcott, London Coroner and father of the Golden Dawn? Westcott had strong ties with the occult Temple of Horus in Bradford. A place he visited before and after the boy's death. Two founders of the Golden Dawn, Westcott and Woodford were among the original nine who, in 1884 founded the first Freemason's research group interested in eastern mysticism including Nimrod's Babylon (Nimrod being 'a hunter of the souls of men'), named the Quatuor Coronati Lodge, 2076, London. Another co-founder of this sect was none other than Police Commissioner *Sir Charles Warren*, Head of the Metropolitan Police, who resigned from his post at the height of the 'Ripper' murders.

Some years after the event, black magician Aleister Crowley, of the Golden Dawn, believed the 'Ripper' had been a dedicated occultist seeking power.

Did the police really know the identity of the killer? Was little John Gill truly the last victim of 'The Ripper'? As a final thought, it is strange to think history repeated itself when a second 'Jack the Ripper', namely Peter Sutcliffe, struck in the same neighbourhood of Bradford almost one hundred years later!

Gunned Down

Who would have believed when the Revd Patrick Brontë christened John Waddington on the 27 March 1837, that the child would end up being murdered by a cowboy in the Wild West?

In 1869 after receiving a letter from his English friend William Hall, who was living in Millsap, Texas, young John got himself a job on board a ship bound for America. A place William wrote, offering free land and great new opportunities. John's wife, a Keighley girl named Mary (nee Hudson) and their six children – all boys – later sailed from Liverpool to join their father in New York. John, a stone-mason by trade had landed a job working on the new railroad bridges. The family claimed a tract of land at Seymour in the State of Texas after leading a nomadic lifestyle and having added another five children (two of whom died young) to their number.

As it happened, John's estate was divided by the Texas and Pacific Railroad's right-of-way. The Railway Company offered John good money for his land, which he accepted. When a local cattle baron heard of the deal he put a price on the Yorkshireman's head. As a result, John Waddington, late of Hainworth Village near Haworth fell victim to a vicious range war. On the 21 August 1880, at the age of forty-five, he was shot in the back by a gunman and buried in Seymour, Texas. John's eldest son Eli was granted guardianship of his siblings, including the only girl – little six-year-old Mary Jane. All were left to the mercy of God and good neighbours.

Burned Alive

Bears were trained to 'dance' by placing the animal in a large copper container and setting a light beneath it. When the metal became hot, a drum was beaten and thus the bear learned to 'dance' when hearing the sound of a drum, for the poor creature thought it was going to suffer the heat of fire under its feet.

Donna the dancing bear was brought to Keighley in the spring of 1884 by her owners, a foreign couple who travelled the country with her as their prize exhibit. Leaving the animal locked for the night in the old smithy next to the Cross Roads Inn near Haworth, the couple retired to bed in a rented cottage close by. Under the cloak of darkness, curious village boys climbed onto the roof and removed some slates so that they could see Donna. The candle stump employed to shed light on the creature, accidentally fell between the wooden rafters, igniting the animal's straw bedding. The hapless bear was roasted alive long before the key holder could be summoned. Her charred remains were buried at Sugden Swamp off Hardgate Lane. The culprits were apprehended and convicted after a reward of ten pounds was offered and claimed and Donna's owners were suitably compensated, using the money to travel the length and breath of England selling crude poems detailing her horrible end.

The smithy was demolished and now serves as a car park next to the Cross Roads Inn – one of Branwell's favourite haunts.

On A Lighter Note

This comical story is culled from Walter White's *A Month in Yorkshire, 1859.*

'Not far from Bradford, an old couple lived in their farm. The good man had been ill for some time, when the doctor who attended him advised that a physician should be called in from Bradford for a consultation. The physician came, looked into the case, gave his opinion, and descended from the room to the kitchen, and was there accosted by the old woman with, "Well, doctor, what's your charge?" "My fee is a guinea!" "A guinea, doctor, a guinea! An' if ye come ageean will it be another guinea?" "Yes, but I shall hardly have to come again, I have given my opinion, and I leave him in good hands." "A guinea, doctor, hey!" The old woman rose, went upstairs to her husband, and the doctor heard her say, "He charged me a guinea, an' if he comes ageean it will be another guinea. Now what do ye say? If I were ye, I'd say no like a Britoner, and I'd die first.'

7 | *Wizards That Peep*

S axon chroniclers recorded that Prince Haakon, son of King Harold of Norway received an English education at the court of King Athelstan and that while he was there, his father presented him with an enchanted sword that "Haakon the Good" treasured until his death.

Harry Speight described Haakon's, magic, golden-hilted sword *Quernbite*, as having a blade sharp enough to cleft a mill-stone through the centre eye and proclaimed that it is buried somewhere on the lonely moors surrounding the town of Bingley. Unfortunately, Speight does not reveal how he came by this information. The Younger Edda stated that Haakon carried this special sword to Norway with him. Perhaps *Quernbite* had a sister sword *Quernbitter?* Should this be correct then there is a wonderful hidden treasure still waiting to be discovered.

Earthly Influences

There are a number of stone circles and 'magic' stones scattered around and about Brontë country. These circles, far older than man's memory, are mystical places where our forefathers worshipped their Gods, giving rise to legendary stories.

On Stanbury Moor, just west of Haworth, stand the strange-shaped Alcomden Stones, which some say were connected with Druidical worship in ancient times.

Nicholas Size strongly believed that pagans sacrificed human beings to their Gods on Rombolds Moor. A key ley-line of electro-magnetic radiation was found to run right through the moor, linking Ilkley Parish Church to Baildon Moor. From here, the line leads to Bradford Cathedral before ending at Bolling Hall, Bradford – the old home of Robert Bolling who fought under the banner of Lord John Clifford at the bloody battle of Towton in 1461. Using his dowsing rods, radiesthesist Mr Bruce-Copen was able to pick up powerful telluric or earth rays inside the old hall, at the exact spot where a woman committed suicide by flinging herself from the balcony onto the stone floor below and where a bloodstain can still be made out.

In medieval days, the powerful stargazer and alchemist Lord Henry Clifford – Yorkshire's Merlin and Lord of Skipton Castle – used to meet with his coven at a secret location on the heart of Ilkley Moor where an energy path linked earth and sky. This mustering place was near the summit of the moor at what is now known as the Twelve Apostles, a stone circle 'psychic power grid'.

In October 1999, I did a spot of novice dowsing at the Twelve Apostles myself, and was surprised to find the rods I was holding were both pulled to the right side of my body by a strong earth current (ley line) that passed through the centre of the circle.

Pagan Practitioners

Around the year 1120, William de Paganell (Lord of Bingley) gave Bingley church to the Black Canons of the Order of Saint Augustine of Drax Abbey, Selby. The abbey, having been erected by Paganell, was situated on the south side of the River Ouse, almost opposite to where the River Derwent empties. So steeped in black rites was Drax Abbey that it was razed to the ground, in order that no man would be able to find it.

It is a matter of record that at least two sixteenth-century Bingley priests who had been instructed at Drax, were severely punished for dabbling in the Black Arts to further their own ends. Word has it that in 1510 Lord Henry Clifford actually arrested one corrupt Bingley chaplain by the name of Richard Greenwood, whose spell book was mysteriously "spirited away from him".

This 'Man of God' was caught seeking a treasure chest filled with all manner of precious metals and jewels, which had been lost at Mountain, near Bradford. Tradition tells that six greedy men, led by Greenwood and a fortuneteller, formed a magic circle and plotted to find the hidden booty with the aid of demons. To this end, the searchers split into two groups, agreeing to meet at Soil Hill (Sol Hid) – which happened to be a favourite walk of Patrick Brontë's – high above Bradshaw, under the cloak of darkness. At the designated mustering place and at the elected hour, a dense fog suddenly descended. Apparently, when the fog vanished, so too had some of the would-be plunderers! The following day, the remaining men met at Harden Wood, St Ives, where they quarrelled. The plot was uncovered and the transgressors were forced by the Archbishop's Court at York to carry banners in the streets and suffer the indignity of being flogged in public for practising witchcraft. They say that the Devil still guards the treasure. Find it if you dare!

Found within the pages of a rare folio volume published in 1677, is John Webster's advice on dealing with the Devil and his cronies: 'The displaying of supposed Witchcraft: wherein it is affirmed that there are many sorts of deceivers and impostors and divers persons under a passive delusion of melancholy and fancy. But that there is a corporeal league made betwixt the Devil and the Witch...or that witches are turned into cats, dogs, raise tempests or the like is utterly denied and disproved, wherein also is handled the existence of Angels and Spirits, the truth of Apparitions, the nature of Astral and Sidereal Spirits, the force of Charms and Philtres'.Webster also wrote a *Treatise on Alchemy* dealing with the properties of mystical chemistry in 1671. He claimed to have published this document to 'counteract the effects of Dr Casaubon's '*Treatise proving Spirits and Witches, & Co*'.

In the days when church font covers were used to stop witches stealing holy water for use in their satanic rituals, one such ritual was known as the *Mass of the Holy Ghost*. It was performed under the influence of the planet Mercury, when an astrologer donned a priest's robe and sprinkled holy water over a pentacle. Quite often seers were in collusion with the parish clerk; a good example of this being Timothy Crowther, Skipton's Parish Clerk who was a well-known magician too!

A scene from Harrison Ainsworth's novel *Lancashire Witches* reveals that the infamous Pendle Witches were drawn to Rombolds Moor in the early 1600s, when mother Demdike declares: 'My worship is paid to the Prince of Darkness…countless Sabbaths have I attended…upon Rumbles Moor'. A single grain of pollen from enchanters' nightshade was found in peat here, at Woofa Bank, by Ilkley archaeologists in September 1983.

I have in my possession a copy of a very curious, hand-drawn geographical type map, which appears to relate to the coven's exact meeting place at the Twelve Apostles. It was situated on the moor's summit where, on a clear day, one can see across Keighley, Bingley, Baildon, Ilkley and Bolton Abbey – over towards the American 'spy' base at Menwith Hill and on into Lancashire.

At the centre of this unusual plan is a triangle within a circle. Outside the triangle is a castle depicting Skipton, a Knight's Templar lantern for Keighley – this shows the top of the old market cross, an open book for Bingley and a hilltop fire for Baildon. Then comes a drawing of the ancient and rare Swastika Stone for Ilkley and finally, there is the ruined priory of Bolton Abbey. The rest of the map is littered with fantastic creatures such as fire dragons, wolfs, a priest and demons. Luckily this item, along with other weird and wonderful documents, was rescued after being destined for the Bradford dump back in the 1970s. Is this a plan of an occult map of the mystical Land of the Dragon, where Cowper's Cross stands at Keighley Gate? Victorian psychic Nicholas Size said this cross was a refuge from the supernatural agencies that roam these moors.

The following piece concerning the treatment of witches in the town of Bradford comes from the pages of *The Yorkshireman* dated 20 September 1879:

> Not long ago a wandering gipsy-woman, with a child slung on her back, was apprehended by the local police, and afterwards sent to prison for a few months by the magistrates, having obtained money and articles of dress from some servant girls on the pretence of telling their fortunes. The offender was treated as a wench and an impostor, and indignant justice visited her with a severe punishment.

> This present week Nancy Bennett, who has for the last quarter of a century been doing openly and notoriously in Bradford the very thing for which the poor gipsy-woman was sent to prison, was had up before the same bench of magistrates and allowed to go free on the prisoner and her husband entering into recognisance's for good behaviour for twelve months. Nay more, the magistrates almost apologised to her for having to deal with her at all, and the Mayor expressed in his opinion that Nancy was "a respectable person who had been tempted to carry on that sort of thing by rewards in money and other forms."

> Now, what I want to make clear is this, that the wandering gipsy-woman is just as innocent and respectable a person as Nancy Bennett. Indeed, if the two are to be judged by the amount of harm they have respectively done, then the prophetess of Green Lane is assuredly the more guilty of the two, for it is well known, and could have been abundantly proved, that Nance has carried on a

very extensive and profitable fortune-telling business for a large number of years. It is not sufficient excuse to say that the ignorant and silly people upon woman such as Nance Bennett feed and fatten are rightly served and beyond the pale of pity. The tempter has in all laws, divine and human been ever regarded as more guilty than the tempted, and although in such a case it might be allowable in a prisoner's advocate to treat this sentiment in the reverse way, it is scarcely what we should expect from those who are called upon to administer justice.

"The prisoner is evidently not a professional fortune-teller," said the kind-hearted chief magistrate, and on this view the bench acted. But "Nance Bennett," I contend, is as much a professional fortune-teller as any of those numerous impostors whom we so frequently read of being sent to prison, for fortune-telling. Is it not professional to assume to herself the power to read the future and trade upon the credulity of the people? Is it not professional to have in her house the recognised implements and paraphernalia of a fortune-teller. Is it not professional to receive visits and demand payment from servant girls and others, day after day, and year after year, on the pretence of telling their fortunes? Nance did not tell fortunes for "love;" oh, no! she always demanded the money down before she consulted the magic glass and the mystic cards. It has long been looked upon as a disgrace in our police system that a woman like Nance should be permitted to carry on her despicable traffic in such an open manner as she has done; but, now that the magistrates have shown themselves disposed to regard the matter as a thing to be excused rather than punished, the race of fortune-tellers will take heart and the evil will spread.'

The Witch of White Abbey *(The Yorkshireman)*

Another notorious 'clairvoyant' of Bradford fame was the Witch of White Abbey. Visiting Wesleyan preacher William Darney wrote of Bradford in 1751, 'On Bradford likewise look thou down, where Satan keeps his seat. Come by the power LORD him disthrone, for thou art very great.'

Cults and Creeds

Spiritualism

Keighley was the first town in England to embrace modern spiritualism, with the emergence of the *Mother Church of Spiritualism*, a few years before Charlotte Brontë's death.

This sad case concerning a suicide appeared on the pages of the *Keighley Visitor* dated 17 April 1861:

'Suicide – George Normington, a spiritualist, hanged himself, at Lane Ends, Oakworth. He was in the employment of Messrs Haggas and Sons, of Damems and Lane Ends, and had been a very steady man. A few years ago, the death of his wife affected him with melancholy. He was then or soon after became, connected with the Spiritualists, and the report at the time was that one of spirits, through a local medium, informed him that a neighbour of his was destined to become his second wife. He accordingly paid her visits, and made her an offer, which she more than once refused. This so affected his mind that he was sent to an asylum. After his return, he behaved himself well, and showed no symptoms of the malady returning until very recently. Some months ago a spiritual medium from Haworth came to reside next door to him and induced him again to attend meetings of the spirit rappers. He again became low and despondent. Eight or ten days ago he removed from Hermit Hole to Lane Ends, where he has been ill, and hanged himself on the staircase on Saturday.' An inquest held upon the body at the Fleece Inn concluded that he had "hanged himself whilst in a fit of temporary insanity.'

John Henry Benson, a child of the Victorian era was born on 20 June 1875, however, he was born *again* in 1978 – according to his 'host', Keighley girl Nichola Wheater. Her astonishing story attracted a flurry of media attention, and in 1990, a BBC TV documentary was broadcast about her previous life as a boy.

It transpired that memories of a preceding life began to unfold on her second birthday, after her maternal grandmother gave her a puppy. Nichola insisted that the animal must be called Muff – after the dog she had owned when she was a boy. Everyone thought this was just child's prattle but as time went by, she began to talk more freely about her former life and of two sisters (Hephyibah and Sellis?).

Her modern day family became alarmed when they heard her say that as John Henry she had been accidentally knocked down and killed by a train on the Keighley and Worth Valley line. Nichola's mother Kathleen was determined to get to the bottom of the mystery and enlisted the help of Keighley's reference librarian, who made a thorough search of the Haworth and Oakworth census of 1881. To the amazement of all concerned, it turned out that

The grave of John Henry Benson, Dockroyd Cemetery, Oakworth *(Marie Campbell)*

there actually *was* a family named Benson (an unusual surname for the area then) living at 12 Chapel Row, Oakworth, having previously removed from the nearby hamlet of Hawkcliffe! A subsequent visit to Oakworth's Dockroyd Cemetery proved to be of even greater interest, for there was the grave of:

JOHN HENRY
The Beloved Grand-son of
HENRY AND MARY FLETCHER (maternal grandparents)
Of Oakworth
Who died January 17 1878 aged 2 years and 11 months

Next to John's grave are those of his paternal grandparents, Thomas and Nancy Benson of Brook Row, and baby Mary Hannah, daughter of John and Mary Fletcher of Hebble Row, Oakworth, who died August 17 1880, aged four months.

A local journalist who had interviewed the child when she was six, told me that there seemed to be something weird going on and that it had been quite chilling at the time, especially since he discovered the records appeared to match her story. Just to be on the safe side, he had asked the librarian if these particular records had been researched by anyone else in recent years, and was assured they had not.

As Nichola grew older, she began describing memories from other lives, including that of a boy named Paul, who lived over Hermit Hole way. She also said that a group of her friends had died in a terrible railway accident on the Keighley and Worth Valley line in 1932. This last story has never been verified, since there appears to be no record of any accidents or deaths recorded in local newspapers or elsewhere during this period.

Nichola told David Knights, a *Keighley News* reporter that she had the power to summon up "ghost people" whom she had known in previous lives – all she had to do was clap her hands together for them to either come or go.

Was this then a case of genuine reincarnation or just a vivid imagination? An American clairvoyant, having investigated the case, felt Nichola's story could be true. The psychic also claimed that the girl possessed the gift of second sight and that she would protect her mother from future psychic attacks.

The Golden Dawn Movement

The Bradford headquarters of the Golden Dawn movement opened its doors on 10 (or 19?) October 1888. Initiates of this new Hermetic Order secretly met at the Alexandra Hotel and then in a windowless attic at 52 Godwin Street (Narey's Yard). Known as the Temple of Horus, it was under the rule of the Very Honoured Frater 'Vota Vita Mea'. The name of a Bradford Chief, occultist Mr T. H. Pattinson (V.V.M.), appears against a list of temples, naming the Bradford Temple as No. 5. Pattinson had been appointed 'Provincial Hierophant of Yorkshire members' on 10 July 1888, enabling him to gather in like-minded souls – seven of whom he had already recruited, as potential members of the Hermetic Order of the Golden Dawn in March of that year. Five of them were, as he put it, "old occult students." F.D. Harrison and J. Leech Atherson were to be Chiefs alongside Pattinson.

The true mover and shaker behind the Yorkshire scene was the alchemist Revd William Alexander Ayton (1816 to 1909), who taught Pattinson and others

Members of the Horus Bradford Temple of The Golden Dawn used secret signs and passwords to identify each other
(The Yorkshireman)

all he knew of occult tradition, prior to the inception of the Golden Dawn. Ayton had an alchemical laboratory set up in his cellar, unbeknown to his Bishop!

The Golden Dawn Movement was started by three British Master Masons – Dr William Robert Woodman, who died soon after, Samuel Liddel Macgregor Mathers an eccentric and one time occult master to black magician Aleister Crowley, and Dr William Wynn Westcott, M.D., Coroner for N. E. London – the father of the Golden Dawn.

Either Mathers or Westcott travelled personally from the City to consecrate the new Horus Temple, in rooms at the Alexandra Hotel, Great Horton Road. Novices, who had to sign a strict pledge of secrecy on all counts, studied occult sciences, including the Magic of Hermes . In addition, they practised curious ceremonial magic rites, such as the Lesser Banishing Ritual of the Pentagram, performed by Pattinson in his role of Hierophant. The sect also investigated alchemy, kabbalistic truths, tarot and astrology. The three main systems taught were Enochian Magic, Abra-Melin and the Key of Solomon.

In the early days, the Yorkshire group was officially banned from using occult weaponry, even though all fourteen men were experienced Master Freemasons and Kabbalists. Madame Blavatsky, the founder of the Theosophical Society (1875) held these Bradford men in high esteem because of their ability to work as a single unit towards one goal – whatever *that* might have been.

In 1983, the new owners of Gobbles Restaurant, Godwin Street, discovered, to their astonishment, a bizarre wall mural, whilst clearing out the attic. It was attributed to Mather's clairvoyant wife, Moina and depicted a setting sun over the great sea, as well as a boat carrying *khu* to the 'Tribunal of Osiris'. According to Egyptian lore, Khu was a wandering spirit whose life ended suddenly, either by suicide, the executioner's rope or accident.

The restaurateurs also noticed what they believed to be some sort of occult initiation oath, written above the entrance to a possible inner temple room. After reading a newspaper article about the forgotten room, two Bradford workmen, Malcolm Brook and Harry Fryer came forward, claiming that they were paid by

Freemasons to restore the unusual painting in the 1950s. On 24 November 1983, Mr Fryer told the *Bradford Star* that he had performed many tasks in a variety of locations but this job was the "weirdest place" he had ever worked. Mr Fryer admitted he would be afraid to be alone in the attic at night, adding that it was a "mysterious place" with its ornate pillars painted with bizarre half-man half-beast creatures. There was a throne, he said abandoned in a corner of the room and a strange patterned carpet on the floor, incorporated in which were a circle and several occult-like symbols (created by Moina Mathers?). Neither Mr Brook nor Fryer ever knew who it was that actually commissioned the work which, I am told, has since been destroyed.

As for Mathers – one of the movement's three originators, his wife claimed he died in Paris exactly as the clock struck the hour of midnight between Thursday 19 and Wednesday 20 November 1918, however it seems there are no official records confirming the true cause of death and neither is there a grave ...

The Theosophical Society and 'Bogus Brotherhoods'

In 1891, watchmaker Thomas Henry Pattinson of Baildon, whose work premises were at 6 Globe Chambers, Piccadilly, Bradford was to become one of the first members of Bradford's Theosophical Society. He was chosen to represent the Bradford movement at Madame Blavatsky's funeral in May 1901.

His daughter followed in his footsteps, taking the lead in establishing an astrological group within the movement during the 1920s. F. D. Harrison and Oliver Firth (who were both Theosophists and Rosicrusians) created a certain amount of trouble for the Golden Dawn in August 1892. Annie Horniman of the Isis Urania Temple in London came up to chastise them for bad behaviour. Two months later the founder, Westcott was forced to act as Horus' Imperator in order to sort out problems at Bradford. Things did not go well, for in March the following year Mathers found himself in Bradford trying to mediate. In the end, Harrison joined forces with ex-Theosophist Annie Besant, when she formed a Universal Co-Masonry group.

In February 1898, the Bradford Temple rejected actress Florence Farr as their leader, petitioning Mathers to keep control of their group – which he declined to do.

At a time when David Weatherhead's Keighley Spiritualist Church was packed to the rafters, David Lund acted as secretary to a bizarre Keighley Occult Order – the Society of the Dew and Light – possibly named after a text found in *Isaiah 26 v. 1* 'For the dew of light is your dew...' This sect produced a journal entitled *The Lamp of Thoth*, dealing with occult subjects, delving deeply into Indian magic, mystical matters and nature rites. The Ros. Crux Fraters, as they termed themselves probably met for a short time at Parkwood Street, Keighley.

Lund's home, first at 190 Spring Garden's Lane and then Fern Cottage, was brought to the attention of the public in a letter from Mathers of the Golden Dawn to *Lucifer* – an occult journal published 15 June 1889. Having heard about what he considered a rogue organisation, he implored his members to have nothing to do with 'The Dew of Light', because they would be led away from the true path of enlightenment.

Madam Blavatsky, founder of the Theosophical Society, wrote an article in 1888, entitled *Lodges of Magic*. In it, she referred to bogus Brotherhoods and Armley Jail, almost in the same breath. (Ironically, a newspaper article of May 1890 reported that Lund was the first theosophist to be imprisoned in Armley). Blavatsky said she had heard a rumour that Yorkshire was "overrun with fraudulent astrologers and fortune-tellers, who pretend to be Theosophists...who swindle a higher class of credulous patrons..." – surely a direct reference to David Lund and the Society of Dew and Light?

Very little is known about the rituals and aims of the Society of Dew and Light, its journal *The Lamp of Thoth*, or its membership, other than what I have gleaned about David Lund. Does someone, somewhere own a copy of *Thoth* or possess any of the books from his extensive occult library?

Another possible member was the mysterious Daniel Murgatroyd, who discovered a copy of Lord Henry Clifford's spell book.

This chief among astrologers bequeathed most of his estate to his niece Mary Robertshaw Lund of Allerton near Bradford, after his death in 1903. The *Keighley Herald's* obituary told of how he was 'a remarkable character besides being interested in astrological research, he was a well known Theosophist...turned his attention to higher philosophical pursuits, which particular branch of scientific or philosophical study determined his decision to enter upon a dubious career of a fortune-teller and charter of horoscopes is not clear...but the result...was not unattended with danger...In his peculiar calling he had the patronage of a large number of persons, mostly females, though his clientele were not entirely confined to the weaker sex, even hard-headed business men occasionally seeking guidance from the "stars" in their speculations'. No doubt Oakworth's Sir Isaac Holden – Liberal M.P numbered amongst these men, for he made his fortune from a vision he had one night – 'His fees were moderate, but so numerous were his 'clients' that his financial gains were, as it is believed, considerable...'

By 1902, adept T.H. Pattinson and Dr B.E.J. Edwards had founded the August and Oriental Order of Light Garuda, which had been a defunct cult until then. It was resurrected after the two men carefully modified the old ceremonial rituals, basing its belief system on the words of Maurice Vidal Portman – a friend of both Lord Lytton and Ayton. Eighteen men (sixteen from the Horus Temple, whose total membership was then twenty-one) attended the inaugural meeting in rooms at 81 King's Parade, Bradford on 9 January the same year ... they subsequently removed to Godwin Street sometime in the 1930s or 1940s. This Bradford based Order continued to operate in its hometown until 1971, when it re-located to York. Today it is referred to as the 'August Order of Light', studying Oriental mystic cultures, and boasts followers in both London and America.

Lord Edward Bulwer-Lytton, freemason and author of *Eugene Aram* was *not* a member of this mystical cult, as some believe. This honour goes to Edward Robert Bulwer-Lytton (1831 to1891).

Astrology

A Victorian astrologer and herbalist who lost his liberty was David Lund of Fern Cottage, Highfield Lane. Lund was a mechanic who also taught Keighley boys higher mathematics on a private basis. He was not a lucky man, being sentenced by Keighley Magistrates to at least one term of imprisonment in Armley Jail, Leeds for persistent fortune-telling (the Chaplain here seemed curious about David's description of the principles of Theosophy). He was also heavily fined on several occasions. Meanwhile, Bradford astrologers publicly advertised their craft in the *Keighley News*!

Townsfolk dubbed the police and magistrates "the greatest of tyrants" for their unjust treatment towards this well-respected stargazer who, according to the mysterious "E.S.", was 'the best educated man in our town'. Lund, a self-educated man, had successfully completed a course in political economy, backed by the Oxford University Extension scheme. He was defended in court by solicitor Mr Robinson (late of 11 Belle Vue, Manningham?). On release from prison in January 1889, Lund and fellow astrologer "Albertus Magnus" (M.E.) of Dolly Hill, Wilsden, set up *The Astrological Defence Association*, to fight against prejudice and ignorance. David Lund wanted the same laws that Methodists and Independents enjoyed, to apply to students of the occult. It is amusing to think that the first time Lund was arrested in 1887, Keighley police were forced to consult Bradford's Antiquarian Society in order to find a copy of the absolute law with which to convict the astrologer! Our Yorkshire 'Magnus' rightly pointed out that, 'People come to us of their own accord, we do not ask them and we are fined 5, 7, 10 pounds for answering a question, while another kills his wife and is let off by paying a sum of 2s 6d (12½p).'

The *Keighley Herald* sprang to Lund's defence writing: 'Astrologers, at least in this district, are men of intelligence, thought and reason.' It is easy to see why some folk were suspicious of this practice, though. One Bradfordian purchased a book on palmistry, intending to learn the art of hand reading. After a careful study of his own hand lines he found the following amusing and contradictory results:

✳ He was nervous and sensitive.

✳ He should live to be ninety-seven years of age, six months and five days.

✳ ... Or die before he reached the age of forty, from cholera infantum.

✳ Marry a rich woman when twenty-one.

✳ Be the mother of twins.

✳ His husband (?) would have red hair and a wooden arm.

✳ Never be a parent, but wife will be a widow with eight fatherless children.

✳ Fitted for the ministry or bank-burgling.

✳ The mount of Jupiter warned him that he had cold feet.

✳ His will would be contested by a lawyer with one glass-eye!

David's obituary claimed he was a well-known Theosophist and it appears that he was directly related to the Theosophist and leading Bradford photographer Percy Lund, who, in 1908, sought to enter Arthur Edward Waite's Holy Order of the Golden Dawn.

Following in David Lund's footsteps was Keighley's renowned but alas, now forgotten, Florry Moorehouse (nee Moody), born in about 1872, who kept a

Florry Moorehouse who operated a flourishing fortune telling business in Keighley posing with her three sons *(Courtesy of Brian Moorehouse)*

lodging house on or near Wellington Street at one time. The fortune telling business boomed throughout the war years, because folk wanted to know if "our Albert" or "Tommy" had survived the wrath of the German Kaiser.

The first time Florry's ten-year-old son Frederick, or Teddy as he was better known, accompanied her to a client's home was towards the end of the First World War. Florry couldn't see anything in the crystal ball except clouds. This prompted the lady of the house to ask, "Is it because you have got your little boy with you?" Florry called out to Teddy, "Come here, come and look into this crystal ball, see if you can see anything." So, he went over and looked into it. "Oh yes, mam, I can see something." Describing the scene before his eyes he said, "I can see a big ship with railing at the back of it and there is a man covered in bandages. And there are a lot of kit bags and other stuff. "

What the woman did not know was that her husband, about whom she was most anxious, had been wounded in France. Shortly after, she sent word to Florry to say that her husband had unexpectedly arrived home from the war, *by ship and covered in bandages*

At the age of 49, and by then a widow, Florry was married again on 23 June 1919 to Billy Hogkinson of 3 College Street at Keighley Parish Church, where she continued to practise her predictions.

*   *   *   *

Mr Steven Wood of Haworth drew my attention to an interesting eighteenth-century hand-written recipe book entitled *Rush Isles Commonplace Book*, dating around 1808 and thought to be in the hand of herbalist William Heaton of Rush Isles, Ponden. In it is a horoscope of a child born in October 1798. Nativities or horoscopes drawn up by astrologers like Jack Kay mapped a person's future destiny. Such a horoscope chart was done immediately follow-ing the death of a young suicide victim born on 16 June 1811.

After she was pulled lifeless from the river on the evening of 17 May 1828, her mother, desperate to discover the reason for her daughter's unexpected and sudden death, consulted the village wise man. As a result of careful consider-ation, the astrologer told her that he could see evil, danger and sorrow in her daughter's chart, for the Sun was in exact opposition to Saturn, and Mars in opposition to the planet Venus, with Saturn's body touching Jupiter. Taking this information into account, an untimely end was to have been expected. Thus, cruel death could not be escaped. The mother confided in the seer that, "On the fatal evening wherein baleful planetary orbs prompted the idea of self-destruction, it appears she (the girl) observed her step-father, (a wicked and desolate man,) come from a house of ill-fame, and observing her watching him, he threatened some personal violence." Having been struck by him, she ran to the river and drowned herself, thereby fulfilling the astrological prophecy.

The Countryman and the Astrologer

A countryman wishing to know
The future mysterious events his life –
What Fate had in store, whether pleasure or woe,
And when Susan would deign to be called his wife;
Having long been persuaded that none could excel her,
He resolved to consult a renown'd fortune-teller.
Ten miles from his cottage resided a man
Whose fame as a sage was extensively spread,
And Hodge with celerity nine of them ran,
To learn when the stars would allow him to wed,
Believing the wiseman, without any cavil,
Would the clue to his fortune completely unravel.
Having stolen from the rustic the state of his mind,
The wiseman, assuming mysterious looks,
Began to examine what the stars were combin'd
To favour or injure the man in his books;
Then told him that Susan her husband would call him,
And everything else that in life would befall him.

J. Jowett, Keighley, 1856.

Haworth's favourite interpreter of dreams and star-lore was Jack Kay. Ignorant folk thought people like Jack sold their souls to the Devil in exchange for forbid-den knowledge, yet he was a devout Christian. Others, such as the Independent politician/astrologer Joseph Blackburn, Keighley (a Capricorn town) believed that "Man gets his soul from the stars."

Those who knew the Haworth prophet intimately said that Jack steadfastly refused to lay claim to any kind of mediumistic abilities. He preferred to believe that a person's destiny lay in their heavenly chart, established at the time of birth. Jack was blessed with a deep understanding of stars, weather and country lore.

The old soothsayer took leave of this world in January 1847 and was buried by Revd Patrick Brontë. Nobody knows exactly where his grave is, but his bones lie somewhere in old Haworth graveyard. According to his death certificate the cause of death was 'unknown'.

Jack was missed in the district for a long time after his passing, as this letter published on 18 August 1862 demonstrates, 'To Heditur o' th' Keithley News, Sur, Thare used to be a wise man at Haworth thay calld Jack Kaye...' signed A Keighley News Reader, Haworth.

The opening of the Keighley and Worth Valley Railway was severely delayed due to several calamities, including the original plans being eaten by a hungry cow. Twenty years after the old man's death, Sir Isaac Holden, of Oakworth House, cut the first sod at Haworth, marking the coming of the new railway The late astrologer was so well respected and remembered that village denizens thought the digging ceremony ought to have been "dug on a gurt wind-day in memory o' oud Jack Kaye".

Halliwell Sutcliffe, in his book *By Moor and Fell*, described the Haworth soothsayer as: 'A fragrant lore, the thought of which takes us back to herb-doctors of the moorside, who could tell a fortune, or cure a fever, or heal cattle of the Evil Eye. Shrewd fellows, these, in worldly as in occult wisdom; their skill in fortune-telling the weather was eclipsed only by their power to read the most innermost secret's of men's hearts: and parson and leech alike played second fiddle to them when a child or a cow, a troubled soul or a tangled love-affair, had to be righted. Jack Kay, however, whose influence as a wise man was paramount in Haworth parish seventy odd years ago, was of a different type: he counted it sinful to claim the power of fortune-telling, and he studied astrology with a reverence that was altogether religious. A quiet and gentle-mannered enthusiast, he laid no claim to supernatural knowledge: what he had learned of star-lore, he was wont to say, any other man could learn by study and by long vigils on the hill-tops: but the moor folk who measure no man by his own valuation, gave to Jack Kay such honour and respect as have left their mark on the history of Haworth moorside...The moor folk were always susceptible to weather-tokens, and Jack Kay, long after Grimshaw's time, uttered many a prophecy touching rain and snow, sleet and hail and wind, which gave him some sort of hold over his neighbours' minds that the parson had acquired by prayer.'

Those who consulted him believed Kay to be a great and wonderful mystic and his special abilities in this direction were documented in Thomas Wood's *Autobiography 1822 to 1880*. Wood, a devout Wesleyan, wrote: 'It seems to me strange to look back over my childhood and youth and let memory call up the serious consultations held in dimly lighted rooms carried on in subdued whispers, with solemn shakings of the head and furtive glances around over the case of a sickly young woman, or, it might be, a man with a broken leg, or some other breakdown in health or limb. Most things of this sort were ascribed to a supernatural agency, to the effect of witchcraft or demonology. "She's just done poor thing, she's wasting away like a sweating candle. She used to be a young lass as ever the sun shone on till she were 'wished.' It's no use that doctor's stuff it'll do no good while that's lifted. Better go to Jack Kaye's and he'll make t'aud witch squeak at's done it." And the man who broke his leg did so because a spell was thrown over him which no care or human effort could avert. Cattle died in the field or sickened in the stall because the evil eye had looked upon them and dried up the fountain of health. Sanitary laws were violated recklessly, hygiene not understood or dreamt of, and when these laws exacted the penalty for their breach, the powers of darkness were credited with the result and in defiance of the old teaching ... Wise men or wise women were sought to exorcise the evil spirit by charms as ludicrous as harmless either for good or ill, but perhaps not harmless in their working or in their latent effects ... The life-long feuds engendered by the suspicion of the evil eye or the power to "wish" often bequeathed from family to family ... all this has passed away or only lingers in isolated places. Even in such cases it appears in a mild and modified form whose outward sign is a horseshoe nailed on the inside of the door, or in more pronounced cases over the mantle shelf, to keep out the witches or quench the evil eye.'

Jack and others in his line of work ran the risk of imprisonment under the *Repeal of the Former Witchcraft Act 9 Geo. 11. 1736*, 'For the more effectual preventing and punishing any pretences to which arts and powers ... whereby ignorant persons are frequently deceived and defrauded, be it further enacted that if any person pretend to exercise or use any kind of Witchcraft, Sorcery, or Incantment or Conjuration, or undertake to tell fortunes or pretend from his or her skill or knowledge in any occult or crafty science to discern where or in what manner any Goods or Chattels Supposed to have been stolen or lost may be found, every person so offending shall for every such offence suffer imprisonment by the space of one whole year.'

Nevertheless, Jack Kay's fame continued to spread far and wide, drawing curious visitors to his humble cottage door like bees to a honeypot. They came in the new-fangled carriages that village folk dubbed "ovens on wheels". Rich folk were shown into his cosy study to have their horoscopes cast, while the poorer clientele waited patiently in the tiny kitchen.

* * * *

Did Haworth oracle Jack count members of the Brontë household amongst his most favoured clientele? They lived but a step or two away from his humble stone cottage. It is evident from the novels of Charlotte and Emily Brontës that they acquired knowledge of the occult from someone who possessed a deep and intimate understanding of such clandestine things. In the pages of *Jane Eyre* we can discover something of Charlotte's understanding of the supernatural, by her description of an old witch-like crone admitted to Thornfield Hall, dressed in a long red mantle (fairies also favoured red cloaks) and wearing a black bonnet.

Charlotte described the Sybil as being a 'shockingly ugly old creature ... almost as black as a crock'. The soothsayer is escorted to the library where she is visited in turn by some of the guests, including Blanch Ingram, who later announces that the old crone was a "genuine witch", practising the "science of palmistry." Whilst Amy and Louisa Eshton and their friend Mary believe that the woman divined their very thoughts, and that she had, 'whispered in the ear of each the name of the person she liked best in the world, and informed them of what they most wished for'. Jane cannot wait for her turn to visit the candle-lit library where the witch sits waiting for her by the fire. Upon entering the room, she finds the old woman muttering words from a "little black book." Jane tells us, 'She shut her book and slowly looked up, her hat-brim partially shaded her face, yet I could see as she raised it, that it was a strange one. It looked all brown and black: elf-locks bristled out from beneath a white band which passed under her chin...her eye confronted me at once, with a bold direct gaze.' Taking a silver shilling (5p) from Jane, the fortune-teller ordered her to hold out her hand. At this point Charlotte used her comprehension of phrenology to describe how the girl's future was being told by the examination of the contours of her head and her facial features.

Sadly, the old skywatcher's rented stone cottage at 6 Acton Street, Haworth (opposite the Edinburgh Wool Shop) was destroyed in 1970 to make way for a wider road and eventually, a tourist car park – "an act of sheer vandalism on the part of Keighley Council", said the late Councillor Smith Midgley. In the process of demolition, workmen uncovered a branch from a magic rowan tree (a witch's broomstick?) – woven into the gable end of the roof under the rafters of a cottage on North Street, close to Jack's home.

Nobody knows whose hand placed it there, but the purpose of this charm was to prevent injury from midnight witches of air and broom and to protect against evil spirits.

* * * *

Did Emily's spirit find its way back from the grave? In an interview with a reporter from the *Craven Herald* in August 1979, astrologer Isabel Holmes of Cowling, revealed that she was sure Emily Brontë had helped her to write a modern sequel to *Wuthering Heights*. Isabel, who had never written a novel before, inexplicably felt compelled to put pen to paper as soon as she had drawn up Emily's birth chart. She was unable to stem the artistic flow from the spirit world and the manuscript was completed within a matter of weeks.

The equivalent of Emily's main characters, Cathy and Heathcliff, were Rockcliff and Maureen, whose tormented souls roamed the wilds around High Rigg rocks. Eventually, a professor interested in psychic research tells the earth bound lovers they must accept their deaths and leave for a higher plane, to be reincarnated and reunited in a new life together. Many years later, the ill-fated couple happily re-emerge as Rowena and Clifford Heath. Sadly, worried that the Brontë Society might disapprove of the book, Isabel did not get her manuscript published.

The Brontë Birth Charts

Given that the actual birth *times* of the Brontë family were never recorded, it is impossible to calculate the true ascendants of their nativity or birth charts, with the exception of Branwell, who, Mrs Gaskell noted, was born sometime in the early hours of the morning, and for whom some degree of accuracy can be obtained.

In the case of Emily Jane Brontë, astrologer Angela Pearl Curtis used midday as a substitute birth time. Although considerable information about Emily's character can be gathered from this, it cannot give us as clear a picture of her temperament, as if the true birth time had been known. However, a great deal of insight into the Brontës' personalities can be gained by looking at the various aspects the planets were making to each other on their *days* of birth. The planet Pluto was excluded from these calculations as no ephemeris (tables that list the planets positions for any given day of any year) contain details of Pluto as far back as the Brontës' time, since Pluto was not discovered until 1930.

Emily's Leo Sun was in aspect to Uranus when she was born, bestowing upon her an unusual personality. This aspect shows how creative and inventive she was and obviously influenced her writing enormously. Her mind was capable of exploring many paths and she would have had ideas and beliefs that were years ahead of her time. Her Sun was also in aspect to the planet Jupiter, which, in combination with the above would make for someone whose attitude to religion or a belief system was very different from the norm. Emily would have had her own ideas about God and these would almost certainly have been unconventional and not at all compatible with her father's teachings, or the religious tenets of the day. Emily possessed a strong will and a fiery nature. She would have done things her own way, no matter what. She was a little too stubborn and uncompromising at times. Freedom to be and live as she wished meant everything to her. She would have deeply resented any interfering attempts to control her.

At times Emily must have felt lonely and isolated, preferring to keep her own counsel, as her independent and highly original character would have found little common ground with and even less support or acceptance from the majority of her contemporaries. They would have viewed her as quite improper and a little eccentric to say the least!

The Moon, in the sign of Cancer, gave Emily a deep love of her home and family life, as well as the surrounding wild windswept moorlands, which took up so much of her time. These things represented security to her, as her emotional nature was one that could not easily adapt to change. The familiarity of Emily's everyday surroundings would have provided her with a great source of comfort and solace.

Venus and Mars, conjoined in the sign of Virgo, made Emily capable of developing fantastic crushes on people she most admired. In relationships, she would have had high standards, coupled with strong desires and deep emotions. In short, she sought the ideal in a partner. She wanted the perfect love, a true soul mate that could merge as one with her in body, mind and soul – as Heathcliff did with Cathy. She would probably have preferred a solitary life, for it is doubtful that she would have accepted anything less than her ideal in a potential partner. Venus and Mars, forming stressful aspects to Saturn and Uranus, confirm this, for they demonstrate that Emily possessed a serious attitude towards love and romance, being very cautious when forming relationships.

She had something of an inner conflict regarding the established male/female roles, because of which, it is likely she suffered from feelings of guilt and consequently, great disappointment in love. At some level, she did not feel as if she deserved to be loved and was unnecessarily hard on herself at times. She would have been drawn into relationships with 'strange types', or those who were either unavailable or unreliable in some way, making secure relationships

Birth Chart

Name EMILY BRONTE

No. ſ .

House System EQUAL .

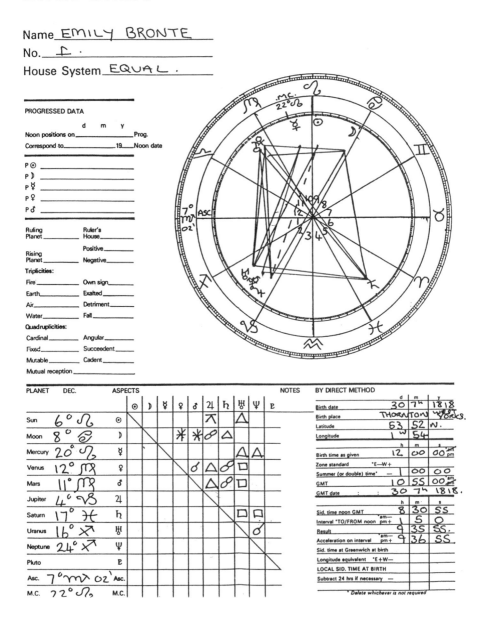

PROGRESSED DATA

d   m   y

Noon positions on _____ Prog.

Correspond to _____ 19__ Noon date

P ☉ _____
P ☽ _____
P ☿ _____
P ♀ _____
P ♂ _____

Ruling Planet _____   Ruler's House _____

Rising Planet _____   Positive _____   Negative _____

Triplicities:

Fire _____   Own sign _____
Earth _____   Exalted _____
Air _____   Detriment _____
Water _____   Fall _____

Quadruplicities:

Cardinal _____   Angular _____
Fixed _____   Succeedent _____
Mutable _____   Cadent _____

Mutual reception _____

PLANET	DEC.	ASPECTS											NOTES	BY DIRECT METHOD			
			☉	☽	☿	♀	♂	♃	♄	♅	♆	♇			d	m	y
														Birth date	30	7ʰ	1818
Sun	6° ♌	☉						⊼		△				Birth place	THORNTON		W. YORKS.
														Latitude	53	52	N.
Moon	8° ♋	☽				⚹	⚹☍	△						Longitude	1	54	W
																h	m	
Mercury	20° ♌	☿					△	△						Birth time as given	12	00	00 pm
Venus	12° ♍	♀				☌	△ ☍	□						Zone standard *E—W+			
														Summer (or double) time* —		00	00
Mars	11° ♍	♂					△ ☍	□						GMT	10	55	00 am
														GMT date	30	7ʰ	1818.
Jupiter	4° ♑	♃														h	m	s
Saturn	17° ♓	♄						□	□					Sid. time noon GMT	8	30	55
														Interval *TO/FROM noon — am pm+		5	0
Uranus	16° ♐	♅							♂					Result	9	35	55.
Neptune	24° ♐	♆												Acceleration on interval — am pm+		36	55
Pluto		♇												Sid. time at Greenwich at birth			
														Longitude equivalent *E+W—			
Asc.	7° ♏ 02'	Asc.												LOCAL SID. TIME AT BIRTH			
M.C.	22° ♌	M.C.												Subtract 24 hrs if necessary —			
														*Delete whichever is not required			

Emily Brontë's birth chart by astrologer Angela Pearl Curtis *(Courtesy of Angela Pearl Curtis)*

Birth Chart

Name___3RANWELL BRONTE___

No.___2___

House System___EQUAL.___

PROGRESSED DATA

	d	m	y
Noon positions on			Prog.
Correspond to		19	Noon date

P ⊙ _____
P ☽ _____
P ☿ _____
P ♀ _____
P ♂ _____

Ruling Planet _____ Ruler's House _____

Rising Planet _____ Positive _____ Negative _____

Triplicities:

Fire _____ Own sign _____
Earth _____ Exalted _____
Air _____ Detriment _____
Water _____ Fall _____

Quadruplicities:

Cardinal _____ Angular _____
Fixed _____ Succeedent _____
Mutable _____ Cadent _____

Mutual reception _____

PLANET	DEC.	ASPECTS											NOTES	BY DIRECT METHOD			
		⊙	☽	☿	♀	♂	♃	♄	♅	♆	♇				d	m	y
													Birth date				
Sun	4° ♋	⊙						⊼△					Birth place				
													Latitude				
Moon	24° ♍	☽				♋⊼♂							Longitude				
															h	m	s
Mercury	16° ♊	☿				. ♋♋						Birth time as given				ᵃᵐ/ₚₘ
Venus	25° ♉	♀				♋		⊼				Zone standard °E—W+				
												Summer (or double) time° —				
Mars	24° ♈	♂					△					GMT				ᵃᵐ/ₚₘ
												GMT date : :				
Jupiter	7° ♐	♃				□ ♂								h	m	s
Saturn	5° ♓	♄				□ ♂					Sid. time noon GMT				
												Interval °TO/FROM noon ᵃᵐ—/ₚₘ+				
Uranus	12° ♐	♅										Result				
												Acceleration on interval ᵃᵐ—/ₚₘ+				
Neptune	22° ♐	♆										Sid. time at Greenwich at birth				
Pluto		♇										Longitude equivalent °E+W—				
												LOCAL SID. TIME AT BIRTH				
Asc.	7° ♊	Asc.										Subtract 24 hrs if necessary —			°
M.C.		M.C.										* Delete whichever is not required			

Branwell Brontë's birth chart as drawn by Angela Pearl Curtis *(Courtesy of Angela Pearl Curtis)* difficult to maintain. Despite her religious upbringing, Emily would have felt very differently from the rest of her family, in many respects.

The most revealing planetary configuration in Emily's chart is that of Uranus, conjoined with Neptune and Mercury, creating a strong positive link with these two planets. These aspects gave Emily her great talent for writing and a mystical imagination. If not a psychic, she was without doubt highly intuitive and something of a visionary. She would have felt rather a misfit amongst the down-to-earth Haworth villagers, but her strong spirit and faith in her own unique beliefs and ideals gave her comfort and enabled her to endure the loneliness she felt. Emily held fast to these beliefs throughout her short life and they, in turn, provided her creative imagination with its main source of inspiration.

* * * *

The Sun, quincunx Jupiter, shows that Branwell Brontë liked to enjoy life but had little self-control. He would have had a tendency to expect things to come to him, without making any effort. To a great extent, he'd have been unwilling to work for long at anything, feeling that he deserved to have everything done for him. There was more than a hint of arrogance to his character but in addition, optimism and generosity of spirit – for Branwell would have been the first person to help anyone in need.

The Sun in trine to Saturn adds a serious note. His father's influence would have taught Branwell how to express himself positively and given him a strong desire to achieve success. In many ways, Branwell was very sure of himself and his natural abilities.

The Moon, in opposition to Venus, shows how much the loss of his mother affected him. His feeling responses would have been very inhibited, creating difficulty within all his relationships – especially with those of the opposite sex. It is more than likely he would have felt uncomfortable with females – feeling that he must always be the one to compromise in order to maintain harmony. Branwell would have gone to great lengths to gain approval and affection, even attaching himself to inferior types, because they seemed to offer the attention he craved. The Moon, quincunx Mars, would have made Branwell highly-strung and touchy, causing temper tantrums when he became emotionally upset. Branwell's Moon, in conjunction with Jupiter, reveals that he had very strong emotional reactions and a deep understanding of many of the social problems of the day. He was emotionally open and capable of great warmth, with a sincere concern for those less fortunate than himself towards whom he was truly generous.

Mercury, in conjunction with the ascendant, shows Branwell had a great ability to communicate and could easily put his thoughts into action. He was a very talkative person, bright and witty, but could burst out with rash statements when provoked. A quick learner, Branwell would have absorbed information easily and found no difficulty in dominating a conversation, as he was an original thinker and a creative speaker, dramatising whatever he said. Branwell would have not been afraid to speak up, whenever he believed himself to be in the right. He would probably have become indignant and argumentative, if criticised.

The negative side of his personality was due to Mercury, in opposition to Neptune and Uranus, which promoted an eccentric way of relating to others. Poorly thought out and impetuous speech may have sounded irrational to others, for he had a tendency to babble inanely at times, when under emotional stress. He possessed a sharp mind and much creative ability but would tend to assume that his opinions were the only valid ones. He would have been stubborn with a refusal to see anyone else's side of things. His know-it-all attitude is likely to have alienated him from others. Branwell's family would have found difficulty in communicating easily or constructively with him at times. It is most likely that his father would have made decisions concerning Branwell's future, based on his son's eccentric or wilful attitudes.

The imaginative and creative Branwell had high aspirations but somewhat unrealistic dreams. He was quite naïve at times and his thoughts would have ranged very much from the inspirational to the delusional. When unduly upset, he could easily have become paranoid and would very probably have suffered at the hands of deceptive and dishonest people.

Venus in opposition to Jupiter made Branwell extravagant and obsessive in love. Somewhat selfish, he would have demanded immediate satisfaction for all his wants. Often confused, he was bound to experience difficulty in reaching his goals and ambitions and Venus, quincunx Neptune, shows that he was far more likely to just drift and dream at times, than create anything worthwhile.

Jupiter, in Square to Saturn, shows that Branwell's father restricted his enthusiasm for life and he would have alternated between sometimes relating to others excessively and then periodically withdrawing from them. He could turn off and on in quite an unpredictable manner. Branwell may well have felt apprehensive about forming relationships with the right sort of people, for fear of rejection, but would have been unwilling to accept responsibility for his relationships and their conditions. Jupiter in conjunction with Uranus shows that Branwell best enjoyed relationships with unusual philosophical types of individuals who had original ideas. Although very rash and excitable at times, he was certainly a highly intelligent and interesting person.

Saturn in Square to Uranus would probably have made Branwell very rebellious and anti-tradition. Overall, he would have had a very difficult relationship with his father and would have insisted on doing his own thing. His erratic self-willed behaviour showed little respect for authority. For all the boy's considerable talents, originality and creative ability, deep down he suffered from an acute lack of self-confidence. Branwell chose to project an eccentric and unconventional persona to the world in order to mask his feelings of inferiority.

Numerology

Astrologer Angela Pearl Curtis used the noted ancient Chaldean system of numerology, attributed to astrologer Zoroaster (parts of which were incorporated into the rituals of the occult Order of the Golden Dawn), in the following analysis of the Brontë family. She believes this gives a truer picture of the individual's character than other numerological systems. Note that this system gives a numerical value for each letter of the alphabet, but there is no number nine included. This is because the ancient wise ones believed number nine to represent the nine-lettered name of GOD and out of respect, no single letter was ever ascribed to it.

Numerical Alphabet:

A – 1	H – 5	O – 7	V– 6
B – 2	I – 1	P – 8	W – 6
C – 3	J – 1	Q – 1	X – 5
D – 4	K – 2	R – 2	Y – 1
E – 5	L – 3	S – 3	Z – 7
F – 8	M – 4	T – 4	
G – 3	N – 5	U – 6	

Now let us see how to find the compound number of a name. For example:

CHARLOTTE BRONTË
351237445 227545

The letters in Charlotte add up to 34:

3 + 4 = 7

The letters in Brontë add up to 25:

2 + 5 = 7
7 + 7 = 14

Thus, the compound number of the name Charlotte Brontë is 14. In a similar fashion, the Compound Birth Number is obtained by adding together each digit in the numerical birthdate. This is what the ancient Chaldean system had to say about each member of the Brontë family:

Charlotte Brontë, born 21 April 1816

Compound name number 14 – Movement – Challenge.

The number fourteen is associated with change and a strong connection with the public. This person will gain success in all matters concerned with writing, publishing and anything media related. There will be many changes of occupation and any kind of partnership usually works to this person's advantage. Gambling and speculation can bring this person much luck; also, foreign travel, especially connected to persons abroad will be beneficial. This individual's fortune may be somewhat changeable, thus instability is never far from the door. Fourteen warns of danger from accidents due to nature's elements – fire, flood, and earthquake – and not to rely too heavily on the word of false prophets. This person must be self-contained and learn to develop their intuition and judgement. Fourteen brings luck in money matters and a degree of self-confidence.

Compound birth number 23 – The Royal Star of the Lion.

This – obtained by adding the digits in 21/4/1816 - is one of the most fortunate numbers of karmic reward. It promises success in career and personal endeavours. People in high places will be a helpful and protective influence on the life of twenty-three. This person has been greatly blessed, not only with grace but also with good luck.

Birthdate

Twenty-one – this was known as 'The Crown of Magi' by the ancient Chaldeans, a number of advancement, honours and elevation in life and in career. It indicates victory after a long fight, for the 'Crown of the Magi' is only gained after lengthy initiation and tests of determination.

Branwell Brontë born 26 June 1817

Compound name number – 16 – The Shattered Citadel.

This number warns of a strange fatality, danger from accidents and failed plans. To avoid the fatalistic tendency of this number, where possible, careful plans should be made well in advance. This person will often desperately seek out positions of power and leadership. However, seeking happiness in other ways, i.e. renouncing fame and celebrity status, will do much to lessen the negative vibration of this number.

Compound birth number 31 – The Recluse – The Hermit.

Genius or high intelligence is often present in persons under the influence of this number. Here is an individual who cannot help but feel separate from the crowd – eventually leading to a degree of withdrawal from society. The thirty-one ruled person is very often opinionated and can be an advocate of political change. This person will always feel like a stranger in his own world always on the outside looking in even when in the company of his closest family and friends.

Birthdate

Twenty-six – brings the gravest warnings for the future. It foreshadows disasters brought about by association with others, and ruin by bad speculations – such as unsuitable partnerships and unions, or acting on inferior advice.

    Poor old Branwell Brontë never stood a chance! According to his friend Francis Grundy, Branwell was fond of visiting soothsayers and crystal gazers – perhaps to get a more favourable forecast!

Emily Brontë, born 30 July 1818

Compound name number 12 – The Sacrifice – The Victim.

There is a need to be continually on the lookout for intrigue. The number twelve warns of false friends and flattery. This individual will suffer a high degree of mental stress and anxiety, caused by sacrificing their own needs, to cater for others.

    Twelve also represents education – the teacher and the student. This person has the willpower necessary to achieve a high level of success and gain knowledge on both intellectual and spiritual levels. This type of person will sacrifice their emotional nature in order to find the answer they seek – with or without their peers' approval.

Compound birth number 10 – The Wheel of Fortune.

Ten is a number of rise and fall according to personal desire. This person's will arouses extreme responses in others – there is no middle ground. A strong willed character who will self-determine every event in their personal life. Through the power of their extraordinary will, they have the ability to bring creative concepts into reality. However, this gift must be used wisely, since, if misused, it can easily wreak destruction upon itself. Ten is a number of honour, faith and self-confidence.

Birthdate

Thirty – Emily's powers of mental superiority over her fellows. Thirty is a number of thoughtful deduction and retrospection but seems to belong completely to the mental plane. Any person the number thirty represents is likely to put all material things to one side, not because they have to but because they wish to. For this reason it is neither fortunate nor unfortunate, for either depends upon the person the number represents. It can be all-powerful but it is just as often indifferent, according to the will or desire of the person. This person can count few people as friends. They tend to be taciturn loners. Social functions and gatherings are not their forte. Fulfilment is found more often in retreating from the chaos of the market place so that one's mental superiority may be used to develop something worthwhile to the world either to write ideas, which may change the world, or to protect and develop one's personal talents. It indicates a lonely yet frequently rewarding life pattern.

Anne Brontë, born 17 January 1820

Compound name number 14 – Movement – Challenge

Refer to Charlotte Brontë.

Compound birth number 20 – The Awakening or Judgement.

At some time in the life of this person there will be a powerful awakening, bringing ambition, new plans and strong purpose. This is someone who will strive for some ideal or cause – in Anne's case, this was her religious faith, which saw her through difficult times. Obstacles and delays to this person's plans can be frustrating but patience and tolerance will help develop character. The number twenty brings with it vivid dreams and pre-cognitive ability. This is someone who can transform his or her life through positive thinking. Persons under the number ten vibration, seldom care about money as long as they have enough to provide the basic necessities of life.

Birthdate

Seventeen – Those born on the seventeenth of any month like Anne and her father Patrick are destined to be superior in spirit to the trials and difficulties of life and career. This number was called 'the Star of the Magi' a highly spiritual number – the image of peace and love. It is considered a number of immortality, ensuring that in one way or another the person's name will live on after them.

Patrick Brontë, born St. Patrick's Day – 17 March 1777

Compound name number 35

This number has the exact same meaning as Branwell's birthdate number twenty-six.

Compound birth number 33 – Love – Money – Creativity.

A kind number, giving karmic reward. Anyone with this number will find assistance comes easily from those better placed in society. The number thirty-three greatly helps facilitate financial success. There will be gains through love, the law or arts. This individual is highly charismatic and finds it easy to attract the opposite sex. The only negative aspect of this vibration is that it sometimes brings with it a tendency towards overindulgence, combined with arrogance. Good things appear to come effortlessly to this individual.

Birthdate

Seventeen – please refer to Anne Brontë for this birthdate.

Note: Angela Pearl points out that when exploring family histories it seems strange how frequently identical numbers seem to keep cropping up. She feels that the Brontës were destined to be together as a family unit in that particular lifetime. This may be an indication of Karma working itself out through a genetic line.

Such Charms

In *Wuthering Heights,* Emily Brontë demonstrates her personal knowledge of the occult, writing, 'This bed is the fairy bed under Peniston Crag (Ponden Kirk) and you are gathering elf bolts to hurt our heifers ... Nelly you witch! So you do seek elf bolts to hurt us.' The enchanted fairy cave she spoke of was the trysting place of ill-starred Cathy and Heathcliff, the elf-bolts the fictional Cathy describes are actually Neolithic arrowheads fashioned from flint, which were seen as magic weapons employed by fairies to kill or wound cattle. If one was found in a live beast, the arrow was immediately removed and plunged into water, which was then given to the animal to drink as an antidote to the evil charm.

Wizards such as John Wrightson of Stokesby, Yorkshire in 1820 employed spells such as this against elf-bolts in farm animals, 'A sheep's heart is stuck with nine new pins, nine new needles, nine small nails and roasted on a good fire of coals and ash sticks ... should this fail you need go to no one else as they will not nor can they cure your beast.' A beast's heart such as the one described was retrieved from a house in Starkie Street, Keighley some years ago. Another cure was a pagan recipe named Lacnunga, 'If a horse be elf-shot, then take a knife of which the haft is horn of a fallow ox, and on which are three brass nails, then write upon the horses forehead Christ's mark, and on each of the limbs which thou may feel at: then take the left ear, prick a hole in it in silence, this done thou shalt do, thou shalt take a yard, and write upon the horn of the knife these words, Benedicit omnis opera domine dominum. Be the elf what it may, this is mighty for him to attend.'

Superstitious folk wore these arrowheads on silver mounts, as amulets to ward off evil spirits and protect themselves against illness and plague. The Brontë children, when out rambling on the moors, often searched for elf-bolts.

Common vexations for medieval farmers were witches drawing milk from cows and demons possessing livestock. Wrapped in a piece of thonged leather, a spell, known as the *LEES WITCH SPELL* was found nailed to a beam in the cow house at Lees Farm. It was written in copperplate characters inscribed on faded blue paper, quoting the sixth verse of *Psalm vii v. 6* thus, 'Arise, O Lord, in Thine anger, lift up thyself because of the rage of mine enemies, and awake for me to the judgement that Thou has commanded. Lo, shall the congregation of the people compass thee about for their sakes therefore return thou on high. The Lord shall judge the people, judge me O Lord according to mine...'

The credulous farmer believed that the charm was powerful enough to drive away any lurking witches or demons from his livestock. Numerous other parchment spells came to light after a search was made of the thatch and cracks in the walls here. Another spell was discovered, tucked away in the back of an old Bible, belonging to the late Brontë scholar Jonas Bradley of Stanbury, which found its way to Keighley Library after his death. An enclosed note stated that a Mr Drake of Northbrook Terrace, Leeds, had given the charm to Mr Bradley on 10 June 1912. It was entitled *THE WITCH SPELL AT BORTON* – 'When Borton sat on a marble stone near the gates of Jerusalem. Jesus said unto him what troubleth thee O Borton? He answered and said I am troubled with the toothache. Jesus said Arise and follow me, and thou shalt be healed of thy pain, and not thou only but everyone that shall carry these lines for my sake.' Perhaps the need for such charms was well founded, for there is a story that soon after Scar Top Chapel near Stanbury was erected in 1869, a witch's coven was established close by, in competition. The secret location was somewhere near Upper Heights Farm. Keighley Corporation later commandeered this farm during the Smallpox epidemic of 1913. It had room for two nurses, one ward each for male and female patients, a disinfecting room and an ambulance shed.

Many examples of charms can still be seen around Bradford. The cross of St. Andrew is often embossed upon the wooden beam across a fireplace, to stop witches from entering the room via the chimney! Adder-stones or witch-stones, as they were sometimes known, have natural holes in them and were frequently tied with string, before being suspended from the rafters, to ward off witches. A fine example of such a stone is on view at Keighley's Cliffe Castle Museum, having hung for many years in Keighley's old market place – to prevent fairies from stealing produce. These large pebbles were often attached to the key of a door or dangled on a bed pole, to keep the occupant safe from burglars (holy water was also employed to ward off thieves) and nightmares.

A wax sealed spell, more than two centuries old, was secreted in a wall of a barn at seventeenth-century Hill End Farm, Harden. At Cliffe Castle Museum, there is a charm which was written to keep Samuel Lund from 'Evil Spirits, from witchcraft and fore-speaking and blasting and the cramps x all Diseases whatsoever in the name of the Father, and of the Son and of the Holy Ghost Bless Thee Samuel Lund be Thou whole and guarded by the Angels of God...' A counter charm employed to safeguard a person against evil spells was to carry a written parchment with the words, *Alpha, omega,* IESVM BERONIKH.

Black luggie, hammer head,
Rowan tree, and red thread.
Put the warlocks to their speed.

Old English Charm.

194

Rowan or mountain ash is at its most potent when gathered on St. Helena's Day (18 August). Helena was said to have discovered the true wooden cross on which Jesus died. The Pagans believe the rowan to be a holy tree.

Two rowan trees grew in the parsonage garden throughout the Brontë era, according to Sydney Biddell in 1879. This wood also makes an excellent rod for dowsing. A Haworth water-diviner found himself under attack in 1890, because he failed to find enough water to feed an underground stream.

On the birth of a Yorkshire baby, visitors were expected to bring three gifts: an egg, a piece of silver and a pinch of salt. The child was not to be carried downstairs when a caller arrived, as this would give it a bad start in life and its finger nails must be bitten with teeth not cut with scissors for iron was closely connected to witchcraft.

Once superstition reigned supreme in Yorkshire ... wizards and white witches were common in every village and the natives did little without consulting some occult practitioner.

Fairytales

West Yorkshire has more than its fair share of elemental fairy tales, especially in the towns and villages around Haworth. Mrs Jane Thompson of Sutton who was born in 1819, spoke of seeing a fairy dressed in a bright red coat and black hat (just like Charlotte Brontë's gypsy/witch attire in *Jane Eyre*), when out walking with a companion on Ravenstone Moor. Nudging her friend she said, "Oh, look, there's a fairy!"

The girls knew that elves, goblins, flibbertigibbets and fairies haunted wells, ponds and groups of stones and that spirits roamed the countryside. Remembering their mothers' dire warnings about fairies, elves or boggards stealing children, they ran home as fast as they could.

Grove Hill Dike, high above Sladen Valley reservoir, not far from Tom Stell's seat, was once feared by local children, whose parents warned them that a frightful boggard, which devoured both man and beast alike had made its home there, in the dark, deep waters. Emily Brontë knew of this tale. She re-named the Dike 'Blackhorse Marsh' in *Wuthering Heights*.

At Blackhill, Keighley, and Priesthorpe, Bingley there are two wells named after Jennet, the Queen of Fairies. The little folk played music and hung out their washing at Deep Cliff in Harden Valley. Brontë servant Tabby swore her own mother had seen fairies, adding that they had been driven away by the hustle and bustle of the Industrial Revolution.

Local author Halliwell Sutcliffe, a friend of Sir Arthur Conan Doyle, assured him that fairies had befriended a schoolmaster acquaintance of his. Boys who put on their first pair of long trousers were nipped by their parents to make sure elementals had not changed them. This reminds one of a case in Ireland in 1898 when a husband claimed he had burned his wife because fairies had swapped her!

In his book *Through Airedale from Goole to Malham*, 1891, Harry Speight (alias Johnnie Grey) tells a queer tale about a holed stone, which used to hang in old Keighley Market, employed to keep unwanted fairies away:

195

'If we go back to the early years of the last century,' (1700s) 'superstition and witchery, and all sorts of odd and out-of-the-way beliefs were, in rural districts especially, all prevalent. An ancestress of the writer's, and a native of Craven, relates a wonderful story of an aunt of hers, who was living not so many miles away from Keighley in the early part of this century (1800s), when this event happened, the story of which has been handed down as a perfectly true authenticated account of the existence of fairies at that time, indeed so circumstantially were the facts always narrated, that none of the family dared ever doubt them. This aunt, who lived in a somewhat remote country district, occasionally acted as midwife, and late one very dark night a faint knock summoned her to the door, when she found a surprisingly little grey man on a little grey pony who plaintively asked her to follow him.

Putting on her bonnet and shawl she followed, and by-and-by was led under some cliffs to a small cave, which they entered, and then they passed into an inner chamber where she found several beautiful fairies in attendance. At first, she felt rather afraid, but the pleasant smiles and actions of the sprightly little beings soon put her at her ease. When the child was born, a little feather and bottle were given to her with which to annoint the infant's eyes, and wondering what the effect would be, the woman, like a true daughter of Eve, slyly brushed the feather across her own eyes, when she instantly saw the apartment quite filled with fairies! It happened, however, that her action was not observed, and the little grey man soon saw her safe home again, rewarding her well for her services. Some weeks afterwards the midwife happened to be in Keighley market, when she observed the little grey man going about taking handfuls of corn, &co., out of the open sacks! She was the more surprised as no one appeared to notice the theft. But she went up to the fairy and asked him how he was and how his wife and baby were. The grey man looked puzzled, but answered they were well, adding "but which eye do you see me with?" She touched the eye, for she thought it best to be truthful, having a wholesome fear of the power of the little people.

The little man instantly blew into her eye, and she saw him no more – the fairy power of sight was lost! The same matronly individual always declared that she knew from her own personal experience that fairies were not imaginary beings, for she had *seen* their clothes laid on the heather to dry, very much like the clothes worn by ordinary mortals, only remarkably small and white, proving too that little folk had washing days! Perhaps after all, she was one of those fated beings who are said to be gifted with second-sight. It used to be a common belief that children born during the hour of midnight possessed through life the strange power of being able to see the spirits of the departed. The fairies, of course, preferred this uncanny hour of birth; ordinary folk, however were generally very anxious to avoid such a calamity befalling their little ones.'

Sir Arthur Conan Doyle (a notable Freemason) said "You must believe in fairies to be able to see them." Well, there are many folk who continue to believe in the famous Cottingley fairies. When Elsie Hill (nee Wright) – one of the girls who took the world-famous fairy photographs in 1917, reached the age of eighty-two she decided she did not want her experiences with little folk to cause anyone to meddle with spiritualism, which she viewed as being highly dangerous. She therefore claimed that the whole fairy thing had been a hoax and that the photo-

Fairies and demons *(The Yorkshireman)*

graphs were faked – just cutout fairies stuck into the ground with hatpins. However, Doyle submitted the negatives to Kodak and experts there had failed to find evidence of any tampering with the original sealed glass photographic plates.

In 1921, Mr Geoffrey Hodson, a psychic clairvoyant visited Elsie's home at Lynwood Terrace, Cottingley near Bingley. He spent some hours wandering the Cottingley Glen, which he claimed was rife with semi-transparent fairies and other types of elemental beings. Mrs Rose Hallem, a childhood friend of Elsie's was always convinced that fairies lived in the Fairy Dell, stripped bare of its trees in 1935 without explanation.

After many years, Francis, Elsie's cousin, finally broke her silence, agreeing with Elsie that all the fairy pictures they had taken together were faked *except* the last of a set of three taken in 1920, which she insisted was absolutely genuine! In 1971, Kodak's curator Mr Brian Coe re-examined the Cottingley pictures, but was unable to shed any further light on the matter. In 1985, some of the lost "fairy" negatives turned up after the death of Mr Rider, one of the girl's uncles. A neighbour of his, a Mrs Mavis Davey of Bolton Road, Bradford, took them to the National Museum of Photography who, after examination, claimed they *had* been tampered with. We shall probably never know now whether the two girls managed to stage an elaborate hoax that was skilful enough to fool the inventor of *Sherlock Holmes* and several Kodak experts, or if they truly did play with nature sprites at the bottom of their garden ...

It was in the early twenties that photographer Dot Inman (a friend of Elsie's), of Manningham Photographic Studios took a photograph of the sun in Bradford's Lister Park. Taking the film home, she developed it in a biscuit tin that same evening. Lo and behold...there were fairies on the photographic plate! Ms Inman never revealed how she got her picture and she refused to part with the negative, even though she had been offered a great deal of money for it. A few years ago, a little girl playing in Lister Park, ran home to tell her family she had seen fairies there, but of course no one believed her.

Another Cottingley resident, woodman Ronnie Bennett of Beckfield Road, knew fairies existed because he saw three of them in Cottingley Glen. He described them as being "ten-inch high, elf-like figures", moving easily amongst the greenery. Catching sight of him, the little folk stopped and stared back at him for a few moments through the fine showery rain.

The gates at Cottingley Manor House remind us of Cottingley's fairy connection, whilst the local Conservative Club assumed the gnome as their official emblem. Stone circle expert, Paul Bennet of Hebden Bridge, told me that he had stumbled across a cup and ring stone in the Glen, similar to those on Rombold's Moor.

An early nineteenth-century fairy tale connected to White Wells, Ilkley, stated that the bath-keeper, William Butterfield, was unable to open the bathhouse door early one summer's morning. Each time he tried, it was quickly pushed back, until he gave an almighty shove. On entering, Butterfield was astonished to see lots of excited little creatures, none of them taller than eighteen inches high, dressed from tip to toe in forest green, playing around the glistening spring water and making a whirring sound. As soon as William made a sound, they all scurried off like squirrels "tumbling head-over-heals".

A former tenant of White Wells, Mrs Barbara Lister, said in 1977, that living there was like living at Wuthering Heights. The track at the rear of White Wells leads close to the Backstone Circle and on to the Bronze Age Twelve Apostle stone circle near the summit of Ilkley Moor. This is a place well known for UFO sightings and fairies dancing within the circle. There is also a legendary tale of "Owd Nick" sending out his demons from here, to harvest newly dead souls for hell. Several members of the Royal Observer Corps reported a strange white light hovering directly above the circle, late one evening in 1976. In 1990, a ball of brilliant white light was spotted floating above the stones before vanishing into thin air ...

At a meeting held at Leeds University in 1963, by the Society for Folk Life Studies, it was suggested that fairies might descend to earth in flying saucers!

I myself have a vivid memory of lying in bed as a child on the night of a full Harvest moon, watching the antics of several fairies dancing on top of the cot rail before drifting off to sleep. One must remember that should the moon peep into a child's bedroom window at night, tradition says. that to avert harm, the child must be taught the following rhyme:

I see the moon,
The moon sees me.
God Bless the Priest
That christened me.

Traditionally Wednesday is the fairies' Sabbath day – my lucky day!

Postscript

Allan, resident Tarot reader, dowser and teacher of psychometry at Spooks of Haworth *(Marie Campbell)*

Have you ever noticed just how many dragon icons appear in West Yorkshire towns, including Haworth and Ilkley Parish Church, on the ground outside Leeds Market and in Keighley – where dragons guard the entrance to the railway station. This town boasts a splendid modern Dragon, which can be seen on the ground at the end of North Street, between Whitegates Estate Agents and the Parish Church.

Spooks of Haworth opened in May 1983, and can be found at 22 Main Street, where one can discover how to calculate a birth chart, or visit modern day Tarot readers. The proprietor, Stan, is friendly and the shop well stocked with all manner of psychic material.

Allan, the shop's resident Tarot reader, dowser and teacher of psychometry, has been a devotee of Wicca for many years, but prefers not to call himself a Witch or Shaman. He simply follows the main creed of the Craft and likes to look after nature, follow his own ideals and beliefs, and help others, if he can. "Now and again", Allan says "it involves a little bit of ritual, perhaps a couple of spells, but mainly it is working with the good side." His staff, given to him by a friend many years ago, is fashioned from mountain ash (very good for dowsing), grown in a Welsh forest, and is bound with natural hand-spun dyed wool. At the end is the tip of a stag's horn. "It's much better to make your own tools, as you put a bit of yourself into it", explained Allan.

On the subject of local hauntings, Allan told me a spooky story, which occurred when the Rotary Club invited both him and the owner of *Spooks*, to give a talk on ghosts at the Old Hall. They decided that they should lead a party of strapping rugby players up the cobbled thoroughfare of Main Street, having first explained what to look out for – for example cold spots, etc. This they did, stopping and starting all the way up the hill, until they reached the old cemetery, when suddenly one of their number got the jitters. Allan asked what was wrong. Pointing to a flat stone the man said, "I don't know what's happening, but it's trying to suck me in." Allan immediately went over to the gravestone, took out his pendulum and settled "it" down by putting "it" back to sleep. Motioning the frightened rugby player over he shouted, "Come and try it now." "Not blooming likely," came back the reply. "Come and try it." Allan insisted. Gingerly the frightened fellow went over and was relieved to find the "thing" had gone. Allan explained that something had been disturbed. He thought a spirit had latched onto the man, simply because he was sensitive to such things. I asked if he had taken note of the name on the grave but Allan said that since it was a moonless night, it was too dark to see whose name the gravestone bore.

8 | *Strange Ways*

There are many rites and rituals associated with Brontë-land. One of these was the ancient custom of ringing what was known as the Soul or Passing-bell at the close of day, whenever there was a death in the Worth Valley area. This curious ceremony, which ended around 1740, was performed in order to guide the newly departed soul safely heavenwards. The doleful sound of the death-knoll was slowly tolled, in the hope of frightening away any lurking demons that might be waiting to steal the spirit. Taken from an ancient manuscript, the formula for the passing ceremony was as follows:

> After the time of his passinge,
> To ringe no more,
> But one shorte peal,
> A one before and after the buriall.
> On the departure of a soul,
> At dead of night the bell to toll.

The peals of the bell were also designed to denote the deceased's sex – twice for a woman, thrice for a man.

Halliwell Sutcliffe described the faith Worth Valley folk had in this quaint custom, in his book *Shameless Wayne:* 'The little old woman sat up in the belfry tower, knitting a woollen stocking, and tolling the death-bell with her foot. She took two and seventy stitches between each stroke of the bell, and not the church-clock itself could reckon a minute more truly. Sharp of face she was, the Sexton's wife, and her lips were forever moving in time to the click of her knitting needles. "By th' Heart, 'tis little care his wife hed for him," she muttered presently. "Nobbut a poor half-hour o' the bell, an' him wi' a lang, cold journey afore him. Does she think a man's soul can racket up to Heaven at that speed? What will 'ull he do when he gets to th' Gate an' th' bell has stopped tolling, an' there's no Christian music to waft him in? Well, I've a'most done wi' th' ringing – save I war to gi'e him another half-hour for nought."

"What art doing Nanny? The bell has been silent these five minutes past," cried the girl ... how little she seemed to care aught save for such matters as concerned her father, whose body was lying cold and stiff in an oak-lined hall at Marsh, whose soul was journeying wearily toward an insubstantial Heaven. Yet the superstition of her folk held her, and the bell's silence was a horror near akin to crime, since it robbed the dead man of whatever cheer the next world held. The Sexton's wife said nothing at all, but took up her knitting and slid her foot into the loop of the bell-rope ... "Better talk to a body dearie, 'twill drive th' devils out," she said.'

*   *   *   *

A Haworth working man may have been partly responsible for ending the old custom of bell ringing in Brontëland. One October night, James Lee – a chimney sweep, was in the midst of a group of revellers at the Dog and Gun, Oxenhope, when he suddenly fell from his seat. They thought he must be dead and the flow of ale and chatter along with the clatter of tankards silenced, as the sweep was examined. Not fond of being poked and prodded, Lee was soon upon his feet. The jape caused much merriment and ale flowed freely once more. The joke was such a good one that Lee and his intoxicated friends hatched a cunning plan.

Urgent cries of "Oh David, David; James Lee's dead!" roused the elderly church sexton from his slumbers. "Dead," quoth the sexton, "how can it be? I talked with him but yesterday". Getting out of his nice warm bed by the light of a candle, the arthritic sexton shuffled uncertainly down a dark winding path towards the church. Shadows rose and then fell from his light, as he wearily climbed the narrow stairwell up to the tower, before going through a creaking oak door into the belfry. Somewhere in the distance an owl hooted and a lone dog howled. On the stroke of two, the Passing-bell tolled out its dreary tidings across the valley.

Meanwhile, James Lee stealthily and quietly mounted the stairs. After reaching the top, he put his grimy, sooty head into the room and in a hollow tone of voice asked the old sexton "I pray thee David who is dead?" 'Old David', not known for observing pious devotion in any form, sank to his knees crying, "Good heaven! What do I see?" Gawping at the sweep, he managed to stammer, "Art thou alive?" "Aye, and healthy too," Lee replied, "Art thou a ghost?" he asked, "Nor spirit risen from the dead?" The sweep offered his hand to prove he was flesh and blood. "T'is v-v-very cold", 'Old David' said, still on his knees. From that time onwards, the sexton refused to ring the Passing-bell after the stroke of midnight.

*   *   *   *

In the days when it was safe to leave house doors open, there was a custom among Yorkshire folk that when a family member was buried, the front door must not be barred for several successive nights. This was because the departed spirit might have felt it had been locked out of its old home. I wonder if Patrick Brontë left the door open at the parsonage?

> When winds were loud and snow lay white,
> And storm clouds drifted black,
> I've heard his step – for heart can hear;
> I know he's coming back.
> What if he comes this very night,
> And the house-door he tried,
> And found that we had turned the key,
> And our bairn outside!
> The good man trimmed the candle light,
> Threw on another log,
> Then suddenly, he said: "Good wife!
> What ails – what ails the dog?
> And what ails you? What do you hear?
> She raised her eyes and cried:

Wide open fling the house-door now,
For my bairn's outside!

Joseph Horsfall Turner, *Yorkshire Folk Lore, 1880*

From an old song sung in Bradford's Market Place by ballad singers in the 1890s, comes this chorus:

Then, young man, think how awful,
'Tis in a gloomy cell to lie,
And to know the day and hour
And the moment you must die.

It was customary for mourners to carry a sprig of Rosemary, to ward off infection from the copse, when following a coffin to the graveside. Once the coffin had been lowered down into its bed of earth, the sprigs were thrown in after it.

A Handful of Pleasant Delites

Rosemary is for remembrance,
Between us daie and night,
Wishing that I might always have,
You present in my sight.

Clement Robinson, 1584.

An anonymous writer to the *Athenaeum* told of yet another odd Yorkshire country practice: 'I can tell you of a fancy that some people have in the wilder parts of Craven, that the mark of a dead person (the body, however, not being cold) being put in a will, is valid in law. A few years ago a case of this nature occurred. A farmer had omitted to make his will; he died, and, before the body was cold, a will was prepared by some relative (of course in his own favour), and a mark, purporting to be that of the deceased, was made by putting the pen in the hand of a dead man, and so making his mark on the will. The body of the man was not then cold. The will was contested by some parties, and, I believe, proceeded to trial at law, when the circumstance of the belief of the parties came out in evidence.'

The children's game of hopscotch is derived from a religious rite once practised at funerals to symbolise the passing of a soul to heaven. The custom dated back to Roman times.

An old Haworth resident writing to the *Keighley News* on the16 May 1964, explained that the saying, "Aye, he has all his chairs at home" came from a mourning ritual. Most folk did not have enough chairs to seat all the guests at a funeral tea, so they often borrowed from neighbours who had "all their chairs at home" – meaning they were well off and had the benefit of a fully furnished house.

Posset was once a popular choice of funeral fare. An eighteenth-century cook's recipe for this dish was to blanch and beat three-quarters of a pound of almonds so fine that they spread betwixt fingers like butter. Put in water as you beat. Take a pint of sack, cherry or gooseberry wine, and sweeten it to your taste with double refined sugar, make it boiling hot. Take the almonds, put to them a little water, and boil the wine and almonds together. Take the yolks of four eggs, and beat them very well, put to them three or four spoonfuls of wine. Then put it into your pan by degrees, stirring it all the while; when it begins to thicken take it off, and stir it a little, put it in a china dish, and serve it up.

Throughout the Victorian era, a funeral tea usually consisted of sponge biscuits and homemade wine. Guests receiving a card bidding them to attend the funeral were charged a shilling (5p) if they failed to put in an appearance, whether they knew the deceased or not!

Bradford's Primitive Methodists worshipped at Manchester Road Chapel. Their burial ground was still in use when a decision was made to tear it up, in order to extend the nearby Methodist School. The sepulchres were ruthlessly desecrated, coffins were sliced in half by workmen's pickaxes and the dead were dragged from their silent tombs. Skeletons and bodies were tossed and shovelled into one stinking heap and re-buried in a large communal pit.

One shocked observer said, "In at least one case...the bones were reviled, for a person who certainly ought to have known better actually went so far as to kneel in mock prayer over one poor skull, and after making hideous fun of it proceeded to smash it to atoms by dashing a huge stone upon it ... It is a disgrace to the town. That respect which every right-feeling man has for the dead, that reverence for the ashes of our ancestors which holds almost a religious, certainly a sacred, place with us, has been rudely, and I cannot but think illegally violated."

The Grave

Se yonder hallow'd fane; – the pious work
Of names once fam'd now dubious or forgot,
And bury'd'midst the wreak of things which were;
There lie interr'd the more illustrious dead.
The wind is up-hark! How it howls! Methinks
Till now I never heard a sound so dreary;
Doors creak, and windows clap, and night's foul birds
Rook's in the spire, screams loud: the gloomy ailes
Black plaster'd, and hung round with shreds of 'scutcheon
And tatter'd coats of arms, send back the sound
Laden with heavier airs, from the low vaults,
The mansions of the dead. – Rous'd from their slumber
In grim array the grisly spectres rise,
Grim, horrible, and obstinately sullen,
Pass and repass, hush'd as the foot of night.
Again the screech-owl shrieks: ungracious sound!
I'll hear no more; it makes one's blood run chill.

Robert Blair, 1818.

Time-Honoured Traditions

In medieval times, it was usual on the eve of a patron saint's festival, or on the day of a church's consecration, for the populace to collect freshly cut rushes and sweet herbs to spread upon the mud floor of the church. Rushbearing was practised with great reverence, for this was when Yorkshire and Lancashire folk held a feast, in readiness for the onset of winter. Haworth people dressed their carts with gaily-coloured garlands of flowers, flags and ribbons and the women prepared special puddings for their Tide Feast. After the floor of little Haworth church was paved over, this age-old observance was abandoned.

When the Rushbearing service was revived at Haworth, during the nineteenth century, not one person could actually remember the last one. The oldest worshipper amongst them stated he had heard his grandmother say that when she was very young, the floors of the Old Hall – a relic from the De Lacie family, whose lands stretched from Haworth to Doncaster, was spread with rushes and sweet herbs. After yet another lapse, the Rushbearing service was restored again in 1955, at St. Michael's and All Angels' Church, where it is still practised. The only original feature of the ceremony that remains today, is children carrying sheaves of rushes collected from the moors into the church.

* * * *

July of 1867 brought hundreds of Bradford folk to Haworth's Tide, by way of the newly opened Worth Valley line. Keighley's bellman was there to greet them, decked out in his smart uniform, topped with a stylish, feathered, cocked hat. The old churchyard was packed for most of the day with folk showing off their best finery, which for some reason caused a newspaper correspondent to comment, "The effect was not pleasing to the eye." At the end of the church service the crowd lustily sang the hymn *Blessed be God the Father*, by John Wesley.

As the day proceeded, several teetotal advocates from the Temperance Society took advantage of the crowds in Main Street to expound upon the evils of liquor, but in the midst of the sermon a sudden heavy downpour of rain caused the multitudes to seek immediate asylum – where? In the nearest tavern of course!

In preparation for the Haworth Feast, the women of the village banded together to share the task of pudding making. One year, they received a message that a body had been dragged from a nearby reservoir and that the condition of the bloated corpse indicated it had been in the water for several days. Since the feast puddings had been boiled in the same water that the decomposing body had lain in, they were tossed into the midden, condemned as not even fit for consumption by pigs. This was the first time the Rushbearing celebrations went pudding-less. It seems Haworth lost its taste for feast pudding after this unsavoury episode and the famous tradition of feast pudding making died out.

After Rushbearing Sunday, came riotous Cromor Monday, a description of which was noted down by preacher Oliver Heywood, in 1680:

> 'Their Tyde (as they call it) on which multitudes of people meet, feast, drink, and commit many outrages in revellings, in rantings, riding without fear of restraint – that Monday which is the day after, they call Cromors day, (Crow Moor?) then they make (horse) races and continue the drinkings, vanitys, it may be longer. Oh, dreadful!'

* * * *

The recipe for Haworth's traditional, but alas forgotten Feast Pudding, was almost lost, until re-discovered in an old local recipe book. In those days village women boiled and then simmered the muslin wrapped puddings for eight to ten hours inside a huge copper pan, before resting them in a warm oven all night. Here are two different versions of the pudding:

Haworth Feast Pudding
8oz (250g) flour or Barley Meal
8oz (250g) suet
8oz (250g) brown sugar
16oz (500g) raisins and currants and ¼lb (125g) of sultanas
2 eggs
1oz (30g) candied peel
8oz (250g) breadcrumbs
¼ teaspoon of salt
Pinch of cinnamon

Put all the dry ingredients into a large bowl. Add milk and eggs to moisten. Mix the whole together until the mixture is stiff. Steam slowly for four to six hours in a muslin cloth. Then leave in the bottom of a warm oven overnight before serving.

The second recipe has been adapted for modern day cooks by Susan Brookes after a plea from the author to Yorkshire Television's *Tonight Programme*. Mrs Susan Jones of Baildon, West Yorkshire kindly sent in the following recipe, which is enough for six servings:

Haworth Feast/Plum Pudding
12oz (325g) of old bread cutting off the crusty bits
4oz (125g) raisins
1 fresh egg
2oz (25g) mixed peel and 2oz sugar
4oz (125g) grated suet
1 level teaspoon of grated nutmeg or a pinch of cinnamon, whichever you prefer.

Cut bread into square cubes and soak in water until bread swells. Drain off excess liquid before mixing the whole of the ingredients together in a large bowl. Grease a shallow tin, pour in mixture and cover top. Bake in a moderate oven, Gas Mark 4 (350F, 180C) for about one hour. Reduce heat to Gas Mark 1 (275F, 140C) for a further two hours. This dish can be eaten either hot or cold.

* * * *

On the first Sunday in May, there was a long-established custom of visiting 'The Spa' springs on Haworth Moor, some two miles west of Haworth. A party of musicians from Denholme performed sacred music whilst leading a large, enthusiastic crowd to The Spa in 1867.

An old resident, Richard Ratcliffe had performed the age-old ritual of letting in the Christmas and the New Year regularly at his house for twenty-two years in succession. No other person was allowed to enter the house until Dick had made the traditional entry and conveyed an expression of good wishes.

On 31 October each year, the festival of All Hallow's Eve or Nutcrack Night – a remnant of pagan times – is still observed today. Traditionally, this is the night when witches and ghosts walk the earth.

It was once common practice to sit around the fire with friends at this time, to crack nuts, bob apples and whisper dark tales. According to Brand's *Popular Antiquities*, young maidens in Ireland (whence the Brontë clan originated), wishing to know if their intended would be true, laid nuts upon the bars of a fire grate. Naming one nut after herself and the other after her lover, she would wait in anticipation to see if the nut jumped or cracked; if so, he could not be trusted, but if it burned, he liked her. If both nuts burned, the pair would exchange wedding vows.

Herbal Health

Moor dwellers possessed an intimate knowledge of herbal remedies and their virtues. They substituted various concoctions of 'simples' (herbs) for the rich man's cocoa, coffee and tea. Amongst the herbs employed as remedies were betony, agrimony, gentian, ground ivy, nettles, passion docks and dandelion leaves.

According to Halliwell Sutcliffe, alternative treatments for ill health consisted of many weird and wonderful potions. Imagine giving a child with whooping cough a lightly grilled mouse or mouse pie to eat! Sutcliffe himself vouched for a tried and tested cure for gout, which was to place a fresh trout over the affected part of the foot. This fish had other uses too, for a trout pulled alive from flowing water was supposed to help stave off consumption. The patient had to 'put his lips to the mouth of the fish, and draw in its breath as it gasped for air'; if this remedy failed, then the sufferer was sure to die. A repugnant solution for a sore mouth was to pop a live frog in and then draw it out slowly by its legs!

Billy Lambert, *alias* 'Billy Boy', lived out his days in a tumbledown two-storey cottage at Ponden Brig, a stone's throw from Ponden Mill. Frugal Billy had green fingers and grew the best vegetables and herbs in the area. His highly aromatic pennyroyal or pudding grass, with its tiny lilac flowers was sought by many as a solution to tainted water and was excellent for the treatment of sickness, bruising, hysteria and headaches, amongst other things. *Gerard's Herbal* of 1636 held that a 'garland of Pennie Royall made and worne about the head is of great force against the swimming in the head, and the paines and giddiness thereof'. It also eliminated fleas and insects and helped to 'expell the dead child and afterbirth', according to the herbalist Culpeper.

After testing each recipe, Billy's neighbour – William Heaton, of Rush Isles Farm, Ponden – set down on paper his unusual collection of medicinal recipes for the benefit of mankind, beginning in May 1808. These remedies, collected from such sources as the 'Blue Doctor of Leeds', 'old woman at Field Head near Heptonstall' and 'owd Watson of Ickornshaw' included antidotes for fits, snake-bites and 'a bull that has got the clap'. A sufferer of the 'rheumaticks' was advised to gather eighteen black snails, boil them in a pint of water over a gentle fire, until the lot gelled together; then strain the gunk through a clean white cloth and rub the afflicted part with the salve, each night. William's painless cure for toothache was to take a piece of red hot wire and stick it into the hollow of the affected tooth!

The original book was last seen some twenty years ago (before the days of the modern photocopier), when Keighley historian Dr Ian Dewhirst copied down the recipes in long hand, before returning the book to its keeper. Haworth historian Steven Wood recently identified a photocopied document at Bradford

District Archives as a reproduction of this book. Archivists had found the photo-copy amongst papers on a colleague's desk, after his death. There was no clue to its provenance and the whereabouts of the original book are still unknown. The burning question is: where is William's recipe book now?

Leechdoms & Wortcunning & Starcraft of Early England (published in 1857) argued that a man could be cured of delusions and temptations of the Devil by making an infusion of betony, fennel, lupins and holy water from a church. He must sing "Deus! In nomine tuo salvum me fac" over the mixture, three times, before drinking the liquid. Might this cure have saved poor, mad Branwell Brontë? Somehow, I think not. Haworth ramblers, discussing cures for rheuma-tism, were told of how a Durham witch had advised a fellow walker to take the juice of dandelion in tea, brewed from the whole plant including the roots. Acting on her advice, he claimed he had not suffered from muscular rheuma-tism from that day onwards.

There was a real threat of contracting rabies from mad dogs and cats in the Brontës' day. Emily, having been bitten whilst parting two fighting dogs, hurried into the kitchen, took a red-hot iron and burnt the wound to stop it becoming infected – an action, which may have saved her life.

More than thirty years after the event two men and a boy were badly bitten by a rabid dog in Haworth. The animal was seen again during the evening, at Bridge Bottom, on Lord Lane between Haworth and Oakworth. Here, it encountered a man named Akeroyd. The mad mongrel chased him to Townend, where, despite trying to seek refuge in a doorway, he was bitten. The dog ran off towards Well and West Lanes, stopping only to bite seven-year-old Arthur Howker and savage several other dogs. At 8pm, it ran in and out of two or three cottages on Stubbing Lane and in the process, bit Fred Walker, a young woolsorter. Villagers, running after the demented animal, managed to drive it into a barn at North Ives Farm, near Marsh Lane bottom, where it was shot dead.

The injured parties travelled to a quack doctor at Colne, who had a reputation for dealing with cases of hydrophobia and since there were no reports of any of the victims dying, we must presume the homespun treatment was successful, or that the dog was not rabid at all!

What A Crime!

Old Time Crime

Watch, Ward, and keepe thy Garments tight,
For I come thiefe-like at Midnight.

Wm. Hone, Every Day Book, 1830

An ancient, plain and roughly-built single storey construction, known as the 'Dungeon' stands at White Hill, Oakworth. The exact date of its creation and the Medieval hands that built it remain unknown. The precise location can be seen on old Ordnance maps, in an area just a little beyond Broadhead Lane. This godforsaken place of enforced confinement lies off the beaten track, on the edge of a bleak and windswept moor. The jail must have been a miserable place, when a small fireplace heated only the side housing the Lord of the Manor's turnkey and the sole source of light was a tiny window.

Legend has it that Oliver Cromwell sought shelter here one night, during the terrible days of the Civil War. I am told that the dungeon now forms part of Springfield Boarding Kennels and Cattery.

An anonymous Haworth antique collector friend of Pierrepoint – Britain's last official hangman – acquired a long, thin wooden stick belonging to the latter, after his death in the mid 1970s. Albert Pierrepoint used this weapon on the heads of some of the country's most notorious murderers. Its owner explained to the *Keighley News* in June 1980,

> 'If he felt sorry for his victim, or even got to like them, he'd give 'em a sharp crack on the back of the head with the club so they were either unconscious or already dead when he hanged them. He used to call it his 'nawping stick' – nawp being an old Yorkshire word meaning 'hit'. So he'd get them on the gallows, knock them on the head-and down they went.'

* * * *

Committed at York Assizes on 4 January 1810, fifty-year-old escaped convict Thomas Milner stood charged upon the oath of Keighley men Joseph Sharpe and John Ramsden, some seven years after being sentenced to transportation at Wakefield Assizes. Milner had been caught and arrested in the town long after the advertisement warning of his escape had appeared in the *Hue and Cry* four years previously, on 13 August 1806. The fugitive had run away from a Convict ship, docked at Portsmouth harbour, waiting to set sail on the next tide.

The hour was late when William Cammidge of York was returning to his Haworth lodgings from a business trip to Bradford, on 15 September 1869. Having only reached Keighley by the last train, he was forced to set off on foot for the village. All was well until he neared Ebor House, where he was set upon by a short, stiff-set man, sporting a black beard and moustache, and attired in a round cut coat. The robber demanded Cammidge's cash, while at the same time attempting to seize the gold watch and chain from his waistcoat pocket. Understandably, Mr Cammidge took exception to this and a fight broke out, in which the robber was kicked and beaten to the ground. At this point, an accomplice rose from behind a wall, seizing Cammidge from behind but he too lost his fight. Cammidge limped away leaving the would-be thieves empty handed. *Note:* Robbers, according to old tradition, were always born on the twenty-first day of the moon.

* * * *

In 1864, an Ingrow widow, removing from Paper Mill Bridge, stole another's husband. The pair packed up their respective belongings, piled them onto a cart and left all their children behind, without a single thought other than for themselves. The neighbours, on hearing of the abandoned families' plights, marched the couple almost to Bradford. Some rattled cans, one blew a horn, and others banged kettledrums and blew whistles. This was to let everyone know what a shameful thing the pair had done.

* * * *

On the 8 May 1856, Davy Lambert and Timmy Bancroft, both of Cullingworth, were each fined 5s (25p) plus costs for being drunk in the village, their alternative was to sit in Haworth stocks for six hours. Ellis Hartley of Haworth received the same sentence for an identical crime.

The *Keighley Visitor*, a temperance magazine, published the following warning to landlords in 1858:

> To Drink Sellers
>
> If there is a business on earth in which the candidates for hell are labouring, it is yours, and full well you know it. Were it not a conscience killing business you could not take the last sixpence (2½p) from the trembling hand of the drunkard, and give him in return a poison that, ere the next rising sun, may send him to the tomb. Were it not a demoralising traffic, you could not stand by unmoved, and see the last spark of morality and virtue driven from the mind of a man by the poison you administer. Were it not an infernal business, you would not be so assiduous in serving the devil with victims for his abode of endless misery, for he exults over every drunkard you prepare for the drunkard's doom.
>
> Then cease your business of ruin, ere the cry of humanity ceases, and ere the wrath of angry Heaven be poured out upon your head; for God has announced a "Woe to him who putteth the bottle to his neighbour's lips."
>
> *Watchman of the Valley.*

In January 1859, The *Keighley Visitor* offered a handsome Family Bible as a prize to the first person who could prove that a teetotaller had spent *any* time in the stocks 'since they were set up'. It is not known if the prize was claimed.

*   *   *   *

An amusing photograph of Revd T.W. Story, seated grinning in Haworth's stocks, was taken by Jonas Bradley in 1910. And, Old Tom Parker, a well-known local man who was born in Haworth at about the time of the Franco-Prussian War, could often be found sitting on the old stocks, waiting for his friends to arrive, before repairing to the Liberal Club down the street.

Haworth once boasted its very own ducking pond, situated at Coldshaw, not far from the Old Hall at Sun Street. In 1932, the centuries old well, known fondly as "Ducking Well", which had been devoid of water for many years, was carried away by the Parks Department, to be reinstated in Haworth Central Park. Unfortunately, it seems to have vanished! Thomas Dearden pointed out that "the well, whatever its antiquity...would present very great difficulty in the ducking of any woman of ordinary proportions" and that "it might be necessary to rend the victim to pieces to accomplish the necessary ducking". There is reason to believe that the ducking pond itself was no more than a trough fed by a small stream.

The last 'ducking' at Coldshaw took place in the 1960s, when someone from Keighley's Round Table volunteered to be ducked in a tank specially erected on the site of the old Ducking Well, directly after he had been released from the stocks near the Black Bull Inn.

East End of Emmott Hall also known as the Old Hall near to the ducking well. Also well known for its ghostly residents *(William Scruton Scrapbook)*

All that Glitters...

Inhabitants of Stanbury once believed that they had struck gold. Leafing through a back issue of the *Keighley News* I came across the following letter addressed to the Editor, dated 5 May 1866:

> 'Some time ago it was reported that gold had been found in the neighbouring hills (around Stanbury) and most of the male inhabitants especially the bachelor portion, left their lawful employment and rushed to the "diggings" in eager haste...many of the diggers especially the bachelors worked day and night and some had narrow escapes with their lives while undergoing their fatiguing and hazardous labours. After being some time at work many of them were almost besides themselves with joy at the thought of having gathered, as they supposed, enough of the much loved treasure to support them through the remainder of their days. It had the appearance of gold in its bright and glittering aspect but alas it turned out after all to be a spurious and worthless article...'

In other words they had struck fools' gold. I have heard tell that there is at least one body still encased in the defunct Stanbury mine.

Then There Was The One About...

Miss Maria Judson, a little middle-aged body whose home was at No. 7 Prospect Street, Haworth, lived an unremarkable life until one day, while cooking her dinner in a tin over an open fire, she opened her mouth and a water-wolf popped out. The *Keighley Herald* got wind of the story and thinking it 'smacked of witchcraft', dispatched a reporter by train, to interview the lady forthwith (the journalist was later to claim that it was one of the strangest cases he had ever come across). Bracing himself against the cold December day, he found the small house, knocked on the door, explained his mission and was invited in. Miss Judson ushered him into a cosy sitting room, where he settled on a horsehair sofa in front of a welcoming fire.

'Seating herself Maria Judson was quick to reassure him that the story was quite true explaining that she had known for some time that a water-wolf was growing inside her. She had felt the creature slide down her throat when drinking from as spring at Lee Shaw. For six years the "Thing" had grown and wriggled about in her stomach while at night it rested its head on her heart. It was while stirring a "tasty bit" of strong smelling onions and butter Maria claimed, 'Ah could feel this thing getting' heer and heer up mi throit. Ah gat up to tak' h'oonion off 'rib, an' Ah just opponed mi maath when summat comes aht, lowps ower twice and dropped. Ah wor in a reight fullock, but Ah hed t'presence to shut me maath ageean, for Ah'd heeard of a woman at Cross Roads 'at hed t'same thing happened to her. It jumped aht when she oppened her maath but shoo kept it oppen sooa it jumped back ageean.' Apparently water-wolves are very partial to cooked onion. Seizing the tin containing her dinner she dashed the contents out onto the street. During the commotion her black and white tabby cat, which until that point had been happily sleeping on a rug before the fire rushed for the safety of the window ledge knocking over a plant in its terror as the water-wolf sizzled to death in the flames. Miss Judson was so surprised at the appearance of the animal that she was unable to describe it properly, but thought it might resemble a "gra-a-ay frog." "Nah," Miss Judson nodded as her tale ended "it seems a foony story, dosen't it?"

As the man from the *Herald* walked away, he could not help thinking to himself, 'Jonah and his whale have been outdone at Haworth.'

In the 1830s, local men worked coal seams beside South Dene, mid-way between Withens and Stanbury. Samuel Greenwood, alias Sam o' Bills was sent to Wakefield House of Correction for a total of four weeks for some misdemeanour or other, but before leaving his moorland home he piled coal acquired from South Dene mine onto the fire. Upon his return, he was delighted to find the fire still burning in the grate!

John Dolby, a bootmaker by trade, left Haworth to join the military train – a Foot Regiment in Ireland. The plan was that his wife Martha Ann would live with her mother-in-law until he returned from the war, with enough cash to set up in the shoe trade. While he was away, John religiously sent her thirty shillings each month. Returning home in November 1872, he was shocked to find Martha Ann openly living in sin with villager William Winterbottom. Worse still, he found that his wife had given birth to an illegitimate child. After the infant's death in March 1872, Winterbottom had gone to carpenter, Will Brigden, paying him to make a sturdy coffin. He requested that Winterbottom be inscribed on the coffin lid; this was denied and the name Dolby was put there instead. Martha Ann's husband was granted a divorce.

In August 1928, F.E., a wandering pilgrim, stopped an elderly villager and asked, "Could you tell me the way to the Brontë waterfall?" "The what waterfall?" "The Brontë waterfall." "Nay, Ah don't knaw. Ah nobbut knaw one waterfall near here and that's at Sladen Beck, ower yonder" and pointing in that direction, he went on to say "Happen tha means that?" "Haven't you heard of the Brontës?" asked the wayfarer. "Ah seeam ter think Ah hev, somehah. What wor they?" After explaining who the Brontës were, the denizen pondered a while before replying, "Aw, aye? That weean't be nah, though, Ah knaw t'parson theer's called Hirst!" (*Note:* Brontë Falls was formerly known as Harbour Falls.)

Haworth was the first northern village featured on a BBC Radio show broadcasted directly to Africa, entitled *Back Home.* In January 1942, the programme began to the thin strains of an old wind-up musical box, belonging to the Brontë Museum's curator, Mr Mitchell. Then William Binns told the story of how Haworth's Brass Band, returning home in the small hours from a performance at Crystal Palace, decided to play a rousing tune. However, not wishing to wake anyone, they performed in their stocking feet! He also recalled the time when, in 1925, having finished their last musical piece in Manchester, the band set off much later than anticipated. Whilst driving home, their coach driver inadvertently took a wrong turn, ending up in Bury instead of Haworth – and the last tune the band had played before leaving the theatre?... *Show me the way to go home!*

For What We Are About To Receive...

A favourite grace in Yorkshire was that attributed to the Scottish Bard Robbie Burns, and known as the Selkirk grace:

Some hae meat and canna eat,
And some wad eat that want it;
But we hae meat, and we can eat.
And sae the Lord be thankit.

William Grimshaw, horrified that most of his parishioners failed to say grace, told them "You are worse than the very swine, for your pigs will gruff over their victuals, but you will say nothing." Thereafter, an elderly farmer living on the edge of Haworth moor, composed his own personal heartfelt thanks to his Creator:

We thank Thee, Lord,
For what we've getten.
If ther'd been more here
There'd hev' been more etten.

Not to be outdone, a neighbour across the way delivered up these words at meal times:

Lord have mercy upon us.
Three butter-cakes for fower on us.
Thank God there's no more of us.
Wire (tuck) in lads.

An eccentric individual named Willie, rising from his chair at a local Methodist tea party, hands solemnly clasped together in fervent prayer, offered up the following words of thanks, much to the astonishment of all those present:

Roast beef an' bacon
My mouth has forsaken;
Butter an' cheese,
My eyes seldom sees;
If potatoes an' such,
Hadn't stuck I' me guts,
Ah'm just flayed at poor Billy 'ud dee.

Hilarious Hoaxes

The following passage is taken from a humorous story written in 1859 by 'Nathan Hotchops', about a group of Haworth men and their particular version of Haworth pudding:

One Christmas during the 1850s, some Haworth wags got their heads together with a well-known pig breeder and came up with the plan of making an enormous pudding. The pig man, having volunteered to do the job, got some grease, some tally (tallow), and some barley meal. He then blended them all together, before putting the mixture in a large cloth and placing the entire thing into a pan to boil. As it turned out, he had forgotten to add water to the meal and the pudding tasted awful. So... after including the contents of a pepper pot, he boiled it again. However, the thing refused to sink; consequently, a lump of iron was employed to keep it down in the pan.

On realising that the pudding had gone terribly wrong, the pranksters decided to play a joke on the Keighley folk. Enlisting the help of an innkeeper in the town, the Haworth lot ran back to the pig farmer's home, sneaked in and stole the pudding whilst he was out.

One of the jokers, disguised in a pair of spectacles and clean white apron, walked into the inn where several Keighleyites were sitting, and said to them, "If you please gentleman, Mrs says shu will make yo a present of a Kirstmas puddin." At this, he plonked fair sized dollops of the pudding onto plates, provided by the helpful innkeeper. The lucky recipients "began a chewin it, an wen they gat ther teeth thro it, they wor capt – then they supt, an then they luk'd at one another an wor fair capt, an couldn't tell wether it wor ther teeth it wor rang or it wor pudden."

As soon as the pepper kicked in, they knew they had been duped and the chuckling benefactor was forced to flee the scene, clutching the remains of the 'feast', wrapped in cloth. What was left of the pudding was returned to its rightful owner.

It took more than twenty years before Keighlyites got the better of the Haworth bunch...'The way in which Haworth people treated Keighley visitors to the famous "pudding" has long been a standing joke between the two places, but the "Village of the Brontës" has been outdone in the cooking line by a neighbour not far away. On Saturday a party of employees of a large machine shop in Keighley started forth to play a friendly game of cricket with a newly formed club at the head of the Worth Valley. After the game, the players adjourned to a public house to have the expected feed. When they had waited for some time in the principal room, four men were seen struggling at the door with something which, when a view could be obtained, turned out to be a pie. The following may help to convey a faint idea of its size: – It contained 8lbs of flour, 14lbs of meat of various kinds, including liver and sheep's heart, 24lbs of potatoes, and rather more than plenty of seasoning. The whole was baked in a large-sized washing bowl. The "lid" was at least six inches thick, and thoroughly saturated with suet. The pie had been ordered for twelve, but twenty-six persons sat down, and, though the number was more than doubled, only half of the pie was eaten. Delicacy forbids that I should detail the harrowing vividness the nauseating effects of this culinary masterpiece upon the partakers thereof. Suffice that upon the road between the banqueting-hall and the railway station the revellers might have been seen for some time after the feast in various attitudes expressive of acute nausea and agony. A Channel steamboat on a rough passage could not have presented a more distressing picture. One individual who can boast of having on a previous occasion eaten twenty-five pork pies at a sitting, succeeded in retaining his equanimity. Of course, a man who could eat twenty-five pies could stand anything.' But then, the proof is always in the pudding!

On April Fools' Day in 1978, Peter Greenwood – reporter for the *Telegraph & Argus*, wrote a spoof story concerning the tragic burning of the parsonage.

A few months later, a Parisian film crew turned up in Yorkshire wanting to secretly film scenes from the life and times of the Brontës. A quick look at Haworth showed that tourists would get in the way of filming, so Action Films commandeered the empty Burnsall Rectory in Wharfedale, to set the Brontë story – thinking no one would notice the difference! Thus, bemused Burnsall residents awoke to find that rows of ancient looking gravestones had miraculously burst forth overnight in the rector's garden.

Haworth's Fleece Inn snug became a free Brontë museum in the summer of 1988. It commemorated a host of hitherto unknown members of the family. These included the dentist Dockroyd Brontë born at Thornton in 1819, who left these shores for Tombstone, Texas, where he met Wyatt Earp. Sadly, Doc was killed in a shoot-out at the OK Corral. The "actual" bullets that killed him were on view in a glass cabinet; alongside his glasses, retrieved from a second-hand stall at Skipton Market. Other "treasures" included several negatives taken by photographic experimentalist, Maybridge Brontë, which had been found in a fireplace, between the remains of two mummified cats. Then there was the history of Bigglesworth (alias Blue-tit) Brontë, who, it was claimed, had been responsible for the tragic death of Daredevil Rainbow Lily. In addition, there was information relating to Percy Brontë – a failed diplomat held directly responsible for the start of the Crimean War *and* the Indian Mutiny. Last, but not least, came the wayward Aggie Brontë, who shocked Victorian England with her outrageous frolics.

Of course, it was all just a light-hearted jape, put together for amusement by two locals. The spoof exhibition created a real stir within Brontë circles, for it seems some could not see the funny side of it. However a visit to the real Brontë Museum is a must.

For further information on this subject, the reader can contact Burlesque Brontë Exhibition Website: http://freepace.virgin.net/pr.og.

Now, Fancy That!

Mick Holmes, an Irishman, put down roots in the Worth Valley in the early 1800s. He fathered twelve children, who, themselves had large families. They say Mick could boast of having more than a thousand great-grandchildren. Imagine having to remember birthdays in his family! His worn-out wife Betty died in February 1863, in her seventy-eighth year.

"Old Steel", who was born in Haworth, settled at Bingley in 1830. On 7 December 1896, he passed away aged ninety-five years. He had fathered fifteen healthy children, his eldest boy being seventy years old when he died.

Work this one out – a family gathering at Haworth, in November 1862, consisted of one great grandfather, two grandmothers, three fathers, three children, two grandchildren and one great grandchild. Nothing remarkable there – except that there were just *four* people present!

A poor Haworth soul by the name of Mrs Hargreaves gave birth to twins for the fourth time in 1866. Her previous husband had died, leaving her with one child and one pair of twins. She then re-married and gave birth to three further sets. The incumbent Revd W. G. Mayne made the mother's plight known to Queen Victoria and Her Majesty graciously sent Mrs Hargreaves two pounds out of the Privy Purse, thus saving her from the poorhouse.

Not Of This Earth

Christmas 1901 was almost upon the Worth Valley. Snow lay upon the ground, muffling the footsteps of Sergeant John Johnson and Constable Clarke, as they walked round the streets of Haworth on night patrol duty. Leaving behind the Old Hall on Sun Street, they headed out towards the tiny hamlet of Marsh, reaching Marsh Lane at about 12.45am. Everywhere was silent, as snowflakes fell on lanes and houses. Sergeant Johnson paused for a moment, remarking to his companion how unusually bright the sky had suddenly become. Thinking at first that it must be light from the moon, the pair gazed upwards, where they saw a bright light tinged with blue, shimmering in the clear winter sky.

Whatever it was, they soon realised it was not the moon. It was something different; something they had never seen before. Perhaps it was some sort of star. As it drew closer, it shot out strong blue rays. The men stepped back in fear. "What is it?" one whispered to the other. Mesmerised, they watched as the entity hovered over them, rising and falling for a good fifteen minutes or so. Sergeant Johnson described what he saw to the *Keighley News*: "The object was about the size of a ship, bright blue in colour, with occasional flashes of red and white, followed by sparks. It was *long and pointed at both ends, shaped somewhat like a boy's tip-cat*" (Haworth's version of a tip cat was a pigging stick, fashioned from a mill shuttle and shaped like a pencil sharpened at both ends). Remaining above the men at a height of about 100-150ft, the ship moved from east to west and then slowly rose to an estimated height of 500ft, before disappearing as quickly as it had come.

The local press was much intrigued by the story because no one had any idea what this strange thing could be. One school of thought said that it might have been some kind of electrical storm, thus creating a "remarkable atmospheric phenomenon" in the night sky. Others scoffed, believing Johnson and Clarke to have partaken of too much Christmas spirit! Yet, at precisely the same time, Keighley Police Inspector Percival was hurrying back to the station, to report a brilliant light in the sky, which *he* had spotted in the market area of the town, close to the Parish Church. His report coincided exactly with the Haworth policemen's story. Stanbury headmaster, Mr Jonas Bradley, stepped forward to say that he too had witnessed the object, as he walked past Rough Nook Farm on the outskirts of Haworth – at the identical moment as the three police constables. He told of how his attention had been caught by a curious bright object entering the earth's atmosphere, close to the Pole Star. Bradley watched as it travelled in a slanting direction across the sky, until almost reaching the ground, under the constellation of Cassiopeia. However, instead of reaching the earth, it suddenly vanished, leaving a luminous head of brilliant blue behind – probably stretching to 50 or 60 degrees. The light remained visible for at least five minutes, altering its shape considerably as it moved across the night sky.

There the matter might have rested, but for the fact that others also claimed to have seen the UFO casting a radiant blue light. Engine driver Smith Marshall and fireman Mr Oxley saw it over Bentham way, several people saw it near the village of Clapham, Yorkshire and a number of individuals in the towns of Keighley and Shipley said that *they* had witnessed the odd occurrence on the same early morning.

Was this, then, the first written account of UFO activity in Haworth? A perplexed journalist's parting shot of the day, was that it seemed to be "impossible to regard the phenomenon as meteoric and perhaps one might be permitted to hazard a conjecture that this was some electrical display more akin to the aurora borealis. It is quite possible that some scientific meteorologists might be able to throw some light upon a very puzzling phenomena." Yet, three years earlier, on 15 March 1898, a brilliant display of the aurora borealis was seen in the same area. So, what was this mysterious flying object, which changed shape as it crossed the night sky above Haworth?

* * * *

It was during the full moon of September 1977 that David Greenwood and his wife, of 5 Little Street, Haworth drove into Haworth at 12.30am, after a night out. Their attention was suddenly caught by what looked like a green saucer shaped object in the sky. From the safety of their vehicle, the couple watched the stationary spectacle for a few minutes, as it hung above the hillside, before shooting off at high speed. Afterwards, they learned that UFO activity was at a peak that week; for eight other people had reported sightings of unidentified flying objects, including Rodney Harrison of Birchdale Grove, Wilsden, who saw a bright orange ball of light, tinged with red, in the night sky above nearby Harden.

Twenty years later, at about 7.00pm, Dolores and Jack Gillson were standing in their hillside garden at Lower Brow Farm, Haworth. As Mrs Gillson looked across the Worth Valley, she saw a very bright light in the sky, floating directly above the tower of Haworth's ancient parish church. What ever it was remained there, until the approach of an aircraft caused it to hide behind a cloud, before moving away at an immense rate. Mrs Gillson said the clear light appeared to vibrate, making it difficult for her to distinguish the strange object's shape...

Spreading the Legacy

Margery Hunter, a typist from Leeds, discovered a twelve foot citrus tree, known as the 'Friendship' tree, whilst she was visiting Sochi, near the Black Sea, in 1969. This bore forty-five separate citrus fruits (achieved by grafting on branches sent from all over the world). The Mayor explained that the aim was to gather soil from every country where famous people had lived and spread it around the base of the tree. On her return to Yorkshire, Mrs Hunter contacted the Brontë Society to beg a handful of soil from the parsonage garden. Mission accomplished, she received an invitation to hand over the earth to London's Soviet Embassy, from where it would be transported to Russia.

Mrs H. Greene Arnold of New England planted a laburnum sapling, grown from a seed taken from the parsonage garden, in American soil to commemorate the 100th anniversary of Charlotte Brontë's wedding. Another Brontë enthusiast, living in San Francisco, California, requested a seed from this same tree. No doubt, there are now a number of these plants flourishing on the Pacific as well as the Atlantic sides of the States.

Man's Best Friend

When Arthur Nicholls and his new bride Mary Bell returned from their honeymoon, Mary's favourite dog Fairy died of excitement on seeing her mistress again. Nicholls had another dog named Pincher who, like Plato – the late Patrick Brontë's dog – followed him everywhere, but was by nature a bad tempered little mongrel.

New recruits to the Merchant Navy, named Martin, were always dubbed Pincher. This goes back to the time of Admiral Sir William F. Martin – a strict disciplinarian, who regularly 'pinched' ratings, sending them to prison for the least offence.

Pincher The Drunken Dog

I once possessed a faithful friend,
One of the canine race;
Few were the faults ascribed to him,
And little the disgrace.
His breed was bull and mastiff,
His colour red and white.

Pincher had beer and grog too much,
His master was too mellow
His conduct could not be conceal'd,
He was a drunken dog.

Keighley Visitor, January 1869.

In 1944, a tiny white and silver-grey sheepdog puppy was carried down from Virginia Farm, a smallholding nestling below Emily's Wuthering Heights, to begin his new life at the Brontë Guest House, Haworth. Now Pincher was no ordinary dog, for his favourite haunt was the Brontë home. Begging free entrance, he liked nothing better than to sit inside the hallway watching visitors come and go. Pincher was privileged indeed, because only a few dogs have ever been allowed to grace the corridors of this world famous museum with their muddy paws. An irate farmer once blamed him for worrying sheep but as no clear case could be made against him, he was exonerated.

If Pincher went missing, presumably on some doggy errand, guests would enquire worriedly as to his whereabouts. When not employed at the parsonage, he would take it upon himself to accompany visitors on their walks to the Brontë waterfall; and on to Wuthering Heights, whenever he got the chance. If Pincher were lucky, the next stop would be at Ponden Hall, where he would be treated to a drop of tea and a slice of cake. Ponden's old visitors' book confirms his presence on more than one occasion…'Caroline Holt – with Pincher'; 'Caroline Holt – without Pincher', together with other people who, accompanied by their new found canine friend, had also signed the book. Back home in the evening, settled in front of a cosy fire, he would dream of Ponden cakes.

On opening an anonymous second-class package, postmarked October 1961, Geoffrey Beard, the curator of the Brontë Parsonage, was surprised to find a used cornflake packet and a London evening newspaper. Wrapped inside was the brass dog collar worn by Emily Brontë's favourite dog, Keeper, which had been stolen from the Parsonage a month earlier. Before being donated to the museum, the collar had been in the safe keeping of Mrs Greenwood Wood. Keeper was a chief mourner at Emily's funeral, following her coffin into the church and pining after his mistress, until he too, a blind, toothless 'old memento of the past', joined her in death. On a bitterly cold day of December 1851, Charlotte recorded: 'Poor old Keeper died last Monday morning, after being ill one night; he went gently to sleep, we laid his old faithful head in the garden'. Miss Brooksbank of Tyrrel Street, Bradford sent a sketch of Keeper to *The Yorkshireman* in 1879.

Final Forays into 'Brontëland'

The *Bradford Observer* reported an interesting story gleaned from *The Times* in May 1942. It seems a Probate Court had heard that a solicitors' firm, after a severe bombing raid by German aircraft, thought it prudent to remove the Last Will and Testament of a Miss Charlotte Branwell Brontë from their strong room, to somewhere safer. However, upon contact with air the document just *"crumbled to ashes."* Why this happened remained a complete and utter mystery to everyone concerned.

Emily's 'Sobbing' Heights

Emily Brontë was supposed to have been inspired by remote Top Withens; so too was Halliwell Sutcliffe, who used the lonely spot as inspiration for his imaginary *Ricroft of Withens*. This famous building stands three miles from the parsonage, at the end of a long, bleak winding track. Not far away is a lone rock called the Cuckoo Stone, which is supposed to be the petrified head of a wealthy giant, who ate animals and people.

There were three farmsteads at Withens but Lower and Middle Withens (the latter was presumed to have once served as an ale house) were razed to the ground a number of decades ago, whilst Top Withens was left to crumble. Several relics of earlier buildings had been incorporated into the fabric of the farm, including seventeenth-century window jambs and lintels, and part of a medieval cruck in the peat cellar, with another in the barn. Best of all, was a tiny window bearing the legend *Dairy* – thereby ensuring the occupier escaped paying window duty. Exactly when and by whom the house was built is not clear. However, it *is* known that the house was put in trust, in accordance with

Top Withens as it was in June 1955 *(photograph by the late Mr M. Jennings)*

the will (dated 5 March 1723) of the original owner, Lord of the Manor, David Midgley. Emily and Halliwell's gloomy Withens was inhabited until March 1926 when the last tenant, Ernest Roddy – a French polisher and poultry farmer – left to live on Main Street. Hereafter, the abandoned dwelling, which had withstood rain and wind for centuries, began to sink into decay. By 1940, vandals and souvenir hunters had wrecked the property. A *KEEP OUT* notice, drawing attention to the dangerous condition of the farm, was erected and the whole site surrounded by an ugly fence.

Doctor Violet Glover of Manor House, Great Horton Road, Bradford picked up a Roman coin near Withens, when her car was bogged down in marshland in 1961. The bronze coin bearing the words *Maximinus Pius Aug Germ* was minted in the time of Roman emperor Maximus, around AD 235 to 238. Her treasure was valued at 3s (15p).

In 1964, the Brontë Society erected a plaque and Bob Cryer MP – who died tragically in a car crash and is still sadly missed by his constituents – managed to get the building protected in 1971. Regrettably, after twenty years, English Heritage lost interest, having decided that the property was too much of a ruin to remain on the list. August 1996 saw a revival campaign to save Emily's Wuthering Heights, but the fight to have the site re-listed failed in 1999. Alan

The alleged setting for Wuthering Heights still draws tourists as moths to a flame *(Marie Campbell)*

Howarth, Culture and Heritage minister at the time, ignored the fact that count-less Brontë pilgrims from all over the world are drawn as moths to a flame by this lonely farmhouse, and justified its removal from the list by saying that there was no *proof* that Top Withens had been Emily's inspiration for the Earnshaw residence.

A novel land sale took place near Withens in 1969. The new owner, Mr Joseph Westlake of Ancestral Estates Ltd., 86 High Street, Skipton purchased a field, skirted by the stream that flowed under Brontë Bridge. His company, Brontëland Estates offered thirty-six thousand, one square foot plots for sale in the 'Ancient and Historic Parish of Stanbury' – 'twixt Stanbury and Haworth'. A small sum of money would entitle the purchaser to a legal deed of land convey-ance, a right of way on foot to their particular plot, plus a lovely colour brochure – brimming with maps and photographs, describing Haworth. Thus, pilgrims the world over could purchase a lot for the sum of ten dollars (£3.50p) – well worth the price!

Ode To A Businessman

If you can't be the tenant
Of Wildfell Hall,
Or have Jane Eyre
As a governess,
Not to worry -
The price is small,
You can be Heathcliff,
More or less.
Enterprise has got a grip,
On wuthering depths of salesmanship.

R.C. Scriven Yorkshire Evening Post 26 August 1969.

The Manchester Guardian on the 14 May 1960, described its perception of the Earnshaw abode in Emily Brontë's *Wuthering Heights*: 'We know all about its architecture, its entrance (with two shameless little boys), its cellars, its two stairways (one from the parlour and one from the kitchen), its ladders and wooden steps up to the garrets and attics, a roof that had never been underdrawn. The house, as Lockwood, when he is narrating, tells us, was in a coal district. A stony by-road branched off to it. Nearby was a "line of upright stones continued through the whole length of the barren; these were erected and daubed with lime on purpose to serve as guides in the dark. None of this descrip-tive background relates to Top Withens but to windswept High Sunderland."

High Sunderland was a true 'House of Mottos' – a unique half-timbered building, extended and revamped in stone during the year of 1664 by Royalist Abraham Sunderland. Emily came to know the hall well when she worked at Law Hill School. Indeed, she could see the mysterious grime blackened building from her bedroom window, being attracted to it as surely as a moth to a flame.

The hall, nicknamed 't' Castle' stood a mile north of Halifax, between the Bradford and Wakefield roads, where it bordered Shibden Hall's lands. An account of the many inscriptions on the hall may be found in Revd John Watson's the *History and Antiquities of the Parish of Halifax, &c.*, London 1775:

'When the present fabric at High Sunderland was erected, does not appear by any inscription upon the building, but it was either the work of Richard Sunderland, who married Susan Saltonstall, about 1597, or of his son Abraham, who wed Elizabeth Langdale, but more probably the latter. A chamber-window, under the arms of Saltonstall, Langdale, and Thornhill, of Flixby, written in Latin were the words -
HAPPY IS HE WHOM THE ILLUSTRIOUS VIRTUES OF HIS ANCESTORS ADORNS, AND WHO, BY HIS OWN VIRTUE, ADDS L'STRE TO THEIRS.
L. S.

Over the north-door was written, *Ne subeat glis serdus*, a mistake for *surdus;* and over the door on the north-side, *Ne intret amicus hirudo*. At the back part of the house, were four English lines, too coarse to be admitted here. In the hall, the words over the fire-place warned:

HOUSES WHEN LARGE YIELD COMFORT: FIRES AND TONGUES CARRY DESTRUCTION WITH THEM.

Over the south-door,

This place	hates	loves	punishes	preserves	honours
	profligacy	peace	crimes	justice	the good.

Below these lines was written: *Confide Deo, Diffide tibi.*

On the pillar on the left hand of the south-door was carved, *Patria Domus* and a pillar on the right hand of the same bore the words, *Optima Caelum*.

Over the door entrance:

The Almighty grant, that the family of Sunderland may peaceably possess this mansion and preserve the right of its ancestors, till the ant drink up the waters of the sea, and the tortoise traverse the whole world. How vain are our wishes, and how uncertain the continuance of earthly things, may hence be seen, when either the writer of these, or his son, alienated this very estate which the then owner so earnestly wished might continue in the family for ever!

Over the principle gate, as read by Emily:
NUNQUAM HANC PULSET PORTAM QUI VIOLAT AEQUUM.
(Never may he who violates justice seek to enter this gate.)

On a scroll beneath a cherub sounding a trumpet:
THE FAME OF VIRTUOUS DEEDS IS A PERPETUAL TRUMPET.'

(Extracted from the *Northern Star, May 1818* – the same year that Emily Brontë was born).

In 1947, the Ministry of Works felt the hall could be rescued for the sum of £6,000; but as nothing was done, the derelict property was pronounced unfit for habitation. Its Harrogate owner Mrs A. M. Holden offered the strange old house – complete with grotesque sculptures, first to Halifax Corporation and then to the Brontë Society. Both declined the offer, since neither could afford the £20,000 needed for a complete restoration. It was a black day when a Queensbury house-breaking firm, aware of the scarcity of good quality building materials, purchased the decrepit hall in 1950 – when sadly the house of solitude and mystery had weathered its last storm.

In the course of demolition, a secret spiral staircase, which ran up to the roof and down to the cellars below, revealed itself from behind a ground floor stone fireplace. What stories of hapless ghosts these walls might have told, if they could have spoken, including perhaps, that of a priest walled up alive, somewhere within this sinister house, and a great treasure yet to be discovered, buried deep in the vaults below!

Braving barbed wire fencing and the threat of danger from the crumbling property, historian Ivy Holgate managed to retrieve a delicate lady's shoe, complete with its ribbon lacing and a comb, which were tucked behind wainscoting, both dating from the seventeenth century. Geoffrey S. West purchased some of the stone relics amongst which were: Emily's famous 'shameless little boys', a portion of the secret staircase, a witch's window that opened out from above the hall's back entrance, and the great decorated archway, re-erected in the grounds of Mr West's home at Long Fallas, Knowle Road, Brighouse. Portions of stone went to Shibden Hall's Folk Museum and Bankfield Museum, where they were put on display, though what became of the stained glass windows, which were sent off to Halifax Museum but never arrived, has yet to be determined. As for Emily's sighting of the legendary white phantom horse galloping down the lane...?

Today, all trace of the 'strangest house in all England' has been obliterated from the heights, where it proudly stood on the moors at Horley Green for many long centuries.

Stanbury

The *Keighley News* asked in 1959, 'What does the future hold for the village of Stanbury-remote, "end-of-the-worldish," with an ageing population and an ever-growing degree of physical decay?'

Was this place destined to become a ghost village, when its decrepit denizens were fated to be lost in the mists of time; its cottages left to fall into dank decay and famous handloom weaver Timmy Feather forgotten? No, thank goodness Stanbury survived to tell the tale.

The title of Lord of the Manor of Stanbury was offered for sale in 1996. Viscount Mountgarret, who resides near Harrogate, decided to auction off his title at a London sale on 11 December. The Viscount had never been to Stanbury. In fact, he didn't even know where the village was, despite his family having held the title since 1894! The *Keighley News* contacted the Viscount, offering to meet him at the Wuthering Heights Inn, Stanbury, for lunch. After being shown round the village, he was so impressed, he attempted to remove the title from the sale but was told it was too late. American Tom Lee, of Michigan, purchased the title for the sum of £13,250. Since this was double the amount it was expected to fetch, Viscount Mountgarret kindly offered to make a donation to village funds.

Brontë Book Connections

Mary Ann Milligan (*nee* Greenwood), a Haworth woman and wife of doctor/poet John Milligan, claimed that the Brontë sisters often called at her home at 11 South Street – nicknamed Milligan's Hill – situated in the vicinity of Oakworth Road, Keighley. Here, the sisters would browse happily in Dr Milligan's private library. These visits usually happened, Mary Ann said, when the girls were on their way to Mr Hudson's lending library – a few minutes away at High Street, Keighley.

Born at Crosshills, Keighley on 18 January 1812, John Milligan was described as a "walking cyclopaedia" where folklore was concerned. He was very fond of all departments of literature and during his lifetime had amassed a varied and valuable library. His "quaint liking" of the eccentric is confirmed by Keighley Library's collection of Milligan's books, retrieved from branch libraries by Keighley historian Ian Dewhirst, aided by Bob Duckett of Bradford Central Library. They show that the doctor's bookshelves were stuffed with reference works, written as early as the 1700s, on fossils, botany and plant life, not to mention autobiographies and, of course, poetry. Amongst these titles are, *Facts on Mesmerism*, *Opium Trade with China*, *African Slave Trade*, *Philosophy of Mystery* and *Masonry, London and Middlesex, five vols.*

It is a fact that, in March 1876 – his last week of life – John Milligan saved Keighley's ancient Market Cross – the top part being unusually fashioned in the shape of a Knight's Templar lantern – from being lost to the town forever.

Haworth village could boast its own early library for, according to Haworth's Rate Books of 1842, Joseph Redman occupied a property at The Fold that was used as a library. The property itself was owned by Mr John Kay – was this *the* John/Jack Kay, the village soothsayer? Kay's personal library would no doubt have been associated with all things occult, as was apparent in the portrait of him – thought to have been painted by Branwell, in which two books entitled *Astrology* and *Sybil* can be seen.

Years later, a serious fire broke out at Haworth's Mechanics' Institute on Tuesday 5 September 1863. It began in a flue from the premises below. Library books including some of those possibly read by the Brontë family and valued at around £70 to £100 were consumed in the flames. As the building was not insured, Sir Isaac Holden of Oakworth House, Keighley donated £20 and Michael Merrall of Haworth contributed a further £10, in order to replace some of the books that had been destroyed.

In August 1955, George Coombe placed a plaque on the wall near the main door of the old Mechanics' Hall, Keighley, where Jack Kay was once vice president and where members were able to borrow books on a variety of subjects. The plaque reads:

'To this building when it was a Mechanics' Institute
the Brontë family came each week from Haworth
to borrow books: 1835-1855.'

Treasured Timepieces

Brontë Country Clockmakers

The old clock in the gloomy hall
Ticks on, from hour to hour. *Emily Brontë.*

The Barraclough clock making enterprise began prior to the family opening a shop almost opposite the Black Bull on Main Street, after the Heatons of isolated Dalemoor Farm taught their nephew the art of clock making around 1780.

Emily Brontë used the name Mosley Barraclough in *Wuthering Heights*, inspired perhaps by the clockmaker's sign swinging above the shop entrance. Zerubbabel Barraclough, born in July 1799, was the best known of the family in Brontë times and was named after King Zerubabbel (the seed of Babylon). His hands fashioned wonderful mahogany grandfather clocks, standing several feet high and containing enough wood "to make a dining-room suite." His father was a dedicated Mason, holding the office of Worshipful Master at the Haworth Freemasons' lodge, at least four times. Zerubabbel died on St. Valentine's Day 1878. His brother Thomas didn't make clocks. Instead, he made artificial cork legs for maimed persons, said to be "a perfect imitation of a natural one", they were patented by Mann's Legs of Bradford.

A Barraclough grandfather clock stood marking time at the turn of the stairs in the Brontë Parsonage, where Patrick would pause each night on his way to bed, to wind it up in readiness for another day. A Barraclough clock still stands here – bequeathed in a will to the museum in 1983. This particular clock was supposed to have been purchased by a member of the Heaton clan, at the Parsonage sale, after Patrick's death, in 1861. However, another tale alleges that Mr Nicholls took the clock to Ireland with him.

During the 1950s, Yorkshireman Major Skerrit was passing Blompierre's Antiques of St. Samson's on his way to work, when the shopkeeper invited him in. To the Major's delight, he was shown a rather fine grandfather clock, made in West Yorkshire, as was confirmed by the maker's name *Barraclough* and *Haworth* painted onto the clock face. Mr Blompierre said it had originally belonged to the Brontë family of Haworth Parsonage. Pointing to the portrait of a girl inserted above the clock face, he told Major Skerrit that the previous owner had suspected it was a likeness of Anne Brontë, painted by Charlotte, or vice versa. *(See "Curious Tales of Old West Yorkshire" also by Marie Campbell.)*

Major Skerrit displayed the grandfather clock in his dentist's waiting room at Potter's Corner, St. Samson's, where it stayed for the next five years. Eventually, the clock followed the Skerrits back to England. First to Southampton, then to a vicarage near Shepperton Film Studios, Middlesex, before ending up in the home of the Major's daughter Mrs Sandy Pimm, of Sunbury – who, fortunately, took several photographs of it.

Time passed and Sandy separated from her husband. Having remained on friendly terms, Sandy borrowed the sum of £25 from him, against the 'Brontë clock', to enable her to purchase a four cubic feet LEC deep freezer or tax her car – she forgets which. This exchange was on the understanding that as soon as she repaid the loan, the clock would be returned to her, from a lock-up garage in Sunbury. Sadly, she never did get her clock back. Where is that grandfather clock now and how did it come to be in the Channel Isles? Was this really the Brontë clock and could the wistful girl staring out from its face be that of Charlotte, Emily or even Anne, perhaps?

Victorian Brontë Forgery

Back in the early 1950s, the Brontë Society received news of a hitherto 'unknown' book, purportedly written by Charlotte and Anne Brontë. Señor Miguel Arimany, a Spanish publisher, having already released the novel under the title *Adversity*, approached two respected London publishers – hoping to have the work authenticated by them. He told the publishing house that it had originally been written by Acton and Currer Bell but was translated from a German edition published in 1851, which had surfaced after German born Paul Schneider died in Barcelona, where he kept a lending library.

Investigations were instigated by the Brontë Society, who found that the book had first come to light in England apparently, after being published anonymously in 1849 by Henry Colburn, a London publisher and that the novel had later been re-issued in paperback under the title *Rockingham*. At this point fate lends a hand, for Brontë expert Phyllis Bentley remembered, that in the course of her work for the Bradford Literary and Philosophical Society, during the 1920s, *Rockingham* had been amongst a great volume of paperwork she had set aside. A diligent search began and the manuscript retrieved – which turned out to be identical to the German/Spanish work. The British Museum later confirmed that the work was *not* that of the Brontës but of Irish born aristocrat Philippe Ferdinand Auguste de Ro-han Chabot (his official title being Count de Jarnac), who was also known by a pseudonym – Sir Charles Rockingham. The Count died in 1875, so no one really knows why he attributed his work (if it was his) to the Brontë sisters and not himself.

Brontë Beat

In 1964, a new pop group calling themselves 'Branwell and the Brontë Beats with Charlotte' appeared on the music scene. The band came from across the border in Lancashire and played at the Imperial Ballroom in Nelson, decked out in early Victorian costume. The name did not go down too well with shocked Brontë admirers. Brontë Beat, unlike the real Brontës, never did reach the top ten. The *Yorkshire Post* published these amusing lines on the subject,

Haven't they got it
A bit off beat -
Some like the Wimpoles
Of Barrett Street?
The older beat group
went down well -
Ellis, Currer and Acton Bell -
Branwell, too, as some depone
He was a bit
of a rolling stone
They might have drained
Fame's sweetest cup
Had Brian Epstein
Taken 'em up.
Something tells me
The newer lot
Will bite a pace
Which the old did not.
As for the nineteenth
Century clothes
are matched
by the Branwell oaths?

Good luck, say I
(for I'm no hacker) -
Watch out for Heathcliff:
He's a Rocker.

19 August 1964

Three decades later, Mark Cresswell and Adam Kirk made their musical debut as the Brontë Brothers. Although the band had played Glastonbury, Cambridge Folk Festival and other prestigious venues, alongside famous bands like Gerry Rafferty and the Hothouse Flowers, they remained virtually unknown in their native Leeds.

The Last Word

A former inhabitant of Haworth was forced to seek employment elsewhere and on climbing the Brow, turned for one last lingering look upon his beloved village, saying – "Farewell, dear old Haworth, this is our parting; but" (adding with a sigh) "I will never forsake thee."

Appendix 1

Haworth's principal and business inhabitants in 1848

Post Office
William Hartley, *Post Master: – Letters from all parts arrive (from Bradford)* daily, Sunday accepted, at twelve noon, and are despatched thereto in the afternoon.

Gentry and Clergy
Berry, Rev. Abraham; Brontë, Rev. Patrick; Greenwood, Mr. James, Woodlands and Springhead; Greenwood, Joseph, Esq. (Magistrate) Springhead; Greenwood, Mr. Wm. Cockcroft, Springhead; Hartley, Mr. John; Moorhouse, Rev. Joseph; Nicholls, Rev. James Bell, (Arthur); Saunders, Rev. Moses; Winterbottom, Rev. John.

Schools
National School, Haworth-Joseph Purnell, master; Mary Wright, mistress; Wesleyan School, Haworth-William Ramsbottom, master; Mary Ramsbottom, mistress

Blacksmiths
Lund, John; Moore, John; Whitaker, James; Wright, Nathan,

Boot and Shoe Makers
Aykeroyd, Jonathan; Feather, Robert; Hartley, Thomas; Hird, Squire; Hudson, Henry and Isaac; Mozley, John; Newell, Wm; Roper, Abraham; Wilkinson, Thomas

Butchers
Bramley, John; Garnett, Wm, Jun.; Holmes, Joseph and Thomas; Moore, John; Stoney, Robert; Wilson, Greenwood

Clog and Pattern Makers
Fernside, Jonas; Hartley Jn., Stubbing Lane; Murgatroyd, Joseph; Sugden, Robert

Inns and Public Houses
Black Bull, Enoch Thomas; Fleece, James Butterfield; King's Arm's, Greenwood Wilson; Sun, Robert Stoney; White Lion, Betty Wilkinson

Joiners
Murgatroyd, Noah; Roper, James; Wood, William

Linen & Woollen Drapers
Draper, James; Newell, John; Thomas, James; Wright, Mary

Millers
Murgatroyd, Robert

Painters
Greenwood, John; Hudson, John; Lambert, Thomas (and plumber & glazier); Wood, Humphrey (and plumber & glazier)

Shopkeepers & Dealers In Groceries & Sundries
Appleyard, Joseph; Aykroyd, Martha; Brown, Robert; Barwin, James; Driver, James; Feather, John; Hartley, Betty, James, John, Timothy; Hird, John; Hudson, John; Lambert, John; Lambert, Robert, (& Druggist); Lambert, Tobias; Murgatroyd, John;

Roper Abraham, Wm; Shackleton, Joseph; Thornton, Squire; Waddington, John; Whitham, Wm; Wright Edward, James, John

Shuttle Makers
Crabtree, Joseph & Joseph jun.

Stone Masons
Binns, Jonas; Bottomley, James & Brothers; Gregson, James

Straw Bonnet Makers
Hartley, Martha; Moore, Sarah

Surgeons
Armstrong, Wm; Feather, Benjamin; Hall, Edward South; Wheelhouse, John Bateman

Tailors
Binns, Benjamin, George; Greenwood, John; Mitchell, Matthew (and draper); Turner, Wm

Tea & Coffee Dealers
Greenwood, John (and stationer); Holmes, William, (wholesale, and coffee roaster)

Wine & Spirit Merchants
Thomas, Wm. & Sons

Woolstaplers
Aykroyd, Jonathan; Horsfall, Jonas; Newsholme, Robert; Townend, Edward

Worsted Spinners
Craven & Sugden; Greenwood, John & James; Merrall, Hartley & Sons, Lees Mill; Thomas, Wm. jun. Hollings Mill; Williamson, John, Griffe Mill

Worsted Stuff Manufacturers
Lambert, James & John; Williamson, John, Griffe Mill; Wright, James

Miscellaneous
Barraclough, Zerrubabel, ironmonger and watch maker; Craven, Jonas, tin-plate worker; Hartley, Wm., tin-plate worker; Ogden, James, register of births and deaths, and assistant overseer, Far Oxenhope; Parker, Tom. Temperance Hotel; Wright Pickles, wheelwright

Railway
The nearest station is at Hebden Bridge, on the Manchester and Leeds line, 8 miles from Haworth; A car to the above Station, from Mr. Jonathan Whittaker's, Far Oxenhope, every alternative Monday morning at seven, to meet the trains for Rochdale market.

Carriers
To Bradford: John Feather and Joseph Todd, from Haworth, every Monday and Thursday morning at seven. To Colne: John Dugdale, from Stanbury, every Wednesday. To Halifax: John Binns, from Haworth, every Tuesday, Thursday and Saturday. Robert Hartley and Jonathan Whitaker, from Far Oxenhope, every Wednesday and Saturday. To Keighley: John Feather, from Haworth, every Wednesday and Saturday and Widow Hey, from Stanbury, every Wednesday. To Rochdale: Jonathan Whitaker from Far Oxenhope, every alternative Monday. To Todmorden: Joseph Todd, from Haworth, twice a week; goes through Hebden Bridge. *Royal National Directory Slater 1848.*

Appendix 2
Bibliography

Adelphos, 'How often ... ' 1868.
Ainsworth, Harrison William, Lancashire Witches, 1849.
Akeroyd, Keith, 'Hearing a faint rustling ... ' 1974.
Anon, Funeral Dirge, c.1621.
Anon, Witch Spell of Borton.
Athenaeum, 'I can tell ... .'
Baldwin, Joshua, 'I remember Emily ... '
Blackburn, J, 'Man gets his soul ... '.
Blackwood's Edinburgh Magazine, 1827.
Blair, Robert, The Grave, 1818.
Blyth, A. Wynter, 'We might ... ' 1884.
Brierley, Harwood, A flagged causeway, c. 1890.
Brontë, Charlotte, Jane Eyre, 1847, Shirley 1849, 'The Haworth people ... ' 1850, Will of ... 1855.
Brontë Emily, Redbreast in the morning, 1837, Wuthering Heights, 1848.
Brontë, Revd Patrick, Church Reform, Earthquake, and Extraordinary Eruption of Mud and Water, 1824.
Brontë Society Transactions, 'My father-in-law ... ' 1898.
Bulwer-Lytton, Edward, Eugene Aram, 1832.
Burnley, James, 'I stand on the threshold of the Night ... ' 1874-1875.
Burns, Robert, Selkirk grace, Some hae meat ... '
Carr, Revd James, Annals of Colne, 1878.
Clough, Dick o' th', 'I mind th' time ... ' 1899.
Corroner, Marie, J. Ripper letter, 1888.
Craven, Joseph, A Brontë Moorland Village 1907.
Crook, Muriel, Correspondence, 1999.
Crowther, Jonathan, 'Haworth's one of those places ... ' 1812.
Darney, William, 'On Bradford likewise ... ' 1751.
Dearden, William, A Retrospect. 1867.
Dembleby-Malham, John, The Lifting of the Brontë Veil, 1907 and The Key 1911.
Denby, Ethel, A Tragic End.
Dodd, E. E. Bingley, 1958. pg 26-27.
Eccles, J.H. Iconoclast at Haworth, 1879.
Elliott, Thompson, W. Revd, 'They would explain ... '
Field, John, Holy Bible, 1659.
Freemasons, 'History of the Three Graces Lodge, 1792-1913.
Forthrop, B.H, 'There is no portrait of Branwell ... ' 1949.
Gale, Revd Miles, 'Unto his son ... ' c.1714.
Gaskell, Elizabeth, C, Life of Charlotte Brontë, 1860.
Gilbert, R.A, The Golden Dawn and The Esoteric Section, 1987.

Gerard's Herbal, *'garland of Pennie Royall*, 1636.

Greenhill, John, *Report on the Steamship London*, 1866.

Grimshaw, William, *'If ye will go to hell ... '*

Grundy, Francis, *Pictures of the Past*, 1879.

Hale, Charles, *Hale Family Papers, Sophia Smith Collection, Smith Collage, Northampton, Mass. USA*, 1861.

Halley, Revd George, *Life of Edmund Robinson*, 1691.

Hardacre, Joseph, *Lyric & Moral on Various Subjects*, 1822.

Hardy, Spence, R. *Memorials of Jonas Sugden*. 1858.

Harper's Bazaar, *The Wedding*.

Hartley, T.F. *Shadows*, 1886.

Heaton Papers, *Keighley Library, BK 105*.

Heaton, William, *Book of Health Cures*, 1808.

Heywood, Oliver, *Dairy of ... '* 1664-1692.

Hirst, Revd, *'best authority ... '* 1935.

Holdsworth, Alfred, *Lecture*, 1951.

Hone's *Table Book*, 1830.

Hotchops, Nathan, *'Haworth folks ... '* 1858.

Howitt, William, *History of Magic*. 1854.

Ingoldsby, Thomas, *The Ingoldsby Legends*, 1840.

Jackdaw, *'more than 30 years ago ... '* c.1897.

Jersey, F.N, *Dairy of ... '* 1821.

Jessno, *'The ivy-clothed gable ... '* 1879.

Jones, Susan, *Plum Pudding*, 1999.

Jowett, J, The Countryman and the Astrologer, *1856*.

Keighley Spiritualist Pamphlet, *The Voice of Good Spirits*, 1855.

Keighley Visitor, Utopia, *'And art thou dear one ... 'and the Keighley Pudding Eaters*, 1859.

Kilnsey, Miss, *A Pattern of Genius*.

Lavater, John Casper, *Essays on physiognomy*, 1797.

Law, Alice, *Patrick Branwell Brontë*, 1923.

Leach, Pie, *'What did they call his son?'* 1887.

Leechdoms & Wortcunning & Starcraft, 1857.

Lister, Barbara, *'It's like living ... '* 1977.

Lock, John, *Man of Sorrow*, 1979.

Longbridge, Rosamond, *'Personality is largely born of freedom,'* 1929.

Lund, Samuel. *Witch Charm*.

Lush, Elsie, M. *'Thou art all ours ... '*

Myers, S.P.B. *'I found Emily ... '* 1932.

Meeker, Claude, *Home of the Brontës*, 1895.

Montagu, Frederic, *Gleanings of Craven*, 1838.

Moore, Virginia, *The Life and Eager Death of Emily Brontë* 1936.

Olridge-DE-LA-HEY, *Letter to the Brontë Society Transactions*, March 1898.

Pearl, Angela, *Unpublished papers*, 2000.

Pimm, Sandy, *The Brontë Clock*, 1998.

Preston, Albert, *'The description fits ... '* 1974.

Roman Exorcism, *'Go hence ... '*

Robinson, Clement, *A Handful of Pleasant Delites*, 1584

Scriven, R. C, *'Ode to a businessman.'* 1969.

Scruton, William, *'interesting looking girl ... '* 1879.

Shackleton, William, *Four hundred years of a Moorland Family*, 1921.

Shenstone, Will, *'His warmest welcome ... '*

Shorter, K, Clement, *'New manuscript.'* 1902.

Sibree, Mary Mildred Davy, *The Curate's Love Story*, pre 1866.

Simpson, Charles, *'Seldom has a phantom ... '* 1929.

Slater, Frank, *The Spectre Horseman*, 1918.

Smith, Minister Isaac, *'Henry Helliwell takes ... '*

Speight, Harry, (Johnnie Grey), *Airedale*, 1891, *Pleasant Walks around Bingley*, 1890.

Spencer, H.G, *The Suicides Rest*, 1874.

Sutcliffe, Revd John, *Letter to Timothy Sutcliffe*, 1803.

Sutcliffe, Halliwell, *By Moor and Fell*, 1899, *Shameless Wayne*, 1900.

Story, Revd T. W, *Notes on old Haworth Registers*, 1909.

Swain, Charles, *The Betrothed.* 1853.

Tanner, Zenda, *'cobbled stone ... '* 1962.

Thornton, Old Bell Chapel, Burial Register, *'When I can see ... '* 1807-1822.

Trade *Directory*, 1848.

Troubetzkoy, Amelie, Princess, *'Emily Brontë has always seemed ... '*

Turner, Horsfall, Joseph, *Haworth Past and Present*, 1879, *Annals of Wakefield House of Correction*, 1904, *Yorkshire Folk Lore*, 1880.

Tyndall, Professor, *Autobiography of ...*

Watson, Revd John, *History & Antiquities of the Parish of Halifax & co.*, 1775.

W. F. *'For I as usual ... '*

Webster, John, *Treatise of Alchemy*, 1671, *'The Displaying of ... '* 1677.

Wemyss Reid, Sir, *'The fashion ... '* 1877.

Wesleyan Religious Tract, *The Pious Weaver*, 1827.

Westlake, Joseph, *'situated within ... '* 1969.

Whalley, Revd James, *The Wild Moor*, 1869.

White, Walter, *'From an inn ... '* 1859.

Whitefield, George, *'It is appointed ... '*

Williams, Henry, *'When such wonderful creatures ... '* 1924.

Willy's Prayer, *'Roast beef an' bacon ... '*

Wilson, Romer, *All Alone*, 1928.

Witchcraft Act *Repeal of ... '* 1736.

Wright, Joseph, *English Dialect Dictionary*, 1898-1905.

Wrightson, John, *Spell*, 1820.

Wood, Thomas, *Diary of*, 1822-1880.

Index

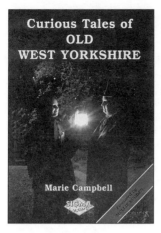

Also of interest . . .

CURIOUS TALES OF OLD WEST YORKSHIRE

Marie Campbell

"A fascinating collection of odd tales of occult doings, curious clergymen, eccentrics and the allsorts of society's fringes." NORTHERN EARTH 1999 "In this fascinating, entertaining, bustling...package of oddities, Marie Campbell ranges far and wide." BRADFORD TELEGRAPH & ARGUS This compendium of 'curious tales' from old West Yorkshire is a first for our times. There has been nothing quite like it since the nineteenth century, when gentleman antiquarians and ghost-hunters took to travelling the country, unearthing the unexplained and the supernatural, and recording their incredible findings as they went. *£7.95*

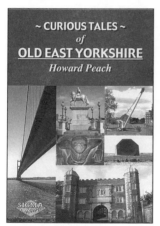

CURIOUS TALES OF OLD EAST YORKSHIRE

Howard Peach

Here is an entertaining guide to the history, folklore, traditions and social institutions of the Old East Riding, arranged in fourteen diverse chapters. Its scope is very wide-ranging, seriously researched and well illustrated bringing a heightened appreciation of the rich heritage of East Yorkshire. Events, personalities and buildings are anecdotally presented. New insights are offered on church life, schooling, punishments, and communications. The highlighting, often humorously, of curiosities/oddities in people, places, unusual death and bizarre dispute - provide an entertaining read. Foreword by David Davis, MP for Cottingham. *£7.95*

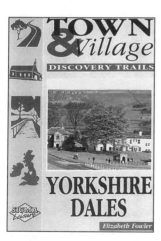

TOWN & VILLAGE DISCOVERY TRAILS: Yorkshire Dales

Elizabeth Fowler

From simple village walks to longer adventures around larger towns, this book is a pure education! Many of the towns and villages are recorded in the Domesday book, and each has a story to tell.
"Leisurely but satisfying walks around some of the most attractive villages in the Dales... a compact well-set out book which should be carried by motorists whenever they visit the area." WHARFEDALE & AIREDALE OBSERVER *£6.95*

WALKS IN THE MYSTERIOUS YORKSHIRE DALES

Graham Dugdale

A new approach to walking in this popular region, with 30 routes which unravel the many varied mysteries of the Yorkshire Dales. These tales dig deep into the region's history and folklore, follow in the macabre footsteps of the Swaledale corpse bearers, challenge the Penhill Giant in his own domain and listen for ghostly revelry at Ribblehead. The author provides his own decorative and extremely detailed maps. This is the fourth in Graham Dugdale's series of guides that transport walkers and armchair travellers into the enigmatic world of mystery and imagination. *£6.95*

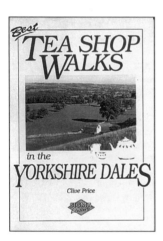

BEST TEA SHOP WALKS IN THE YORKSHIRE DALES

Clive Price

Enjoy a stroll in the Yorkshire Dales rounded off with afternoon tea in a specially selected teashop. Described by the author as "A tantalising mixture of walks and eating places... a delightful concoction of exercise and culinary indulgence."
£6.95

All of our books are available through booksellers. In case of difficulty, or for a free catalogue, please contact:

SIGMA LEISURE, 1 SOUTH OAK LANE, WILMSLOW, CHESHIRE SK9 6AR.
Phone: 01625-531035
Fax: 01625-536800
E-mail: info@sigmapress.co.uk
Web site: http//www.sigmapress.co.uk
MASTERCARD and VISA orders welcome.